Black Feminism
in Education

Cynthia Dillard, *Series Editor*

Rochelle Brock and Richard Greggory Johnson III
Executive Editors

Vol. 69

The Black Studies and Critical Thinking series
is part of the Peter Lang Education list.
Every volume is peer reviewed and meets
the highest quality standards for content and production.

PETER LANG
New York • Bern • Frankfurt • Berlin
Brussels • Vienna • Oxford • Warsaw

Black Feminism in Education

Black Women Speak Back, Up, and Out

Edited by Venus E. Evans-Winters and Bettina L. Love

PETER LANG
New York • Bern • Frankfurt • Berlin
Brussels • Vienna • Oxford • Warsaw

Library of Congress Cataloging-in-Publication Data

Black feminism in education: Black women speak back, up, and out /
edited by Venus E. Evans-Winters, Bettina L. Love.
pages cm. — (Black studies and critical thinking; v. 69)
Includes bibliographical references and index.
1. African American women teachers. 2. African American women scholars.
3. Feminism and education. 4. Educational sociology.
5. Education—Research. I. Evans-Winters, Venus E.
LC2781.B4618   378.1'982996073—dc23   2014040321
ISBN 978-1-4331-2605-5 (hardcover)
ISBN 978-1-4331-2604-8 (paperback)
ISBN 978-1-4539-1462-5 (e-book)
ISSN 1947-5985

Bibliographic information published by **Die Deutsche Nationalbibliothek**.
Die Deutsche Nationalbibliothek lists this publication in the "Deutsche
Nationalbibliografie"; detailed bibliographic data are available
on the Internet at http://dnb.d-nb.de/.

Cover artwork by Amira M. Davis
Photograph by Nailah F. Davis

© 2015 Peter Lang Publishing, Inc., New York
29 Broadway, 18th floor, New York, NY 10006
www.peterlang.com

All rights reserved.
Reprint or reproduction, even partially, in all forms such as microfilm,
xerography, microfiche, microcard, and offset strictly prohibited.

Table of Contents

Acknowledgments ix

Introduction 1

Section I. Black Feminism and Intellectual Spiritual Pursuits 7

Chapter One: A Praisesong for Johnnie 9
    Ruth Nicole Brown

Chapter Two: Navigating Inhibited Spaces: Black Female Scholars'
    Re-articulation of Knowledge Production in the Academy 25
    Lameesa W. Muhammad, Andrea L. Tyler, Adonica Jones-Parks,
    and Lara Chatman

Chapter Three: "Out of the Mouths of Babes": Using Cynthia Dillard's
    Endarkened Feminist Epistemology to Reveal Unseen
    Gendered Passageways 35
    Angela N. Campbell

Chapter Four: Rising Harriett Tubmans: Exploring Intersectionality
    and African American Women Professors 49
    Darlene Russell, Lisa Hobson, and Denise Taliaferro-Baszile

Chapter Five: Eating from the Tree of Life: An Endarkened
   Feminist Revelation 61
   Kyra T. Shahid

Chapter Six: Colorist Dimensions of Black Feminist Knowledge 71
   Carla R. Monroe

Chapter Seven: (Her)story: The Evolution of a Dual Identity as
   an Emerging Black Female and Scholar 81
   Tuwana T. Wingfield

Chapter Eight: Having Our Say in Higher Education: African American
   Women's Stories of "Doing Science" Through Spiritual Capital 93
   Ezella McPherson

Chapter Nine: Truly Professin' Hip-Hop—The Rewind (1996): Makin'
   Black Girls Embodied Musical Play the Teacher 103
   Kyra D. Gaunt

Section II. Black Feminism in Educational Research 119

Chapter Ten: If You Listen, You Will Hear: Race, Place, Gender, and the
   Trauma of Witnessing Through Listening in Research Contexts 121
   Roberta P. Gardner

Chapter Eleven: Black Feminism in Qualitative Education Research:
   A Mosaic for Interpreting Race, Class, and Gender in Education 129
   Venus E. Evans-Winters

Chapter Twelve: Me, Myself, and I: Exploring African American
   Girlhood Through an Endarkened (Photographic) Lens 143
   Karla Manning, Adrienne Duke, and Philip Bostic

Chapter Thirteen: Embodying Dillard's Endarkened Feminist Epistemology 153
   Amira Millicent Davis

Section III. Responsibility for Who and What as a Black
Feminist Educator? 161

Chapter Fourteen: Black Girl Interrupted: A Reflection on the Challenges,
   Contradictions, and Possibilities in Transitioning from
   the Community to the Academy 163
   Monique Lane

Chapter Fifteen: "Oh, You'll Be Back": Bridging Identities of Race,
  Gender, Educator, and Community Partner in Academic Research......... 173
  Billye Sankofa Waters

Chapter Sixteen: Lessons Learned Through Double-Dutch: Black
  Feminism and Intersectionality in Educational Research 183
  Corrie L. Theriault

Chapter Seventeen: Responsibility, Spirituality, and Transformation in
  the (For-Profit) Academy: An Endarkened Feminist Autoethnography 191
  Qiana M. Cutts

Chapter Eighteen: Why We Matter: An Interview with Dr. Cynthia Dillard
  (Nana Mansa II of Mpeasem, Ghana, West Africa)......................... 201
  Bettina L. Love and Venus E. Evans-Winters

Contributors... 211

Acknowledgments

Every book project is a team effort with many individuals providing support and guidance. I would like to express extreme gratitude to my coeditor and sister-friend, Bettina "Bet" Love, for jumping on board with this project with no hesitation, for helping keep me organized, and for adding that extra creative touch to the book. Also, I would like to give much thanks to Cynthia Dillard for hearing, understanding, accepting, and tweaking the vision that Bettina and I had for the book. Undoubtedly, Dr. Dillard, your guidance made this volume a better book than we could have imagined. Thanks for pushing us to think more critically and expressively about what is possible in performing a Black womanist identity in the academy. Also, I wish to acknowledge the unwavering support of the Peter Lang team. Thanks for supporting scholars living at the margins. For my behind-the-scenes support, I would like to thank the entire Winters clan: Steve, Stephen, and Serena. Working on a book project means deadlines, and deadlines mean a distracted spouse and mother. Yet, you all always support this women's work that I do on behalf of the family, community, and nation. Thank you all for always having my back and displaying much needed patience. Lastly, I thank all of the coauthors who have made this book idea a reality. Our spirits are inscribed onto these pages and together we represent our mothers and foremothers well, giving voice to the past, present, and future of endarkened knowledge and activism. —Venus

First and foremost, I would like to thank the creator. Her love is undeniable and abundant. I am humbled that the authors of this book trusted Venus and

me with their impressive work that embodies the love and spirit of Black girls and women everywhere. Thank you for your trust and for holding the work to a standard that would make our ancestors smile. A special shout to my sis, Venus, an amazing scholar who never stops working and fighting for social justice. Thank you for the invitation to join you on this journey. Dr. Dillard (Nana Mansa II of Mpeasem, Ghana): Your love and light are beyond words. You inspire us to reach back and remember our greatest achievements and how we must "do the work" in the present. Thank you for being the light at the end of the sometimes long, dark, and frightening tunnel called life in the academy. I am beyond grateful for your mentorship and love for me and my family. To my family, Chelsey, Chance, and Lauryn, thank you. The ways in which you look at me with love, admiration, and devotion inspire me to be more than I ever could imagine. Love you all!
Peace. —Bettina

Introduction

The authors of this book share with the academic community the ways in which we have learned to embrace, resist, adapt, and reconceptualize education research, teaching, and learning in ways to better serve our personal growth, individuals, our cultural communities, nation, and all of humanity. Although books are available on how Black women navigate the academy, what makes this book unique is that contributing authors intentionally and creatively reflect on how they use *endarkened feminist epistemological frameworks*, a term coined by Cynthia Dillard (Nana Mansa II of Mpeasem, Ghana, West Africa) to construct stories on educational transformation as raced, gendered, and cultural embodied work.

In her book *On Spiritual Strivings: Transforming an African American Woman's Academic Life*, Dillard (2006) explains,

> I use the term "endarkened" feminist epistemology to articulate how reality is known when based in the historical roots of Black feminist thought, embodying a distinguishable difference in cultural standpoint, located in the intersection/overlap of the culturally constructed socializations of race, gender, and other identities, and the historical and contemporary contexts of oppressions and resistance for African American women. (p. 3)

While Black feminism and writings have long traditions, Dillard's theoretical and methodological writings are some of the first works in the field of *education* that successfully interweaved Black feminists' politics, spirituality, and Africanism with traditional education research, curriculum, and practice.

Historically, women of African ancestry, such as Gwendolyn Brooks, Septima P. Clark, Anna Julius Cooper, Fanny Lou Hamer, Elizabeth Higginbotham, and Mary Church Terrell, among many others (see Giddings, 1996; Guy-Sheftall, 1995; Phillips, 2006, for an extensive overview and collections of Black feminist thought), have extensively written or publicly spoken about the significance of Black women's experiences in developing meaningful educational philosophies and practices that are culturally (and politically) relevant to those of the African Diaspora. The message conveyed by African women scholar-activists across the world was that Black women as laborers and nurturers, of our own children and other people's children, have an ontological way of being, viewing, and conveying the social world that could simultaneously contribute to social theory and serve democratic purposes.

Many Black women in the field of education find themselves at once culturally isolated and politically embattled as scholars. Thus, besides developing a critical consciousness out of our historical experiences of marginalization (and the forms of resistance that Black women have drawn upon to adapt and survive) as Black and woman and poor/working class, those of us located within the academy also have developed an endarkened feminist epistemology often out of our solitary confinement in the white ivory tower.

Similar to other Black womanist scholars, the editors' intellectual pursuits and articulations here have been certainly shaped by the philosophies of Black feminists Patricia Hill-Collins, Angela Davis, bell hooks, Clenora Hudson-Weems, Audre Lorde, and Alice Walker. The aforementioned Black feminists remind us that women of African ancestry's multiple identities create a multiple consciousness (King, 1988) that is informed by resistance against racism, sexism, and class inequality. In relationship to this book, what Hudson-Weems's (*Africana Womanist Literary Theory*), hooks's (*Ain't I a Woman*), Walker's (*In Search of My Mother's Garden*), Davis's (*Women, Race, and Class*), Lorde's (*Sister Outsider*), and Collins's (*Black Feminist Thought*) theoretical cogitations provided for us theoretically, methodologically, pedagogically, and spiritually nearly a decade ago, is what Cynthia Dillard's endarkened feminist epistemology is doing for the next generation of Black women, emerging and budding scholars in the field of education—it provides a more global perspective on Black women's ways of knowing.

As Evans-Winters discussed in *Teaching Black Girls* (2011), Black women of our generation never experienced de jure segregation, the civil rights movement, or Baptist church teachings, which are the experiences that many Black feminists declared informed their identities as feminist scholars. While many younger Black women scholars have been reared and influenced by other women's and community members' stories of Jim Crow segregation, the women's and civil rights movements, and the religious practices of the Black church, we are ultimately a part of a generation that has mostly experienced de facto segregation in urban communities *and* suburban integration. Another difference between Black women scholars matriculating through the academy more recently and those Black feminists who came before us? We are accessing the formal marketplace in the midst of internationalization and a neoliberal post–civil rights academic climate. Therefore, we tend to be curious about an identity that extends beyond U.S. borders, an identity that is possibly accorded more acceptance and freedom. In this book, many of the authors speak to locating their identities as scholars in *communities of affinity* (Dillard, 2006) for spiritual preservation.

Nevertheless, different from many of our Black feminist predecessors, we have benefited from *Brown v. Board of Education*, the Civil Rights Act of 1964, Title IX, ethnic studies and gender studies programs in higher education, and multicultural curriculum. Also, Black women scholars today live in a historical moment where most Americans remain skeptical of organized religion and have disengaged from formal institutions of worship, yet, Black women are also a part of an ethnic group that is the most religious in this country. Demographic patterns, cultural shifts, and political mandates indubitably shape present-day Black women scholars' worldviews.

Along these same lines, Love (2012) emphasizes in *Hip Hop's Li'l Sistas Speak* that Black girls' and young women's identities have been shaped by more than simply history. Today's generation of African ascended women are shaped by contemporary images of Black women that are constructed by popular media, including rap music and hip-hop culture. For the editors of the volume and the authors of this book, popular culture has shaped our racial and gender identities as scholars, activists, and critical pedagogues. Contradictorily, pop culture has been a site of both cultural affinity and, simultaneously, a site of resistance. Readers will certainly be able to identify within this text where the authors accept and reject the complexities of popular culture, and how an endarkened feminist perspective helps all of us to disentangle the web of culture (Geertz, 1973). The messages conveyed in the book's chapters are undoubtedly shaped as much by a historically constituted racialized gender paradigm as they are by a creative imagination often characterized by the rhythm and blues that accompanies Black girlhood in the post–civil rights world.

As readers will discover in the chapters presented in *Black Feminism in Education*, many Black women scholars exist in a liminal space between the traditional and the modern. Many Black women scholars in this volume are synchronously questioning the intentions of White feminism and patriarchy, while also embracing a multicultural/multiethnic, multi-vocular, and multigenerational Black feminist epistemology that crosses multiple (cultural, political, and geographical) borders. In other words, contemporary Black women scholars are even pushing traditional Black feminism forward by adding their own experiences and perspectives to the dialogue.

As Dillard articulates in *Learning to (Re)member the Things We've Learned to Forget: Endarkened Feminisms, Spirituality, and the Sacred Nature of Research and Teaching* (2012),

> What is needed are models of inquiry that truly honor the complexities of memories. Of indigenous and "modern" time, experienced not just in our minds, but in our bodies and spirits as well. Frameworks that approach teaching and research as sacred practices, worthy of reverence. (p. 10)

The scholars in this book merge past lived experiences with their learned knowledge to bring forth a more complex reality of what it means to be a scholar in a White supremacist patriarchal imperialist society (for example, see hooks, 2013, for an explanation of using more veracious language to name racism). Propitiously, Dillard's notion of *endarkened feminism* brings forth a framing or language that may be more conducive and representative of how many 21st-century Black women engage theory, research, and practice. Below is a concise outline of the conceptualization of endarkened feminist epistemology (Dillard, 2000, 2006, 2012) and its major themes that have noticeably emerged across chapters presented within this book.

1. Endarkened women scholars' ideas, conceptualizations of the social world, and aesthetics are grounded in a historical and/or global Black feminist thought.
2. A Black feminist epistemology culturally and ontologically differs from traditional White feminist thought.
3. A Black feminist epistemology is located in Black women's existence at the intersections of race, class, and gender oppression in a society that privileges whiteness, maleness, and wealth.
4. An endarkened feminist epistemology challenges, and at times necessarily rejects, Eurocentric Western canons and research methodologies.
5. An endarkened feminist epistemology is purposefully activist and community-engaged.
6. Spirituality is an underlying theme of a Black woman's scholarly identity and is connected to the types of research and relationships one seeks out in (and outside) academe.
7. An endarkened feminist worldview is connected to a transnational identity that exceeds borders and connects histories, cultures, and ways of being in the social world.

Our standpoint is simultaneously located in seeking to better identify, understand, and name Black girls' and women's vulnerabilities, resilience, and forms of resistance across the African Diaspora. Many women of African ancestry also seek to challenge traditional Eurocentric positivist ways of knowing and inscription of the social world; we seek to turn to alternative indigenous knowledges to read the self, community, and spiritual world. Thus, Black feminist theorists tend to draw upon alternative research methodologies, and pedagogies that are possibly transformative and healing for all involved in the research, teaching, and service experience.

In this volume, the authors explore and discuss how endarkened feminist epistemological frameworks are woven into our education research, teaching, and mentoring. Throughout the book, we take up a central question: *How is Black feminist thought and/or an endarkened feminist epistemology (EFE) being used in pre-K through higher education contexts and scholarship to marshal new research methodologies, frameworks, and pedagogies?* The contributing authors address this question from multiple perspectives. Readers will find that the authors' endarkened perspectives align with Nana Cynthia Dillard's assertions that a cultural standpoint is present among women of African ancestry. In this volume, the authors conscientiously excavate these standpoints.

SECTIONS OF THE BOOK

In Section I of the book, "Black Feminism and Intellectual Spiritual Pursuits," the authors highlight the ways in which researchers, teachers, and students make sense of, and explore, their identities as "other" in a context that privileges whiteness, maleness, and Eurocentric ways of knowing and being. Attention is particularly given to the multiple ways of seeking to know and exist in spaces that have not been traditionally carved out for non-Whites and women of color. In Section II of the book, the dialogue focuses on methodological implications of "Black Feminism in Educational Research." Essays in this section illuminate how research is concomitantly a contested site, an opportunity for refuge and an act of service for Black women. This section also foregrounds the multi-vocal cultural and gendered perspectives that Black women bring to research paradigms that endarken these methodologies and paradigms.

Finally, chapters in Section III of the book, titled "Responsibility for Who and What as a Black Feminist Educator?," explore the kinds of research that endarkened feminists of color engage in (e.g., research, teaching, community advocacy, etc.) that revitalize our souls and serve to empower and be empowered by those whom we serve. The book closes with an interview dialogue with Dr. Cynthia Dillard and the editors of this book that points to the future of endarkened feminist perspectives and epistemologies and how we might put our work to work on behalf of communities we care deeply about. We proclaim that our endarkened voices will be the flame that lights the path to educational transformation and liberation.

REFERENCES

Collins, P. H. (2000). *Black feminist thought: Knowledge, consciousness, and the politics of empowerment* (2nd ed.). New York: Routledge.
Davis, A. (1983). *Women, race, and gender*. New York: Vintage.
Dillard, C. B. (2000). The substance of things hoped for, the evidence of things not seen: Examining an endarkened feminist epistemology in educational research and leadership. *International Journal of Qualitative Research in Education*, *13*(6), 661–681.
Dillard, C. B. (2006). *On spiritual strivings: Transforming an African American woman's academic life*. Albany, NY: State University of New York Press.
Dillard, C. B. (2012). *Learning to (re)member the things we've learned to forget: Endarkened feminisms, spirituality, and the sacred nature of research and teaching*. New York: Peter Lang.
Evans-Winters, V. E. (2011). *Teaching Black girls: Resiliency in urban classrooms* (2nd ed.). New York: Peter Lang.
Geertz, C. (1973). *The interpretations of culture*. New York: Basic Books.
Giddings, P. (1996). *When and where I enter: The impact of Black women on race and sex in America*. New York: HarperCollins.
Guy-Sheftall, B. (1995). *Words of fire: An anthology of African-American feminist thought*. New York: New Press.
hooks, b. (1999). *Ain't I a woman: Black women and feminism*. Cambridge, MA: South End Press.
hooks, b. (2013). *Writing beyond race: Living theory and practice*. New York: Routledge.
Hudson-Weems, C. (2004). *Africana womanist literary theory*. Trenton, NJ: Africa World Press.
King, D. (1988). Multiple jeopardy, multiple consciousness: The context of a Black feminist ideology. *Signs, 14*(1), 42–72.
Lorde, A. (1984). *Sister outsider: Essays and speeches by Audre Lorde*. New York: Crossing Press.
Love, B. L. (2012). *Hip hop's li'l sistas speak: Negotiating identities and politics in the new south*. New York: Peter Lang.
Phillips, L. (2006). *The womanist reader*. New York: Routledge.
Walker, A. (1983). *In search of our mother's garden: Womanist prose*. San Diego: Harcourt Brace.

SECTION I

Black Feminism and Intellectual Spiritual Pursuits

CHAPTER ONE

A Praisesong for Johnnie

RUTH NICOLE BROWN

I want you to know and remember Johnnie Summerset.

Johnnie Summerset, deejay, father, husband, veteran, educator, and my first cousin died at 33 years of age after fighting cancer for the third time. In this chapter, I present *A Praisesong for Johnnie*, a performance I wrote about his life and our relationship. I first performed this praisesong at the Independent Media Center in Urbana, Illinois, as a part of a public performance associated with my research on Black girlhood (Brown, 2014). Following the praisesong, I discuss what I learned from the experience of performing it. Notably, performing my cousin's praisesong allowed me to teach two lessons. First, when I show up, so too does my cousin. Second, sometimes what I have to teach and learn is more than academic. Cynthia Dillard (2012) instructs, "praisesongs can be used to celebrate or affirm triumph over adversity, bravery, and courage both in life and death" (p. 7). *A Praisesong for Johnnie* was my intervention into the gapping pause grief conjures and allowed me to go on. I felt more concerned for the world he left behind and more certain that I myself could continue on this journey living with greater integrity by wholly accepting and sharing more of myself as I know myself to be, Johnnie's little cousin. *A Praisesong for Johnnie* is but one more example from which to address the role of extra-academic labor Black women professors such as myself so often perform. To praise someone like my cousin Johnnie, whose story you probably have not heard before reading this chapter, has proven both a spiritual and pedagogical project with profound implications that converge at the intersections of Black girlhood, endarkened feminist epistemologies, education, and performance studies.

A PRAISESONG FOR JOHNNIE

My first trip to the motherland was in May 2000. As a student of performance studies, I was awarded a $3,000 scholarship to travel the world. To go anywhere in the world.

> But I am from Chicago's southern most suburbs
> The windy city... where we stayyyyyyyyyyyyyyyyyyy and never leave.
> But I am a woman of the wind.
> Constantly changing...

> Anywhere in the world, you mean?
> It took Dr. Frank Gunderson to say... go to Africa.
> But where?
> I asked like it was a dare.

I was/am first generation, after all, and my world was between Chicago Heights and Park Forest, Illinois with 14th Street or what the White folks call Lincoln Highway in between.

> Tanzania?

After a while, I came to think of it as my idea. I went to Africa for the first time. I went to Tanzania for my whole family. I was the first to travel outside of these United States sponsored by a university fellowship, not the military industrial complex.

> We partied.

Johnnie sent me off with these words:

Nicole,

I am so very proud of you. Always remember you can accomplish anything you set your mind to...

Anything you strive for worth any value always has a difficulty factor attached to it. So when you achieve great things the road along the way will make you a better person.

Whenever you get down in spirit always remember: you as a Black woman are the greatest of God's creation! You are the mother of the Universe. The secret of God and all his mysteries is all wrapped up inside you. So get to know Nicole and bring out the best of yourself!

I love you

Johnnie

My cuz ended his letter with a postscript:

A Nation Can Rise No Higher Than its Women. When you teach a man you teach an individual. When you teach a woman you teach a nation!

Because the woman is the first teacher of her child. Peace be with you always!

As-Salamu Alaykum
As-Salamu Alaykum
As-Salamu Alaykum

I told you I was from the Windy City. My cousin was NOI.

As-Salamu Alaykum

Saved his life.

In 1994, Johnnie joined the Nation of Islam under the teachings of the One Honorable Minister Louis Farrakhan.

Before that, he was a vet of the Desert Storm war.

On the morning of August 2, 1990 the mechanized infantry, armor, and tank units of the Iraqi Republican Guard invaded Kuwait and seized control of that country. The invasion triggered a

> United States response, Operation DESERT SHIELD, to deter any invasion of Kuwait's oil rich neighbor, Saudi Arabia. On August 7, deployment of U.S. forces began."[1]
>
> Our "liberation of Kuwait" resulted in 148 U.S. battle deaths, and 145 nonbattle deaths, including 15 women. Number of U.S. soldiers wounded in action: 467. Of Iraq's 545,000 troops in Kuwait an estimated 100,000 were killed, and 300,000 were wounded.[2]

Anddddddddd

Johnnie came back. Johnnie came back. Johnnie came back.

We partied!

He brought me Persian money!

He got married. Had a son. And Lived.

Made a living as deejay—house music was his life.

Deejayed for the love of it.

Deejayed for the joy of it.

Taught others how to deejay at Columbia College to make a steady income of it.

We are from Chicago Heights. Our family settled in the suburbs, do you hear me. We did not move to the city then to the suburbs. Our family hailed from different parts of Kentucky and moved to Chicago Heights because of the factories. Steel. Working class. Where kinds of people were divided by railroad tracks. We are still here. Generations, three to be exact, claim Chicago Heights as home, though we still live like we in Kentucky making business outta sittin on porches and buying homes with breezeways. We still keep our speech, that's why I say a bid (bed) is something you sleep in not something you bargain for, and a dawl (doll) is a toy, nothing more. But Our Chicago South Suburban living family intersected with the city, in one very simple way:

House music is our confession.

House music was his obsession.

House music was ours, and Johnnie gave it back with so much love.

My cuz

In between the drum and the bass, the kick machine and the analog synthesizers

Johnnie. Came down with a cough (cough).

I am sorry to have to bring you this story. I wish it wasn't true. I wish that I could protect you from what you are going to hear tonight, because it has taken me a year to investigate this story. During that time, I went through the worst depression you can imagine. I finally came to the conclusion one day that—yes, our country had provided the biologicals to Saddam Hussein that were used on our troops. Our troops are sick and they are dying.—Captain Joyce Riley[3]

A well-kept secret known to only a handful of leaders, Iraq's BW program—approved by Saddam Husayn, overseen by Husayn Kamil Hasan Al Majid, guided by Dr. 'Amir Hamudi Hasan Al Sa'adi, and closely linked to the IIS—culminated in the first Gulf war in January 1991, by which point Iraq had developed a small but impressive arsenal of BW weapons comprising over 100 bombs, at least 25 Al Husayn warheads filled with anthrax spores, botulinum toxin and aflatoxin, as well as many thousands of liters of these agents stored in bulk, for use in Iraq's unsophisticated delivery systems.—US CIA.[4]

Germ warfare was used by Saddam Hussein against the Americans and their alliances—biologicals which were illegally manufactured in America and sold illegally to Iraq from 1985 to 1990 with the approval and blessings of the Reagan and Bush Administrations.

Our servicemen and women were exposed to deadly chemical and biological agents supplied to our enemies by our own government.—Donald S. McAlvaney[5]

Johnnie had cancer.

"Give birth and see."

Remission.

House music all night long!

Johnnie had cancer again.

"You cannot tell a mother how to act."

Remission.

House music all night long!

Johnnie had cancer for a third time.

Sometimes I feel like a motherless child a long way from home.

That's when he said:

"You don't even know that you know God unless you are striving to make the impossible possible."

In a NOI lecture he wanted to give since his first diagnosis

Battling cancer for a third time, my cousin questioned…

"How many of us are daring to do something different? Not just different, but something that you know you were called to do? Even if it seems difficult, or impossible. Taking risks and making a difference—how many of us are achieving our dreams?

It is in the doing of our dreams that we become most intimately acquainted with God.

It should NOT have to be the worst of the worst before we decide to get sincere." Johnnie said, "the Kingdom of God is right here."

House music all night long.

House music all night long.

House music all night long.

"How many people do you know who can say they have survived cancer three times? If it is His Will, He will save me again. But if He decided to allow me to pass on then I pray to die the death of a Muslim. And I thank Him for the time he has allowed me to be alive."

My cousin died the death of a Muslim at 33 years of age on April 21, 2003.

He died prematurely.

He died with his son a living legacy.

He died a part of Chicago's house music history.

He LIVES!

House music all night long!

He LIVES!

House music all night long!

He LIVES!

House music all night long!

I want you to know and remember my cousin deejay Johnnie Summerset.

***

My world stopped when Johnnie passed. It seemed odd to me that life did not stop for us all. I thought it only right that the universe acknowledge his transition in a big, even if momentary, way. To show its respect, I fully expected time to stand still, trees to bow down and maybe even red, black, and green sunshine. Since none of that happened, I wrote. As a way to begin, I recollected some of Johnnie's "life notes," including the "letters, stories, journal entries, reflections, poetry, music, and other artful forms" (Dillard, 2000, p. 664) he gave to me, to direct my memory and the writing process. I reread and retraced the now artifacts of our relationship. I cried over all the family celebrations he would never deejay. I stared at pictures. I tried to console my grieving aunt who seemed to have disappeared right in front of us. I used Google to search for some public trace of his existence and learned of his impact as a teacher of house music. I remembered one of the many times he babysat my cousin (his little brother) and me and let us play hide and seek in the house. I laughed at the remembrance of him grabbing our ankles from behind the steps as we tiptoed down into the basement seeking him as "it." I listened to his mix-tapes and danced. It took me a long time to listen to his Nation of Islam (NOI) lecture, because the truth in his voice required more preparation of me. It required a kind of listening that demanded movement.

THE CREATIVE PROCESS: TEACHER AS SELECTOR

I first shared this praisesong in a university classroom setting. I instructed students to write poems set to music and I did the same. The soundtrack of my praisesong was one of Johnnie's house music mix-tapes. My presentation was more of relief, then grief. The sharing of it resulted in the kind of joy that comes from truth-telling. Johnnie's praisesong carved out a space for me to say, "Where I am from, cousins are everything." So many different relationships are privileged in research literature, in daily conversations, and via national hallmark holidays, but cousins always seem to me undervalued. In my class, as in my life, I want it to be known that cousins, vulnerability, grief, house music, memory, and our family histories have a place. In decolonizing the relationship between student and teacher, I teach that who we are in relationship to other people, often non-iconic, matters as I learn about those who are important to my students. If you know that I am Johnnie's cousin, well then, I thought, my students too may tell a story about who they know themselves to be in relation to someone, place, or thing important to them. We bring all kinds of things to class with us beyond books and computers. Our memories can and do teach; our memories can and do inform our research.

Writing about my cousin and performing the praisesong was a personal and pedagogical exercise with political implications. Calling attention to the politics of personal narrative performance, Langellier (1999) wrote:

> Approaching personal narrative as performance requires theory which takes context as seriously as it does text, which takes the social relations of power as seriously as it does individual reflexivity, and which therefore examines the cultural production and reproduction of identities and experience. (p. 128)

To perform Johnnie's praisesong I made the bold choice to "embrace all of me for the good of all of us," especially my students (Dillard, 2000, p. 42). By performing I was "cricking to crack like those who came before me" (Ulysse, 2012, p. 4). In my own way speaking in my mother tongue that is performance, I was saying, "Not yet big bird of prey not yet," because some of us did not die (Jordan, 2002, p. 15). The personal, pedagogical, and political comingle in performance—they are not to be collapsed.

A Praisesong for Johnnie created a space where I could differently think about the culpability of inequality, death as pedagogy, the power of grief, urgency as telling, spirituality and/as house music, duty, and the kind of teacher I want to be. Of her cousin's premature death, Lisa Cacho (2012) wrote, "to make the unthinkable not just plausible but necessary, we have to reckon with restless ghosts and living people who share the status of 'dead-to-others' and demand from us nothing less than transformation" (p. 168). I fully embraced Johnnie's gift of moving the crowd, hoping I could do the same. In the non-negotiables of my partial telling and full being, spirit spun Johnnie's passion, our history, and my calling to a life as action beat intended to uncover those memories that do work toward creating better days now and ahead.

Compelling stories are often told in a way that contains internal arguments, multiple meanings, and implicit understandings (Feldman, Sköldberg, Brown, & Horner, 2004). The underlying premise in my praisesong about my cousin was the provision of spirit. Spiritual literacies of expressive cultures include linking honesty and eloquence in body talking to a purity of intention in motion (DeFrantz, 2004, p. 73). The music, the actors on stage, the audience, the words, the costume, the altar, the prayers and offerings to my ancestors, the props used and given created a force to which my schoolbook expertise submitted. I recognize that force within myself as spirit. According to Dillard (2006a), spirituality "involves consciousness" and "choosing to be in a relationship with the divine power of all things" (p. 41). Awareness, honesty, presence, contact, dialogue, touch, and collective remembering are not necessarily required in a traditional classroom setup, but I knew that to be consciousness of these things as they mattered on the dance floor, after service, in hospice, and at any one of our family's Sunday dinners would make the kind of power Johnnie demanded of the living. Critical co-presences, nuance readings of bodies, an attentiveness to emotionality and interior constructions is advanced praxis that requires more than book smarts. Some of my students have been waiting a long time for this kind of instruction and are more than prepared, ready. My students who are disconnected from the source of what they know to be life will not learn the lesson of Johnnie's praisesong. The forces of the profession that suggest disassociation as preferable pedagogy too often leave me thinking "forget it then" in mid-demonstration. Then, when, and because of what is at stake, Johnnie's praisesong reminds me that I am a better teacher and student when I am answerable to the source many of us call spirit. This work is extra-academic and also not academic at all.

CREATIVE UNKNOWING DISRUPTS

Doing performance disrupts academic routines and one promise of such disruption is the revelation of creative unknowing (Brown, Carducci, & Kuby, 2014). Creative unknowing engages the senses, transforms the self, brings wisdom into conversations about knowledge, and invites inclusion. Perhaps most critically, performance allows for the betrayal of sense typically taken for granted, and thus opens up space to think and reflect (Jagodzinski & Wallin, 2013). As deep and profound as knowing can be, it is often productive to dwell in the unknown, the not yet, the horrific, and the dream. What it feels like to think and learn has become so synonymous with punishment and control that dreaming, creating, and even fun often registers in our body as something other than instructive. Unknowing enables creative disruption. Johnnie taught me how to lovingly embrace the unknown and yet-to-be known. I want my students to survive and live, just as I desire this for myself—and teaching us how to linger in the unknown is a useful skill for theorizing. Praising my cousin through performance was a reconciliation of parts, pieces, and fragments in favor of a labor that I was connected to because I ran not away, but to what I could not count on or render tangible with absolute certainty.

It is exactly the already humanized subjectivity of African ascendant women educators that Dillard (2000) theorized as already intelligible when she wrote, "our choices for methodology become a form of agency, a way to learn, think, and imagine something different, that is to transform taken-for-granted ways of knowing, especially in the academy" (p. 131). Spirituality, then, becomes one mechanism to resist a hegemonic knowing premised on faulty assumptions of White supremacist logics of recognition because, as Dillard (2006b) emphasized, an endarkened feminist epistemological space "centers reciprocity and necessitates a different relationship between ourselves as the researcher and the researched, between knowing and the production of knowledge" (p. 70). To insist on spirituality as an interdisciplinary interpretive strategy, *A Praisesong for Johnnie* refused hierarchal and border maintenance approaches to educational research—purchase the book/read the book, teacher/student binary, acting by the book, with the printed word as privileged authority. The university remains structured in such a way that the discipline and segregation of people and ideas work to privilege the life of the mind over life. About academic routine, bell hooks (2003) wrote, "Many of students come to our classrooms believing that real brilliance is revealed by the will to disconnect and disassociate. They see this state as crucial to the maintenance of objectivism. They fear wholeness will lead them to be considered less 'brilliant.'" (p. 180). In the academy, motivation to disassociate is everywhere and the push and pull to compartmentalize is rabid. Even among those of us who want to do things differently, fear is present as are those practices that reproduce myths of objectivity. For this reason, I call out brilliance when I see students making connections and reconnecting—especially when the linkages feel counterintuitive and seem threatening. As Johnnie would lecture, we cannot let the hard work scare us to death as an acceptable choice.

In a praisesong written about my cousin, I performed, and—in between our differences—the performative enactment of spirit enlivened associations and provided occasions for solidarity not premised on sameness, status, or professional norms. Performing Johnnie's praisesong made it possible to discuss some of what I've known about him in relation to things, people, and places that are typically assumed very distant and out of reach—war, spirit, healing, and education. These subjects are assumed to occur "outside of ourselves" and are too often determined by someone else with more power and privilege, who holds a certain position. Moreover, performing the praisesong allowed me to make significant associations within myself. Often the professor part of me feels displaced by the performing artist and vice versa. If I act out of my training and discipline, I easily compartmentalize my body from what I know from what I feel from my spirit. When I am fully present, what I do is inherently interdisciplinary in the best possible way. Through my praisesong, I remember not only my cousin but also that my people are a race for theory, following Barbara Christian (1988) who made it plain:

> For people of color have always theorized—but in forms quite different from the Western form of abstract logic. And I am inclined to say that our theorizing (and I intentionally use the verb rather than the noun) is often in narrative form, in the stories we create, in riddles and proverbs, in the play with language, because dynamic rather than fixed ideas seem more to our liking. How else have we managed to survive with such spiritedness the assault on our bodies, social institutions, countries, our very humanity? (p. 68)

Theory also and often emerges in the form of kitchen prayers, dreams, visions, and maxims (Mattis, 2000). Theory may emerge in the form of soulful gospel house or in regional hip-hop rhythms. To explain what I sometimes do not have the words for, and to incite singular hearts to beat collectively together, are lessons I sometimes do not even know how big and how much mine they are to teach until I danced, well after it is taught.

As a researcher of Black girlhood, when I work with Black girls we routinely call the names of people we want known and remembered. It is often during this ritual that I am most clear how research with Black girls recalls Black boys (and ideally vice versa). It was in this ritualized cipher of remembering that I first called Johnnie's name, foreshadowing the tribute to my cousin I would perform publically with students whom I needed to trust for it to work. The idea that Black girlhood studies is relational to Black boyhood is a lesson often met with skepticism and critical resistance; however, calling Johnnie's name iteratively and repeatedly became a teachable practice that suggests categories of difference need not be mutually exclusive or rendered significant only through negation and comparison.

While fully engaged in the labor of celebrating Black girlhood, Durell Callier (2009) poetically penned,

> This work is dirty work... and not in the sense of soiled pampers or blood stained underwear.
>
> No, this work is dirty because these girls come to us....

So as we come to them

> Half-whole-but already whole just needing someone to help us connect our disconnected parts… to explore with us and awaken in us our rightfully divined god/goddess.… Needing just a touch… yes a laying on of hands to witness this beauty I/we sometimes hide and run from… this beauty I/we sometimes don't see.

Though "dirty work" it may be, when the connections across and because of difference are made it can produce a kind of beautiful recognition that sameness either takes for granted or discounts. For example, in doing research on Black girlhood and working with Black girls in community spaces with Black women the idea that a Black man could also homegirl was initially suspect. Many homegirls have been told their research and everyday practice of working with Black girls was antithetical to and presumably less important work than most everything, especially work that occurred in schools in alignment with core standards and that primarily addressed Black boys. This particular line of patriarchal logic was used to reduce homegirl labor and to diminish their impact and presence. To resist, some Black women homegirls, well familiar with the master's tools of exclusion, suggested we use them in the same ways against those who disappeared us. But the "Black boys first and most" line of critique rarely, if ever (meaning never), is made by those willing to do the work with us. Such misguided discourse dissolves the complexity of Black girlhood and looks over the diversity among, within, and between those who identify as Black girls and those who love them. Instead of thinking about how gender is performed within and throughout cultural work with youth and interrogating what intersections matter when, seeing only Black girls as not just gendered but also as singularly and unidimensionally gendered is antiquated and infuriating. Would it not be an asset to us who do the work of Black girlhood celebration to also work with those whose masculinity does not foreclose the dirty work of bringing snacks, doing the practice, and reflecting on who we are together? Would it not be brilliant to understand how a Black girl celebration accounts for and is also accountable to queer bodies, ideas, and politics? That gender structures the lives of all youth, albeit in different ways, is important to interrogate and foreground particularly when gender is always and already at play in programs and services specified by gender. That we were small enough in number to know each other's motivations as they were demonstrated and stated was a gift to our collective organizing that surely we would not turn away from love, in favor of cutting up. The move to embrace complexity was named brilliance and I was unwavering in my insistence that our bodies were necessary but not sufficient. That we are connected and interdependent, gender is unstable and contested, our histories counter pure boundaries and borders, is wisdom that performance reveals twice over. For those of us who are familiar with displacement, disconnection, and disassociation in educational spaces that disembody our memories from our histories, disconnect our heads from our hearts and from our hands, distance our profession from our calling, and disease the spirit through capitalist formations of work performance offers us not only a chance to rehearse what we've forgotten but to also act and bring into existence actions that orientate us toward each other. As I call Johnnie's name in the cipher whether it's in a performance or after school working toward Black girlhood celebration, it is always as an affirmation of spirit, an appeal to the most transgressive formations possible.

Performance allowed me to create anew by (re)membering African wisdom and culture as our activism in the spirit and remembrance of our artists (Dillard, 2012, p. 108). To craft the piece that I believed could honor Johnnie in a way that was spiritually powerful and intellectually responsible, I was glad to have African ascendant students with whom I could co-create. I performed with students who knew spirit, dirty work, and discernment. This performance required a wellness with grief so that I could be clear and uncompromised in my delivery. I needed spirit, or the life force within us all, to connect us to each other, in spite of how I am physically read and perceived. The audience members, when they lit a candle and called the names of their loved ones that they want known and remembered, joined in the process of signification, showing me the lesson learned, heard, and understood.

Building on Gloria Anzaldúa's legacy, AnaLouise Keating (2008) mindfully acknowledged, "spiritual activism entails hard work, with no guarantee of immediate success" (p. 249). *A Praisesong for Johnnie* was personally, pedagogically, and politically productive more than it was successful as a traditional theatrical performance. The praisesong is written as monologue and my performance could have certainly benefited from more direction. While on stage, I wanted more cousinness comraderie among the secondary characters who played bid whist in the background. The card game should have been louder, the players faces more calculating, and I needed some children the ages of my nieces, nephews, and youngest cousins to run through the scene. Mostly, I wanted my aunt in the audience to know that I too remember, but she was not yet ready to make that trip.

As I performed, my cousin became the professor and I the student. What resulted was the creation of a sacred space. It was sacred because it was not merely a performance about praising and affirming my cousin's life that we lost too soon, but it affirmed my cousin, whose life was still teaching and feeding us. Remembering her sister Octavia's death, Dillard (2006a) wrote, "And when we choose to share the contributions and stories of the human journey of those who have died, we usher in a sacred space of relationships with them that recognizes both their life and death as part of the same event" (p. 70). During the final scene when I ask the audience to come up and light a candle about someone they want known and remembered, audience members more diverse than any one of my university classes participated. One Black man announced to the other audience members that before the show began he did not think a performance about Black girls would be relevant to his own life. But as he participated by calling the name of someone who died prematurely and lit the candle, he also said the performance changed his expectations of what Black girlhood is about. He also surprised himself by welcoming the opportunity to be vulnerable in public among people he once thought strangers. This man told us he used to be "in the streets" and how he found his way to our performance, I do not know. However, in his affirmation of the performance was yet another—we can sense ourselves honest teachers of urgent truths who are able to make the impossible possible.

***

Black feminists and Black women performers have placed a significant value on the exploration of meaning related to recognition, remembering, and recovering in theoretically engaged and engaging ways (Brown & Nyong'o, 2006, p. 3). As a Black woman artist-scholar, the praisesong for my cousin Johnnie was a personal way for me to remember him. Additionally, by publicly recalling him through performance, I hoped to make a collective impact. In this chapter, I sought not to make legible how spirit works but, more importantly, to support and encourage those already in the know. That sense-making occurs in the spiritual realm is not a new idea for many of us. That spirit speaks if you let it use you is not an education for those of us who us grew up in communities where book knowledge was not all that mattered and schools could not always be trusted. It comes as no surprise, then, that when we are in the position to teach, sometimes the impeccable repertoire of teaching, knowing, loving, and performing we've benefitted from is forgotten; with the repertoire forgotten, so too are its embodied lessons of life and living, without which academic information means next to nothing.

Dillard (2012) recognized,

> It is from our memories that we can recognize and better answer the question: "Who am I?" and collectively "Who are we?" This isn't just about being able to recognize times past on a calendar or datebook. This is fundamentally to see that our known, unknown, and yet-to-be known lives as human being are deeply imbued with meaning that is based in our memories. (p. 7)

Performing *A Praisesong for Johnnie* required me to remember myself. Johnnie's life lessons were important to me to teach, but I realized they could not be taught in just any way. I used what I call a "wreckless theatrics" that allows for the creation, presentation, and representation of culturally embodied knowledge for the purpose of loving better, including practices that allow for addressing multiple ruptures, intimate contradictions, and new visions (Brown, 2014).

The memory I presented of Johnnie was partial and incomplete. It was minor compared to all that could have been told. It was critical in the sense that I needed to show how the system failed him, and how we are complicit, those of us living with the privileges of Empire (Alexander, 2009). As Cozart (2010) wrote of her husband's deployment to Iraq, "I was filled with contempt, not for my husband, but for President Bush, whom I believed was taking my husband away to participate in an ill-conceived war" (p. 250), which is fully comprehensible to working and poor Black and Brown people whose involvement in the U.S. military is one of survival more than it is about patriotic duty. Those audience members versed in storytelling and Black history understood that the story I was telling was also one that asked them to fill in what I left blank. For example, my spoken mention of Johnnie's conversion to the Nation of Islam should have also brought to their minds and hearts Black men like Malcolm X—who once answered to Detroit Red, lead masses, change themselves, even as they remain faithful. So, while celebratory, Johnnie's praisesong was not uncritical, and it all taught.

I am coming to understand how my performing, my invocation of the spirit, affects students who are now doing their own thing in the academy, who take risk to achieve their dreams as Johnnie encouraged. With greater intention, I am instructing those who saw me call the name of my cousin and witnessed the power of performing research in spite of the academy's continued investments in consumer education and neoliberal public engagements. I know presenting and teaching toward wholeness reveals purpose, transforms the academy, and allows us to remember. I know that, even as we perform, particularly from the location of social sciences and the humanities, we are creating lifelines and disciplines of wellness. Given that the context in which we labor is not yet ready to meet the brilliance that is often our gifts, we perform anyway because the associational force provided by spirit moves us toward a necessary collective healing.

REFERENCES

Alexander, M. J. (2009). *Pedagogies of crossing: Meditations on feminism, sexual politics, memory, and the sacred*. Durham, NC: Duke University Press.

Brown, J., & Nyong'o, T. (2006). Recall and response: Black women performers and the mapping of memory. *Women & Performance: A Journal of Feminist Theory, 16*(1), 3–5. doi:10.1080/07407700600555063

Brown, R. N. (2014). "She came at me wreckless!: Wreckless theatrics as disruptive inquiry." In R. N. Brown, R. Carducci, & C. Kuby (Eds.), *Disrupting qualitative inquiry: Possibilities and tensions in educational research* (pp. 35–52). New York: Peter Lang.

Brown, R. N., Carducci, R., & Kuby, C. (2014). *Disrupting qualitative inquiry: Possibilities and tensions in educational research*. New York: Peter Lang.

Cacho, L. (2012). *Social death, racialized rightlessness, and the criminalization of the unprotected*. New York: New York University Press.

Callier, D. (2009). This work is dirty work. Unpublished paper.

Christian, B. (1988). The race for theory. *Feminist Studies, 14*(1), 67–79.

Cozart, S. (2010). When the spirit shows up: An autoethnography of spiritual reconciliation with the academy. *Educational Studies, 46,* 250–269. doi:10.1080/00131941003614929

DeFrantz, T. (2004). The Black beat made visible: Hip hop dance and body power. In A. Lepecki (Ed.), *Of the presence of the body: Essays on dance and performance theory* (pp. 64–81). Middletown, CT: Wesleyan University Press.

Dillard, C. (2000). The substance of things hoped for, the evidence of things not seen: Examining an endarkened feminist epistemology in educational research and leadership. *International Journal of Qualitative Studies in Education, 13*(6), 661–681. doi:10.1080/09518390050211565

Dillard, C. (2006a). *On spiritual strivings: Transforming an African American women's academic life.* Albany, NY: State University of New York Press.

Dillard, C. (2006b). When the music changes, so should the dance: Cultural and spiritual considerations in paradigm "proliferation." *International Journal of Qualitative Studies in Education, 19*(1), 59–76. doi:10.1080/09518390500450185

Dillard, C. (2012). *Learning to (re)member the things we've learned to forget: Endarkened feminisms, spirituality, and the sacred nature of research and teaching.* New York: Peter Lang.

Feldman, M., Sköldberg, K., Brown, R. N., & Horner, D. (2004). Making sense of stories: A rhetorical approach to narrative analysis. *Journal of Public Administration Research and Theory, 14*(2), 147–170. doi:10.1093/jopart/muh010

hooks, b. (2003). *Teaching community: A pedagogy of hope.* New York: Routledge.

Jagodzinski, J., & Wallin, J. (2013). *Arts-based research: A critique and a proposal.* New York: Sense Publications.

Jordan, J. (2002). *Some of us did not die: New and selected essays of June Jordan.* New York: Basic Civitas Books.

Keating, A. (Ed.). (2008). *Entre mundos/Among worlds: New perspectives on Gloria Anzaldúa.* New York: Palgrave Macmillan.

Langellier, K. (1999). Personal narrative, performance, performativity: Two or three things I know for sure. *Text and Performance Quarterly, 19*(2), 125–144. doi:10.1080/10462939909366255

Mattis, J. S. (2000). African American women's definitions of spirituality and religiosity. *Journal of Black Psychology, 26*(1), 101–122.

Ulysse, G. (2012). Invocation: Excerpts from *Because when God is too busy: Haiti, me, & THE WORLD.* In V. K. Valdés (Ed.), *Let spirit speak!: Cultural journeys through the African diaspora* (pp. 1–6). Albany, NY: State University of New York Press.

ENDNOTES

1. "John Nave: Operation Desert Storm," 11-01, http://www.glynn.k12.ga.us/BHS/Juniorprojects/Durham01/kimberlyn18601/
2. "Desert Storm," http://www.u-s-history.com/pages/h2020.html
3. Gulf War Syndrome. A Lecture by Captain Joyce Riley 1/15/96. http://all-natural.com/riley.html
4. https://www.cia.gov/library/reports/general-reports-1/iraq_wmd_2004/chap6.html
5. Germ Warfare Against America the Desert Storm Plague and Cover up. http://all-natural.com/intro.html

CHAPTER TWO

Navigating Inhibited Spaces

Black Female Scholars' Re-articulation of Knowledge Production in the Academy

LAMEESA W. MUHAMMAD, ANDREA L. TYLER,
ADONICA JONES-PARKS, AND LARA CHATMAN

INTRODUCTION

Black men and women often work in spaces in which they have been historically prohibited and struggle against inequitable and systemic contemporary cultural norms that seek to further suppress and not only prohibit, but inhibit legitimized thinking and practice. Although both the Black male and female bodies face oppressive attitudes and behaviors that seek to delegitimize their very nature, the Black woman, because of both her race and gender, suffers an intersection of oppression that lends itself to multiple marginalization and an experience in which she is treated in a way that marks her struggle persistent, insistent, and unique in the ability to attain acknowledgment and respect in a world that deems her a raced, gendered, and cultural deviant (Turner, 2002). Despite this struggle, the Black woman consciously strives to affirm and celebrate the intersection of raced, gendered, and cultural identities although we continue to find ourselves in places of restrictive vocalization by those who do not share our multiple identity (Tillman, 2012).

There has been an increase in research focused on the impact of race and gender for Black women as we work to achieve academic pursuits in predominantly White institutions (Benjamin, 1997; Berry & Mizelle, 2006; Collins, 1990; Cooper, 2006; Gregory, 1995; Mabokela & Green, 2001; Turner, 2002). Much of this research acknowledges that due to both the race and gender of Black women, our treatment in academic spaces subjects our voices to be filtered, restricted, under-represented, and poorly reflected in curricula in a manner that continues to limit our contribution to offer ways of knowing that run counter to the more normative views (Arya, 2012; Wilson, 2012). Black women not only struggle in this society for self-definition and the ability to be heard, but we fight against stereotypes and oppressive attitudes that limit opportunities, degrade our self-concept, and render us invisible through dual subjugation by both the Black male and by White women (Aronson, 2003; Collins, 1990; Heywood & Drake, 1997).

This work seeks to explore the lived experiences of four Black women who navigate historically prohibited spaces as scholars by showcasing a struggle, rethinking, and re-articulation on how we come to know what we do as rooted in a claim or reclaiming of our own identity. Dillard (2000) posits that the reality from which Black women come to know and articulate our own reality is couched in historical roots of Black feminist thought, which embodies a cultural standpoint located in the intersection and overlap of the social constructions of race, gender, and other identities shrouded in both historical and contemporary oppressive and inhibitive experiences. Endarkened feminist epistemology allows educational research to be an ideological undertaking that is embedded within traditions, perspectives, viewpoints, cultural understandings, and the discourse style of the researcher (Dillard, 1995, 2000; James & Farmer, 1993; Lather, 1986; Packwood & Sikes, 1996; Scheurich & Young, 1997; Stanfield, 1994).

This work embraces performance narrative autoethnographic writing as a manifestation of the dialogical praxis of critical theory and the performing body as self-reflexive, heretically liberating and invocative of a challenge, change, embrace, and interrogation of the performance itself by announcing the process as its own politics and political consensus (Conquergood, 1985; Spry, 2001; Trihn, 1991). Essentially, this work challenges traditional forms of knowledge production by reaching outside of normative parameters by giving voice to the voiceless by providing a platform of re-articulation in an imagined yet liberated space.

THE WAY I KNOW IT TO BE: AN INTERVIEW WITH MYSELF (LIFE NOTE 1—ADONICA)

Me: Why did you want to pursue a doctorate? What moved you in that direction? I think you refer to the pursuit of a doctorate as *the doctoral journey*.

Me: Uhmmm-Yes, it is a journey that can not be explained unless you actually experience it.

I began my pursuit of a doctorate in January 2005. I was an assistant principal at the time at an urban, low-performing, high special education public high school that was "redesigned" with a career technical educational focus. Once there, it struck me that something was wrong with public education. Why didn't this school have the resources needed to improve the plight of a predominantly Black population that was over 60% free/reduced-priced lunch and over 30% special education while many public magnet schools are plentiful in their resources? There were glaring inequities. I was confused, so I thought that researching the root causes would provide me with enlightenment. The more I observed, the angrier I became. I applied for a doctoral program, was accepted, and began the journey.

Me: Did you ever want to walk away from the doctoral journey?

Me: There was a lot of drama including professional and personal setbacks that often had me asking, *Why in the hell did you take this on? Are you insane?*

I had no clue what the doctoral journey would be like, but I was committed. Why? Simple: I pursued a doctorate for the children, for my community, for my people, for me—to be the best teacher and educational leader that I could be. I'm a womanist, which Alice Walker (1983) defines as a woman who is "committed to the survival and wholeness of entire people, male *and* female." Sista Souljah (1992) said, "I'm estrogen first/I'm Black first/I want what's good/For my people first." This is who I am.

Me: Did you find some things out during your journey that you surprised you?

Me: Huhm. Did I! (rolling eyes) While my focus was on the educational genocide of Black males, I observed that Black girls had their own set of issues pertaining to their education and schooling. I never considered myself a feminist, but I became aware that Black women were *very* oppressed, especially in the academy and even in K 12. Because of the alienation I felt in higher ed being a Black woman, I became more tuned in to what Black girls were going through in school and life. They were going through it and were angry. I came into the academy angry because of the educational disenfranchisement of Black children, but I left with my doctorate in hand, angrier. I loved the predominately White institution that I attended, the intellectual stimulation and growth that I experienced, and being around Black people who were emerging scholars. It was empowering. But there was this insidious side to the experience that was stifling. The Black women in the program lacked mentoring and there were sistas who started the program several years before me, who had fallen by the wayside. Myself and a friend, Lameesa, who was also in the program, both noticed that the Black men—yes, the Black *males*—were getting preferential treatment. They were privileged! They were given scholarships, fellowships, encouraged to publish and presented at conferences while the Black women were left in the dark until after the fact. I would *never* have believed that this could happen at a PWI, but it did. The brothas graduated with jobs, too. Another issue was that although I was a K 12 administrator working on an Ed.D. and able to take theory classes along with the Ph.D. students in the program, I still felt as though I was not considered a scholar because of my K 12 experience. It was assumed that I wanted to stay in K 12. Uh, no I wanted out. No one bothered to ask me what I wanted. I graduated having no clue how to navigate the job search for higher ed positions, with no publications, no transition plan, no advising, and no job. I have a doctorate, but I've had to start over and now I'm a triple threat: Black, female, and I hold a terminal degree. I guess the university thought us, Black women, would find a way to survive. Although we get overlooked and made invisible, we are threatening! The struggle is real before, during, and after the doctoral journey. Our struggle is permanent, like racism, but we can be empowered and unleash our silenced voices.

JUNE'S EDITION, IT LOOKS LIKE WE ARE NOT HURTING: PAINFUL PERSEVERANCE (LIFE NOTE 2—LARA)

"We Wear the Mask," a poem written by Paul Dunbar, resonated in my spirit after hours of reading and listening to women share their stories after I defended my dissertation. It appeared to me just as it had to these women, I removed my mask. I wore this mask for years while I managed school. The painful perseverance that I reveal through stories is powerful and elucidates how African American women navigate graduate school. Perseverance means to never give up, but *painful perseverance* means there were several strongholds. By painful perseverance, I speak to the various ways a person perseveres despite the situation and with all the thorns in your back. After reading some of these women's stories that say I was diagnosed with high failure, I kept pushing, I cried until my tear ducts dried up and stayed up all day and night until I could not decipher the difference. The perseverance that graduate school requires for many African American women influences other areas of their lives in painful ways. I will share several incidents that happened to me that caused me to silence myself for the duration of my program.

The day I defended, I faced the reality that I had no plans like many of my White or Black male counterparts. I wondered, What could I have done differently? The reality was, "I have a Ph.D. and no job." I take on some responsibilities for that, but not a lot. The part I own is that I had not properly talked about what I experienced and the part I don't own is that no one bothered to ask. So, I reflected back on my experience and realized that I no longer wear a mask. I knew that whatever kept me in school was going to keep me sane after the Ph.D.

During the doctoral journey, I considered quitting. My thoughts had nothing to do with my grades or finances, but were because of some experiences I had. I questioned why I faced these challenges. I experienced marginalization, social and academic isolation, passive aggressive treatment, and abrasive comments. I confronted these issues and decided that I would not be made "invisible."

As a result, I became furious because my "voice" needed to be heard and no one was listening. I began to silence myself because I felt situated in an environment where I had no power. This silence did not mean I feared speaking, but it was because I felt no one would understand me. I was often in classes taught by White men reading books by White male authors. In these classes, although I knew I was competent, that is not how I was made to feel. I was ignored. People questioned me about the way I dressed and even asked if I believed I could get a job given my fashionista style of dressing. Although, I knew that I would not change my style of dress, I was more bothered by the fact that no one else was being questioned about their appearance or their ability to be professional because of it. I was even told that I smelled like an an optometrist's office. Too afraid to respond or even report how uncomfortable such comments made me feel, I began to think about the various stereotypes that have plagued African American women for centuries. I felt like "mammy" for sacrificing my feelings, but I didn't want to speak up because I did not want to be labeled "sapphire," the angry, loud-talking and emasculating Black woman. I was not free to be me. Although I did finish, the pain I will never forget.

Despite all the suffering, indignities, and ignorance I faced, I was resilient. It was resilience that kept me surviving and strong. Many Black women in pursuit of higher education painfully persevere and display their resilience by using various coping methods. However, the most important aspect remains true; we compromise ourselves and our lives to deal with the various painful stressors we face and we persevere.

I WON'T SETTLE AND YOU CAN'T MAKE ME: A MONOLOGUE (LIFE NOTE 3—ANDREA)

> "If I didn't define myself for myself, I would be crunched into other people's fantasies for me and eaten alive." —*Audre Lorde*

I settled for something that goes against the very thing I stand on, my truth. I thought I could pretend to believe in someone else's explanation of knowledge. I lied to myself. I think the dominant discourse regarding knowledge production and thought is total crap. I believe there is a clear distinction between the way Black and White scholars produce knowledge and thought. I don't believe either position adds up to some perfect equation; however, I feel passionate that evoking the Eurocentric dominant viewpoint is incorrect.

As a counter-narrative to the Eurocentric discourse concerning knowledge production, Black scholars can speak to the scholarly contributions from Black female scholars (e.g., Davis, Collins, Walker, hooks, and Dillard) and how they have made exemplary contributions to Black feminist thought and knowledge production. I rest in their words and expressions because in many ways, they have gone beyond the hegemonic White female experiences of knowledge production. I feel empowered by the counter-narratives of Dillard, Collins, and Walker. I believe in the progression and I remember to articulate the theories and frameworks of these Black feminist scholars in my everyday life.

Feminist theories of the past are not applicable to me as a Black female because my experiences are different and more intense. For example, my Black vernacular about what I have experienced has a resonance that is both cultural and political. Out of necessity, I have spent time delving into the cultural and experiential nature of my academic oppression because for me to overcome the rhetoric, I unravel the multilayered texture of Black women's lives.

My story and how I process knowledge has perpetually been viewed through the lens of a Eurocentric feminist viewpoint. In doing so, this portrays the two lived experiences as somehow equal, harmonious, and interchangeable. These terms misrepresent who I am and the experiences I've had to overcome to arrive at this space and the discourse necessary to understanding significance, presence, intelligence, spirituality, engagement, and voice.

The scholarship of Black feminist thought and knowledge reproduction collides with the inherent "othering" and opposed thought of the dominant narrative. On the basis of such challenges, I desire to capture the process of oppression and "othering." That is why I metaphorically consider myself as a "diamond in the rough." This means that I am Black, female, strong, intelligent, and more knowledgeable than my misrepresentation. I aspire to explain reality and instruct on the ways to showcase the voice of Black females in the academy.

My experiences are like a Broadway stage performance with my life as the main character and the Eurocentric viewpoint the audience. I act out according to the characters in the play and pretend to be someone I am not while I wait for the applause of acceptance. Who are the characters in my struggle? The process of the struggle reveals narratives that explain and articulate the struggle while highlighting the differences in racial, cultural, and gendered identity. Exploring the nature of my existence with my White peers reveals a great divide inimical of a social transgression.

So, how do I position myself to stand, speak, and be heard? I stand in the room screaming at the top of my voice, while others spend a lifetime rejecting my existence. The objectification of my voice allows the oppressor to treat me impersonally and create distance. However, my voice, thought, and intellect are salient to my identity and being. The self-constructed space I create gives me a platform to tell who I am and what I represent and this expression is salient to me and my existence in the academy.

I reject the stance of feminist thought and knowledge production being equal for Black and White female scholars because it is not a viable, plausible testament to my person. There is an increase of criticism and loathing for the scholarship that continues to articulate the notion of equality among Black and White female scholars. I deny it. I choose not to conform and create a platform of freedom from and resistance to the traditional and oppressive norms of the academy that are inequitable and stand on my own stage. I see myself as a bird being let out of a cage; it's a feeling I can't describe—I'm free to speak back, up, and out!

TOO BLACK TO BE A TOKEN: A POETIC SOLILOQUY (LIFE NOTE 4—LAMEESA)

Too Black, No one knows how I feel
Lightened skin on the outside
Makes me a token whom they steal
Or whip on my backside

Rather have me in their classrooms
Teaching all white faces
Denying the blackness of my skin
Marked in red—The inhibited spaces

You don't think I have a doctorate
It has been conferred upon me
Amongst accolades and acquisitions
And two other highly honored and coveted degrees

You noticed me while I was a student
Thought you'd groom me and grace me
To be the only Black woman
In a place you won't take me

I studied and focused
For approximately six years
To leave the academy a little while later
Both jobless and in tears

Who said the doctorate pays off
Was speaking to certain aces
Who don't have to work hard
And are granted positions in high places

A female and Black
I am stigmatized perpetually
To Be Ole' Black Mammie
Whose function is defined as a reproductive key

To unleash and further
The progress of a nation

But you deny and denounce
All of my Black sisters hardened faces

You won't be stealing my cells
Like the late Henrietta Lacks
I remain too strong, too talented
And will always represent Black

My last name is not Johnson, Smith, or Mason
I carry another name
Which is exceedingly profiled
Amongst the bigots and racist

You call me a radical and refuse to believe
My intellect and pride
Wasn't stripped out of me
From the four hundred years cast aside

I always represent Black
And a feminine location
An infinite progeny
Of The Dogon Nation

CONCLUSION

These four distinct performance narrative autoethnographic writings display the singular and unique struggles of four Black women who pursued a terminal degree at a predominantly White institution. Each life note represents a memoir of particular ways of thinking, knowing, and understanding our experiences in spaces that remain restrictive to voices of women whose intersectionality and cultural ethos are stigmatized and delegitimized. These life notes posit each experience as unique, yet grounded in the roots of a shared racial, gender and cultural positioning while self-defining, legitimizing and validating Black female understanding and knowledge production in an alternative manner (Collins, 1990).

While our voices speak up to our own experiences as we travailed prohibited spaces in the academy in our seeking to attain our independent academic goals and aspirations, our words speak out to all others who share an experience of multiple marginalization who wish to achieve acknowledgment and respect in a world that deems our being as a raced, gendered, and cultural deviant. This work declares research as a responsibility in which our lived expressions on how we come to know what we do as answerable and obligated both to and by ourselves as well as the communities that have shaped us (Dillard, 2000). Black female scholarship is not antithetical to the traditional ways of knowing, but rather it is an embrace to acknowledge and respect our raced, gendered, and cultural identities. Our life notes represent a reclaiming of this identity by refusing to be muted, blurred, or ignored and thereby reinventing the self through a rethinking and rearticulation of not only who we claim to be, but who we are by speaking back.

REFERENCES

Aronson, P. (2003). Feminists or "postfeminists"? Young women's attitudes toward feminism and gender relations. *Gender and Society,* 17(6), 321–336.
Arya, R. (2012). Black feminism in the academy. *Equality, Diversity and Inclusion: An International Journal, 31*(5), 556–572.
Benjamin, L. (1997). *Black women in the academy: Promises and perils.* Gainesville: University Press of Florida.
Berry, T. R., & Mizelle, N. D. (2006). *From oppression to grace: Women of color and their dilemmas within the academy.* Sterling, VA: Stylus.
Collins, P. H. (1990). *Black feminist thought: Knowledge, consciousness, and the politics of empowerment.* New York: Routledge.
Conquergood, D. (1985). Performing as a moral act. Ethical dimensions in the ethnography of performance. *Literature in Performance, 5*(2), 1–13.
Cooper, T. L. (2006). *The sista' network: African-American women faculty successfully negotiating the road to tenure.* Boston, MA: Anker.
Dillard, C. B. (1995). Leading with her life: An African American feminist (re)interpretation of leadership for an urban high school principal. *Education Administration Quarterly, 31*(4), 539–563.
Dillard, C. B. (2000). The substance of things hoped for, the evidence of things not seen: Examining an endarkened feminist epistemology in educational research and leadership. *Qualitative Studies in Education, 13*(6), 661–681.
Gregory, S. T. (1995). *Black women in the academy: The secrets to success and achievement.* New York: University Press of America.
Heywood, L., & Drake, J. (1997). Introduction. In L. Heywood & J. Drake (Eds.), *Third wave agenda: Being feminist, doing feminism.* Minneapolis, MN: University of Minnesota Press.
James, J., & Farmer, R. (Eds.). (1993). *Spirit, space, and survival: African American women in (White) academe.* New York: Routledge.
Lather, P. (1986). Issues of validity in openly ideological research. Between a rock and a soft place. *Interchange, 17*(4), 63–84.
Mabokela, R. O., & Green, L. A. (2001). *Sisters of the academy: Emergent black women scholars in higher education.* Sterling, VA: Stylus.
Packwood, A., & Sikes, P. (1996). Adopting a postmodern approach to research. *Qualitative Studies in Education, 9*(3), 335–345.
Scheurich, J. J., & Young, M. D. (1997). Coloring epistemologies: Are our research epistemologies racially biased? *Educational Researcher, 26*(4), 4–16.
Souljah, S. (1992). The hate that hate produced. *360 Degrees of Power* [CD]. New York: Epic/SME Records.
Spry, T. (2001). Performing autoethnography: An embodied methodological praxis. *Qualitative Inquiry, 7*(6), 706–732.

Stanfield, J. H. (1994). Epistemological considerations. In J. H. Stanfield (Ed.), *Race and ethnicity in research methods* (pp. 16–38). Newbury Park, CA: Sage.

Tillman, L. (2012). Inventing ourselves: An informed essay for Black female scholars in educational leadership. *International Journal of Qualitative Studies in Education, 25*(1), 119–126.

Trihn, M. (1991). *When the moon waxes red: Representation, gender, and cultural politics.* New York: Routledge.

Turner, C. S. V. (2002). Women of color in academe: Living with multiple marginality. *Journal of Higher Education, 73*(1), 74–93.

Walker, A. (1983). *In search of our mother's gardens.* Orlando, FL: Harcourt.

Wilson, S. (2012). They forgot mammy had a brain. In G. Muhs, Y. Niemann, C. Gonza'lez, & A. Harris (Eds.), *Presumed incompetent: The intersections of race and class for women in academia* (pp. 65–77). Boulder, CO: University Press of Colorado.

CHAPTER THREE

"Out of the Mouths of Babes"

Using Cynthia Dillard's Endarkened Feminist Epistemology to Reveal Unseen Gendered Passageways

ANGELA N. CAMPBELL

INTRODUCTION

The Ella Baker Rites of Passage study advanced how adolescent Black girls negotiated intersecting identities in the midst of navigating interpersonal relationships in high school (Brown, 2009; Collins, 2000; Evans-Winters, 2005; King, 1988). Rites of passage (ROP) classes at Ella Baker Freedom Academy prepared students to use successful communication strategies to develop mutual trust, resolve peer conflicts, and embrace a healthy self-concept. ROP activities included trust building exercises, lessons on effective interpersonal communication with "other sisters," conflict resolution on the "hot seat," and a series of interactive dialogue about internalized oppression, sexism, male and female relationships, women's issues, domestic violence, and female confidence found in films, book excerpts, poetry, and special guest lectures. These nontraditional classes evoked intense conversation, debate, and challenges about ways to overcome the silences on important adolescent issues. Relational and identity concerns dominated most of these classes. In this context, rites of passage functioned as a female empowerment youth program.

My informants' reflections and counter-narratives revealed important lessons about developing a womanhood and sisterhood consciousness. The term *sisterhood* connotes the development of relational bonds that promote empathy, friendships, and collaboration among same-sex peers. This chapter examines how an endarkened feminist epistemology (EFE) *endarkens* or *deepens* our gendered and cultural understandings of adolescent girls' reflections of rites of passage. Dillard (2012) explains that EFE articulates,

> how reality is known when based in the historical roots of Black feminist thought, embodying a distinguishable difference in cultural standpoint, located in the intersection/overlap of the culturally constructed socializations of race, gender, and other identities and the historical and contemporary contexts of oppressions and resistance for African–American women. (p. 662)

EFE revealed important epistemological implications found in African ascendant[1] girls' voices. EFE embodies an emancipatory imperative that promotes holism and complementarity among men and women, girls and boys. The gender unifying and liberating aspects of EFE also echoed by Hudson-Weems (2003), Steady (1983), and Evans-Winters (2011) have thus shifted the discourse from blaming men and boys for the challenges that women and girls face to focusing on liberating solutions that benefit everyone. EFE directs our attention to the local, community-based, national, and continuity of transnational voices and cultures. This analytic lens focuses on girls' and women's issues using African ascendant females' ways of knowing and being in the world for the purpose of uplifting and healing learning communities. Dillard's perspective advances "a holistic view of the African woman, in relation to her community, echoes pre-colonial African practices and values regarding the physical as well as the spiritual well-being of the community" (p. 72). Dillard's EFE provides a viable theoretical framework to discuss the implications of ROP classes at Ella Baker Freedom Academy.

CONTEXTUALIZING RITES OF PASSAGE

Rites of passages (ROPs) have existed throughout human cultures worldwide (Blumenkrantz & Wasserman, 1998; Mbiti, 1970; Van Gennep, 1908). In contemporary times, ROPs have been important sites for adolescent socialization in Black communities. They have included rituals, traditions, and practices that guide young people through the turbulent terrain of adolescence into adulthood (Alford, 2002; Butler-Derge, 2009; Goggins II, 1996; Hill, 1992). African American ROPs emerged in independent Black institutions as a result of the resurgence of Black community control over schools in the 1980s and an Afrocentric education movement of the 1990s in cities nationwide (Bush, 2004; Murrell, 2002; Pollard & Ajirotutu, 2000). These ROP programs emanated from Black people's struggle to attain a just and equitable education that was also capable of providing the youth positive gendered racial socialization (Brookins, 1996; Hill, 1992; Warfield-Coppock, 1992).

To elaborate, gendered racial socialization refers to a holistic process of training in preparation for human functioning in the family, community, school, and society. It is a process of inculcating youth with the necessary values, principles, and accurate historical and cultural knowledge to resist deracination. Effective gender socialization is rooted in an awareness of *equality*, not necessarily *sameness*, and complimentary roles and responsibilities among men and women who work interdependently to uplift and maintain functional and organized families and communities. In these programs male or female youth are guided in their maturation as socially responsible young adults who learn how to contribute to their families and communities (Brookins, 1996; Warfield-Coppock, 1992; Wilson, 1992).

Over the years, rites of passages have become a cornerstone of African-centered education, reflecting key tenets in African-centered pedagogy[2] (Akoto, 1992; Lee, 1994; Murrell, 2002). Since the late 20th century, ROPs have been offered in community organizations, churches, and urban schools (Blumenkrantz & Gavazzi, 1993; Blumenkrantz & Goldstein, 2010; Warfield-Coppock, 1992, 1994). Literature on ROPs identifies formal and informal rites of passage, as well as school- and community-based ROP programs that buffer the effects of racism, poverty, and sexism among Black youth (Alford, 2002; Blumenkrantz & Wasserman, 1998; Brookins, 1996; Butler-Derge, 2009; Goggins, 1996; Hill, 1992; Lewis, 1988; Rodriguez, 2010; Warfield-Coppock, 1992, 1994). Literature on ROPs explains that they provides instruction on African-centered values,[3] Black history, while promoting positive and empowering gendered ethnic images and messages in single-sex spaces (Brookins, 1996; Butler-Derge, 2009; Hill, 2009; Hilliard, 1997, 2002; Warfield-Coppock, 1992).

In addition, research studies on African American youth programs link healthy ethnic and gender identity development to personal empowerment, academic achievement, and decreased relational aggression among adolescents (Belgrave, 2004; Sears, 2010). ROP programs have historically connected healthy character and identity development to mitigating injustice, resolving community issues, and group empowerment. With increasing reports of bullying, school violence, police brutality, and juveniles entering the criminal justice system, school-based ROP function as sources of youth empowerment and contribute to cultivating a positive, non-violent school culture (Blumenkrantz & Wasserman, 1998; Brookins, 1996; Butler-Derge, 2009; Campbell, 2013). Research on urban African American adolescent girls suggests that culturally relevant learning models promote problem-solving capacities, thus lessening girls' relational aggression (Belgrave, 2004; Leff et al., 2009; Warfield-Coppock, 1994). The Ella Baker ROP Study echoed these findings and more. Next, I narrate what led up to these findings and how the use of an asset-based lens located the funds of cultural knowledge and traditions of the students and staff at the site, and led to revelations about ways to support adolescent girls' same sex peer relationships and transitions into womanhood.

ELLA BAKER RITES OF PASSAGE (ROP) STUDY

My desire to challenge deficit notions of Black women and girls fueled my interest in adolescent rites of passage (ROP) programs. The Ella Baker Rites of Passage study,[4] one of the first of its kind, addressed the dearth of research on female ROPs and produced new insights on ROP as a potentially effective gender socialization and empowerment program. To that end, I conducted a 15-month ethnographic study at Ella Baker Freedom Academy (EBFA) with a group of 26, 11th-grade students, seven of whom were informants. Using multidisciplinary, asset-based approaches, I investigated how EBFA deployed gendered socialization practices through their ROP for adolescent Black girls and Latina who came from primarily lower income families. This study explored the internal and external social influences on Black girls' gendered passageways, and examined the girls' critical reflections of ROP. I used a Black feminist and African centered perspective to examine socialization processes of young women of color. Socialization at Ella Baker was conceptualized as an intergenerational and guided process that supported students' development of healthy identities, peer interactions, and critical consciousness (Campbell, 2013).

Study findings revealed that ROP classes supported many female students by developing (1) a critical awareness of sexism and internalized oppression; (2) an appreciation, esteem, and respect for themselves and each other; (3) positive academic identities through healthy female peer relationships via critical dialogue, trust building, and conflict resolution; (4) personal standards of womanhood; and (5) gendered passageways to womanhood and sisterhood in intergenerational and emotionally safe spaces, and across school contexts. The study illuminated the strengths and challenges of nontraditional adolescent rites of passage programs situated in African-centered institutions and Freedom schools. These study participants identified how ROP contributed to how these adolescent girls developed a sisterhood consciousness and proudly "wore" their womanhood.

STUDY LIMITATIONS

While the ROP classes at Ella Baker did not offer magical solutions for all of the study participants, they afforded most girls a safe space to begin the identity work required to proactively define themselves in the midst of supportive "sisters." More research is needed to verify the extent to which ROP or a combination of factors and school influences contributed to girls' social and academic identities and peer interactions. For example, some students suggested that they wanted to engage issues of sexuality and sexual orientation more often. One informant who self-identified as "bi" admitted that she wanted to discuss issues of sexuality in ROP more often. Some participants critiqued the ROP program by alluding to institutional and pedagogical impediments to them having more consistent and dynamic classes. Moreover, there is a need to understand non-school-related factors and relationships such as parental messages, home life, and SES. Future research is needed to assess the kinds and quality of supports provided to youth in programs such as nontraditional youth programs and rites of passages.

ENDARKENING SISTERHOOD WITH *UBUNTU*

Dillard's (2012) use of *Ubuntu* as an ontological and epistemological framework to restore culturally synchronized and relevant ways of knowing and being in school contexts is also used here to legitimize the voices of African ascendant girls (Ladson-Billings, 2000). As Dillard (2012) referenced Battle's (2009) articulation of *Ubuntu*, I synthesize them to frame the significance and legitimacy of identity work done in ROP classes at EBFA.

As female peers learned to eventually embrace their role and responsibilities to each other as "other sisters," they practiced strategies to resolve conflicts and set and reach goals collaboratively (Collins, 2000). To illustrate, the hot seat activity helped girls accomplish these "sisterhood" objectives. The hot seat was an interactive communication activity that called for clearing the air in a positive, yet intimate, question and answer session. This "air clearing" exercise allowed the girls to ask authentic questions of each other to clarify misunderstandings, build trust, and form bonds through honest dialogue.

While the girls gave the hot seat activity mixed reviews, I witnessed the girls release and learn how to manage negative emotions. This exercise helped them to challenge stereotypical beliefs and assumptions they held about each other. Most of the informants shared with me that the hot seat activity was usually productive, but occasionally incited more drama among the female students than resolved problems. Some informants described instances where they first assumed negative things about their female peers, and after the hot seat session better understood each other. Their comments suggested that the activity helped the girls to generate empathy and compassion. The hot seat activity *endarkened* the girls' understanding of themselves as multidimensional beings, filled with contradictions, insecurities, and myriad possibilities.

Endarkening the Ubuntu principle, "I am because we are" may be translated into "I am because *we are sisters.*" The formulation of sisterhood requires the drama of recognizing and dismantling "seductions" pervasively present in media images and societal messages found in comments such as "I hate girls" and "girls are too catty" (Dillard, 2012). EFE suggests holistic intellectual and spiritual practices that lead to extricating women and girls from seductions manifest in the deeply embedded lies about Black womanhood. ROP challenged the stereotypical assumption that Black women and girls are unable to connect as *other sisters* who can work together productively and get along. *Ubuntu* reflects an understanding of Black women and girls' shared needs, gifts, and power, and supports an intergenerational sisterhood consciousness. ROP girls considered before and after their arguments and verbal disagreements more constructive avenues to handle pressure, gossip, sadness, attention, and rejection from young women and young men. The ROP process of creating sisterhood revealed a paradox. The girls tried to avoid closeness while they yearned for deeper connection. I discerned this much later in the study as the girls' post-study responses confirmed their appreciation for sisterhood in ROP. The girls' resistance to ROP initially suggested a fear or vulnerability in being *sisters*. While a safe space was created for them to reveal themselves, the girls were usually resistant, and those who embraced the process took the most risks.

ROP invoked a process of moving girls and women toward an empowering personal and collective identity rooted in humanization and oneness as an act of the sacred. The concept of self-love is intentionally connected to accepting and embracing the self and others. In *Learning to (Re)member the Things We Learned to Forget*, Dillard (2012) advances lessons for revitalizing African ascendant female relationships. Her work contributed to my research on girls' relational dynamics in secondary school through unveiling the sacred possibilities of sisterhood and womanhood. These narrative exchanges found in interview and ethnographic data illuminated Dillard's notions of *stories as gifts* of the *sacred* and *lessons to remember* the ancestral wisdom analogous to the symbolism of the *beads*. Dillard writes, "Remembering our beads provides us the strength, courage and wisdom to withstand the seductions that do not value who we are and the dignity to affirm ourselves, our memories, and our cultural knowledge and legacies" (p. 49). The "beads" represent African ascendant cultural traditions and rituals. I used Dillard's EFE lessons to analyze the girls' reflections, dialogue, and field observations using knowledges rooted in the African diaspora and local communities.

DEVELOPING A *WOMANHOOD* CONSCIOUSNESS IN *SISTERHOOD*

ROP girls established interdependent connections that allowed them to bond, self-actualize, and reach collective goals. One of the 11th-grade female informants responded to an open-ended question about what she appreciated about her rites of passage classes. Erica shared the following:

> I mean, rites helps us a lot... it's a positive and influential class most times, but not always... I like how it helps us see the importance of bonding with our rites teacher and other women teachers at the school. I model myself after them... watching how they carry themselves... how they teach us, the way they spend time with us... they teach us how to handle situations. (Interview, 4/13/12)

Erica explained further that she and other students frequently go to their female teachers and get advice about their problems and their lives. She admitted that "they teach us about who we are as Black women and how to stay strong and stuff like that. The teachers influence me more I think" (Interview, 4/13/12). Rites of passage classes for adolescent girls facilitated students' building trust and positive interpersonal relationships with peers and adult women. Study participants shared the ways these classes offered guidance and safe space for "real talk." Over time in ROP, they developed a critical awareness of sexism, internalized oppression, and negative racial/gendered stereotypes about Black women and girls in U.S. society and in the media. They learned to use the "community cultural wealth" they were developing in ROP to resist violence, internalized oppression, and "controlling stereotypes" (Collins, 2000; Yosso, 2005).

Patterns in these narratives revealed how these classes supported students' agency (Evans-Winters, 2011), a positive self-concept, and empowering definitions of womanhood. The interview transcript is rich in themes of agency and taking control of the power to define her reality as a woman. Erica suggested the role ROP played in her evolution into the woman that she is today. Her words express a burgeoning sense of agency, critical inquiry, and recognition that she is not alone. Similar to the goals of EFE, Erica's reflections suggest that intergenerational collaboration and communication are important dimensions of sisterhood and womanhood development. Not only does EFE provide the conceptual tools to unpack the students' discourses, it alerts the researcher to allow the girls to speak up and out as they gain confidence in sharing their stories, singing their songs, and embracing their power. The following excerpts address the students' views on how ROP influenced their understandings of womanhood and sisterhood.

> **Rosia**: I think that in itself ROP has been a marvelous type of experience. I don't think anybody in other type of schools have taken a class like that, that actually gives you a chance to be raised in school; it's kind of weird you're being raised you're being taught how to be a woman or be a man in a CLASS.

ROP influenced study participants to develop familial and social capital as they recognized the value of "sisterhood" and developed mutual respect and appreciation for one another in fictive kinship relationship as "other sisters" (Collins, 2000;

Evans-Winters, 2011a and b; Yosso, 2005). The girls' evolving development of a "sisterhood consciousness" and "sisterhood bonds" enabled them to resist relationally aggressive behaviors, and instead resolve and prevent conflicts through positive, critical discourse. These historical markers highlight African Americans' survival through the maintenance of fictive kinship relationships. For example, Risa, another informant, explained,

> Rites of passage helped a lot of us with different situations and these encounters with people can definitely help you develop your maturity and know what the boundaries are like, for instance, fighting here [is] unacceptable, that's one part that prepares you for college and being mature. You cannot just decide I'm gonna punch her in the face... I have better examples here and the school boundaries dictate... how you conduct yourself as a person.... Rites just rounds you, helps us feed off of... positive energy. (Interview, 4/13/12)

ROP provided students a safe space to practice empathy, humanizing differences, remaking "the other" as an extension of the self. Rather than punching a female peer in the face to resolve a problem or project pain or resentment onto another, the girls practiced critical dialogue and problem pose via questioning assumptions and commonly held beliefs. Risa's commentary above spoke of a sisterhood identity most reflective of the freedom school mission of personal and collective transformation. The school culture promotes normative dictates about resolving problems rather than fighting about them. Resolving relational tensions did not occur for the girls instantaneously, but rather iteratively. Several informants commented that ROP cultivated an inner world of freedom in which they created success strategies for themselves and one another collectively. As in the process of bead making, EFE framework, these students' experiences illuminate a process of excavating deeper meanings about their experiential connections with their peers and the role of other adult women in their lives. EFE pushes researchers and practitioners to reach higher levels of critical reflection, mutual understanding, and empathy. The researcher is urged to demonstrate a holistic commitment to re-humanize educational spaces for young women and girls of color.

In the following excerpt, Laura, a student informant, shared a poignant story about her evolving sisterhood consciousness after watching Tyler Perry's film *For Colored Girls*. The film, she confessed,

> made us closer after we watched for colored girls it impacted a lot of people at the same time it caused a confrontation; the boys got there and some boys got in the room and the girls got upset with the girls who cried in front of the boys... a lot of the girls reacted... [and asked] How we can be ourselves and stuff? At that time it brought a lot of girls closer. (Interview, 5/1/12)

As this excerpt reveals, ROP provided a context for girls to liberate themselves from external definitions and directives. They found a space among peers and adult women to share their truths, fears, and need for belonging. They formed bonds through critical and empathetic dialogue on trauma shown in the film, witnessed, or experienced.

In addition, ROP encouraged critical dialogue in support of students' social and academic identities and resiliency. For example, an informant named Erica expressed how ROP inspired her and others to become "intellectual warriors." When I asked her to comment on the relationship between ROP and academics she shared that the classes aided her focus in math class, for instance, since she was no longer focused on her problem, as she described, "fighting a girl after school." Instead, she focused on learning math. This salient response suggested that focus on academics occurred by default, a consequence of ROP participation that imparted how to responsibly resolve or prevent conflicts. In this way, ROP prepared the girls with an "emotional readiness to learn" (Nakkula, 2009; Porterfield, 2013). Erica, as did other informants, expressed how ROP classes set the tone for "sisterhood," which required strategies for maintaining positive feelings about each other. These sessions provided strategies for the girls to take responsibility for their actions and the quality of their interactions. The ROP goals also reinforced the freedom school mission for students to use their academic, intellectual skills and diverse talents for personal and collective transformation and for social justice imperatives.

During the Ella Baker study, the process of data analysis was akin to Dillard's discussion of remembering the lessons we learned to forget as symbolized by the collaborative efforts of bead making. In these lessons, the wisdom "beads" promote preserving intergenerational traditions of Black women and girls. The beads were reminders to stay true to one's calling and purpose. They functioned to challenge oppressive seductions. Dillard's lessons on the "beads" urge Black women and girls to grow, to go beyond their present awareness and evolve in consciousness individually and collectively. The multisensory "beads" symbolized the life enhancing gendered traditions of African women and girls. ROP, like bead making, was a process that invoked clarity and direction from caring mothers and our sisters in community. Beadwork mirrors the process of Black woman's/girl's learning to remember lessons long forgotten in the seductions of Euro-American, middle-class-dominated cultural experience, media, values, and traditional methods of schooling.

WEARING MY WOMANHOOD

Inspired by Trapeta Mason's poem, "How you gonna wear your womanhood?" students created poems about the kind of women they wanted to be. They discussed critical reflections of how they were going to wear their womanhood. The teacher recited,

"Some chicks wear womanhood on the seat of their panties... street style respect.... Always a party in their drawers... but no one's home upstairs... some ladies wear their *womanhood in alligator pumps, will do whatever and whomever* to stay on *top*..." So, now, you all tell me at least three ways you will wear your womanhood. (Field notes, November 18, 2012)

The ROP girls shared their womanhood poems:

Deirdre shared, I wear my womanhood with *self-respect; a wife, a mother*, and a lawyer..." Keisha announced, "I wear my womanhood... *respectfully*... I wear my womanhood with *power... spiritually...* with *Pride, cocky, and with confidence*. (Field notes, November 18, 2011)

The ROP girls asserted their agency and capacity to define themselves in contrast to the stereotypes. They linked holistic aspects to Black femininities in notions of womanhood rooted in confidence, pride, and spirituality. EFE provides a lens to locate Black women's and girls' holistic connections to human and divine experiences, liberating their present experiences in a communal, interdependent context. Dillard's framework also bolsters the meta-meaning making process in feminist ethnography by locating sacred significance of critical, personal reflection.

Reflecting on the beads conceptually spawned my growth as a researcher particularly during member checking of findings. Although I was a researcher during the Ella Baker Study, I was a co-participant in the process of evolving the meanings of sisterhood and womanhood. I diminished my ego and became vulnerable. I opened my heart to learn from my young, novice co-researchers who comprised my study participants. It was their story, not only my analysis that mattered. Their voices answered the research questions. My stories were intertwined with theirs, as I was, too, a Black girl, an evolving African ascendant. I empowered my informants to teach me as I also learned to walk away from the seductions of many colliding worlds from media to academe. Seductions emerged in the form of controlling stereotypes (Collins, 2000), messages, music, and images that influence relational aggression, individualism, materialism, and dehumanization.

The process of *endarkening* the analysis of Black girls' experiences in ROP required recognition of the sacred. Attending to and attaining well-being constitute the sacred found in the spiritual, physical, intellectual, and emotional dimensions of humanity. Sacredness in this context is holistic and multidimensional. Holistic healing was a concept explored in ROP in moments of seductive transcendence. Sacred experiences in ROP did not represent perfection and absolute answers about identity and relational development. Instead, an *endarkened feminism* foregrounded the *sacred dimensions of* female ROP. Sacredness rather than religiosity was restored in ROP. Sacredness was expressed in wisdom sayings, critical reflections, and debates. In tears and laughter new possibilities of sisterhood and womanhood were born. Promise and positivity in our relationships were restored. Space was created in ROP for girls and women to think with and about each other and not for each other. Being *for* rather than *against* each other reflected the *endarkened* sacredness of ROP.

Endarkening the analysis of girls' experiences led to unearthing the possible healing and restorative powers of ROP. Although there were no miraculous cure-alls associated with ROP, these classes encouraged the girls to develop a conscious and contemplative journey with "other sisters" and "other mothers." Over time my informants' seductive resistance to ROP was replaced with a gradual acceptance of sisterhood. *Endarkened feminisms* allowed me to understand how out of girls' challenges hope was restored, and out of existing chaos emerged peace. *Endarkened feminisms* empowered me and the girls and women of Ella Baker Freedom Academy to create beautiful beadwork in rites of passage together.

CONCLUSION

Through a challenging process of getting to know each other at deeper levels and in more authentic ways, ROP girls learned slowly and iteratively over time to value *sisterhood*, and to endure moments of vulnerability to invest deeply in female peer relationships. They disrupted controlling stereotypes about the inability of Black girls to get along in unity and support each other as *other sisters* (Collins, 2000). The girls' tumultuous journeys allowed them to experience the value of sisterhood as they helped one another consider their personal definitions of womanhood. Among the informants at Ella Baker a sisterhood consciousness developed that encouraged these students to shore up an ethic of Black love and care for self and others in intergenerational, sisterhood relationships (Dillard, 2012).

In this way, the Ella Baker ROP research highlights the possibilities for schools to create safe spaces for urban youth to move toward self-actualization through self-acceptance, personal definitions of womanhood, and sisterhood. The keys to unlocking many of the doors and institutional barriers in America may be found in Black women's relationships with each other. It is important for educators to integrate academic and gendered socialization as chief priorities in a holistic education model. Educating the "whole child" requires the integration and cultivation of multiple forms and funds of knowledge, and the active creation of emotionally safe, sacred spaces that supportively prioritize students' gendered ethnic identity and relational development.

REFERENCES

Akoto, K. A. (1992). *Nation building theory & practice in Afrikan centered education*. Washington, DC: Pan Afrikan World Institute.

Alford, K. A. (2002). Cultural themes in rites of passage: Voices of young African American males. *Journal of African-American Studies* 7(1), 3–26.

Battle, M. (2009). *Ubuntu: I in you and you in me*. New York: Seabury Books.

Belgrave, F. Z. (2004, August). An evaluation of Sisters of Nia: A cultural program for African-American girls. *The Journal of African-American Psychology, 30*(3), 329–343.

Blumenkrantz, D. G., & Gavazzi, D. G. (1993). Guiding transitional events for children and adolescents through a modern day rite of passage. *The Journal of Primary Prevention, 13*(3), 199–212.

Blumenkrantz, D. G., & Goldstein, M. B. (2010). Rites of passage as a framework for community interventions with youth. *Global Journal of Community Psychology Practice, 1*(2), 42–50.

Blumenkrantz, D. G., & Wasserman, D. L. (1998). What happens to a community intervention when the community doesn't show up? Restoring rites of passage as a consideration for contemporary community intervention. *Family Science Review, 11*, 239–258.

Brookins, C. (1996). Promoting ethnic identity development in African American youth: The role of rites of passage. *Journal of Black Psychology, 22*(3), 388–417.

Brown, R. N. (2009). *Black girlhood celebration toward a hip-hop feminist pedagogy*. New York: Peter Lang.

Bush, L. V. (2004). Access, school choice, and independent Black institutions: A historical perspective. *Journal of Black Studies, 34*(3), 386–401.

Butler-Derge, S. R. (2009). *Rites of passage: A program for high school African American males*. Lanham, MD: University Press of America.

Campbell, A. N. (2013). *Gendered passageways in Freedom School: An ethnographic study of adolescent girls' journeys to womanhood* (Unpublished doctoral dissertation). Temple University.

Collins, P. H. (2000). *Black feminist thought: Knowledge, consciousness, and the politics of empowerment* (2nd ed.). Cambridge: Routledge.

De Cuir-Gunby, J. T. (2009). A review of the racial identity development of African American adolescents: The role of education. *Review of Educational Research 79*(1), 103–124.

Dillard, C. B. (2012). *Learning to (re)member the things we've learned to forget*. New York: Peter Lang.

Evans-Winters, V. E. (2005). *Teaching Black girls: Resiliency in urban classrooms*. New York: Peter Lang.

Evans-Winters, V. E. (2011a). Critical epistemologies in social foundations: A postwomanist pedagogy. In R. Brock, C. S. Mallot, & L. E. Villaverde (Eds), *Teaching Joe L. Kincheloe* (pp. 145–154). New York: Peter Lang.

Evans-Winters, V. E. (2011b). *Teaching Black girls: Resiliency in urban classrooms* (2nd ed.). New York: Peter Lang.

Goggins, L., II. (1996). *African-centered rites of passage and education*. Chicago, IL: African American Images.

Hill, P. (1992). *Coming of age. Black male rites-of-passage*. Chicago, IL: Black Images.

Hilliard, A. G., III. (1997). *SBA: The reawakening of the African mind*. San Francisco, CA: Makare. Gainesville, FL.

Hilliard, A. G., III. (2002). *African power: Affirming African indigenous socialization in the face of the culture wars*. Gainesville, FL.

Hudson-Weems, C. (2003). Africana womanism. In A. Mazama (Ed.), *The Afrocentric paradigm* (pp. 153–164). Trenton, NJ: Africa World Press.

Karenga, M. (1988). *The African-American holiday of Kwanzaa: A celebration of family, community, and culture*. Los Angeles, CA: University of Sankore Press.

King, D. K. (1988). Multiple jeopardy, multiple consciousness: The context of a Black feminist ideology. *Signs: Journal of Women in Culture and Society, 14*(1), 42–72.

Ladson-Billings, G. (1995). But that's just good teaching! The case for culturally relevant pedagogy. *Theory into Practice, 34*(3), 159–165.

Ladson-Billings, G. (2000). Racialized discourses and ethnic epistemologies. In N. Denzin & Y. Lincoln (Eds.), *Handbook of Qualitative Research* (2nd ed. 257–277). Thousand Oaks, CA: Sage.

Ladson-Billings, G., & Tate, W. F. (1995). Toward a critical race theory of education. *Teachers College Record, 97*(1), 47–68.

Lee, C. D. (1994). African-centered pedagogy: Complexities and possibilities. In M. Shujaa (Ed.), *Too much schooling too little education: A paradox of Black life in White societies* (pp. 295–318). Trenton, NJ: Africa World Press.

Leff, S. S., Gullan, R. L., Paskewich, B. S., Abdul-Kabir, S., Jawad, A. F., & Power, T. J. (2009). An initial evaluation of a culturally-adapted social problem-solving and relational aggression prevention program for urban African-American relationally aggressive girls. *Journal of Prevention & Intervention in the Community, 37*, 260–274.

Lewis, M. (1988). *Herstory: Black female rites of passage*. Chicago, IL: African-American Images.

Mbiti, J. S. (1970). *African philosophy and religion*. New York: Anchor Books.

Murrell, P. C., Jr. (2002). *African-centered pedagogy: Developing schools of achievement for Black children*. Albany, NY: State University of New York Press.

Myers, L. J. (1988). *Understanding an Afrocentric world view: Introduction to an optimal psychology*. Dubuque, IA: Kendall Hunt.

Nakkula, M. (2009). Transforming self control through peer relationships. *Reclaiming Youth at Risk, 17*(4), 35–40.

Pollard, D. S., & Ajirotutu, D. S. (Eds.). (2000). *African-centered schooling in theory and practice*. Westport, CT: Greenwood.

Porterfield, L. (2013). *Hidden in plain sight: Young Black women, place, and visual culture* (Unpublished doctoral dissertation). Temple University.

Rodriguez, J. B. (2010). *The effect of Black rites of passage prevention program on adolescent ethnic identity, drug attitudes, behavior in the classroom and academic performance* (Unpublished doctoral dissertation). The College of William and Mary.

Sears, S. D. (2010). *Imagining Black womanhood: The negotiation of power and identity within the Girls Empowerment Project*. New York: New York University Press.

Skeggs, B. (2001). Feminist ethnography. In P. Atkinson, A. Coffey, S. Delamont, J. Loland, & L. Lofland (Eds.), *Handbook of ethnography*. 426–442 doi:10.4.135/9781848608337

Steady, F. C. (1983, June). African feminism: A global perspective. Keynote Speaker, Association of Black Women Historians Conference on Women of the African Diaspora, Howard University, Washington, DC.

Van Gennep, A. (1908). *The rites of passage*. (M. Vizedom & G. Caffee, Trans.). Chicago, IL: University of Chicago Press. (Original work published 1906)

Warfield-Coppock, N. (1992). The rites of passage movement: A resurgence of African centered practices for socializing Black youth. *Journal of Negro Education, 61*(4), 471–482.

Warfield-Coppock, N. (1994). Images of African sisterhood: Initiation and rites of passage to womanhood. *Baobab Associates*. Washington, DC.

Wilson, A. N. (1992). *Understanding black adolescent male violence: Its prevention and remediation*. New York: Afrikan World Infosystems.

Yosso, T. J. (2005). Whose culture has capital? A critical race theory discussion of community cultural wealth. *Race Ethnicity and Education, 8*(1), 69–91.

ENDNOTES

1. I use Cynthia Dillard's (2012) term "African ascendant," which suggests an identity rooted in and rising upward toward holistic liberation, as opposed to "descendant" connoting an identity rooted in a legacy of oppression. African ascendant and Black in this context are interchangeable. African ascendant denotes ethnic/racial identities of those whose ancestors come from Africa who share African ways of knowing and being in the world. In this case, the term refers to African American, Black, and Brown (Latina and/or mixed race, multiethnic group) female youth.
2. Murrell (2002) defines African-centered pedagogy as "concerned with the acquisition of self-determination and self-sufficiency for African people" (p. 37).
3. Myers (1988) identifies an overarching humanistic African worldview that recognizes unity of spirit, body, and material reality. Karenga (1988) identifies eight principles from the Nguzo Nane including (1) Heshima (Respect); (2) Umoja (Unity); (3) Kujichagulia (Self-Determination); (4) Ujima (Collective Responsibility); (5) Ujamaa (Cooperative Economics); (6) Nia (Purpose); (7) Kuumba (Creativity); and (8) Imani (Faith). Hilliard (1997; p. 2) articulates the ancient kemetic (Egyptian) principles of Djehuty and Maat, that is, truth, justice, harmony, order, balance, and propriety to all humanity.
4. Also titled "Gendered Passageways in Freedom School: An Ethnographic Study of Adolescent Girls' Journeys to Womanhood."

CHAPTER FOUR

Rising Harriett Tubmans

Exploring Intersectionality and African American Women Professors

DARLENE RUSSELL, LISA HOBSON, AND
DENISE TALIAFERRO-BASZILE

INTRODUCTION

This chapter focuses on the experiences of three African American women faculty members employed as tenure-track professors at three universities across the United States. In this auto-ethnographic rendering, we sought to identify challenges, obstacles, strategies, and options of/for tenured and nontenured Black women currently navigating higher education. For this project, we examined (a) how the lack of support mechanisms in research and professional associations often define the experiences and limit the success of African American women professors and (b) how challenging and reversing the past social structures would assist in gaining tenure and promotions.

Through our narratives, we engage and interrogate theories of self, rationality, history, voice, place, power, and knowledge as they are shaped by intersectionality, which is the coinciding and contradicting relations of race, gender, and class. Ultimately, we work within a critical approach where we advocate for emancipatory policies (Creswell, 2007).

Some authors assert the most salient and prevailing of the *multiple* identities of women of color in the academy is race. Ladson-Billings and Tate (1995) discussed how race is at the nucleus of American life—it shapes, defines, and stratifies us. Turner (2002) noted women of color in the professoriate experience *multiple marginality*, which is evidenced in some of the following ways: pressure to conform, social invisibility, isolation, exclusion from informal peer networks, limited sources of power, fewer opportunities for sponsorship, stereotyping, and personal stress.

The vortex of social positions and identities lies within intersectionality. Intersectionality is "the intersection of single dimensions of multiple categories, rather than at the intersection of the full range of dimensions of a full range of categories, and that is how complexity is managed" (McCall, 2005, p. 1781). Brah and Phoenix (2004) describe intersectionality as "signifying the complex, irreducible, varied, and variable effects which ensue when multiple axis of differentiation—economic, political, cultural, psychic, subjective and experiential—intersect in historically specific contexts" (p. 76). Furthermore, these authors assert that the various aspects of social life cannot be compartmentalized in a distinct fashion.

Multiple marginality and *intersectionality* both address and envelop the dynamic experiences reflected in the multiple threads of race, gender, and class in the lives of women of color (McCall, 2005). Thus, Black women and other women of color occupy space in a host of categories as it pertains to race, ethnicity, gender, and class, and within this space conflict, indifference, and/or support can exist.

CONCEPTUAL FRAMEWORK

Collins (1991) stated, "Stories, narratives, and Bible principles are selected for their applicability to the lived experiences of African Americans and become symbolic representations of a whole wealth of experience" (p. 211). In this chapter, we provide a cultural portrait of situations we have experienced as African American women navigating academia. Creswell (2013) states, "How we write is a reflection of our own interpretation based on the cultural, social, gender, class, and personal politics that we bring to research. All writing is 'positioned' and within a stance. All researchers shape the writing that emerges, and qualitative researchers need to accept this interpretation and be open about it in their writings" (p. 215).

The framework used for examination of our experiences evolved from the exploration of the legacy of Harriet Tubman in her work of helping slaves escape to freedom through the Underground Railroad. "The Underground Railroad is also the story of codes and secrets involving cunning systems of visual and oral communication, known only to those involved and reflecting the indomitable spirit of a people's resistance to slavery and desire to be free" (Tobin & Dobard, 1999, p. 66). Harriet Tubman encountered a number of challenges and did not always receive support within her ethnic group. Harriet Tubman had an end goal of helping others reach freedom. In navigating higher education, we have an end goal of reaching the *alleged* freedom of being (i.e., tenured/tenure-able and promoted/promotable).

In subsequent sections, we provide three narratives of intersectionality from our lived experiences as African American women working in higher education. In some instances it is hard to determine which intersection is more prevalent. In other instances, it's quite obvious whether race or gender is the catalyst for an experience. When referring to individuals other than ourselves, we used pseudonyms or omitted names.

PART 1. DARLENE'S STORY: CRITICAL STOPS ALONG THE UNDERGROUND RAILROAD OF ACADEMIA

Araminta was unquestionably stalwart and vigorous in her devotion to her life's work. Harriet Tubman, a thunderous warrior leader, was born Araminta Ross. This indelible iconic female emancipator led countless slaves to freedom, saved soldiers' lives as a nurse during the Civil War, rendered speeches for women's rights, and was a God-fearing woman. Tubman's hands warred, cared, organized, and prayed—all in the name of justice. This is the essence of authentic philanthropy. As an African American female professor, I try to embrace some of Tubman's attributes such as persevering in the midst of opposition (leadership) and reaching back to assist sisters of color to navigate the twirls of inequity in academia (concern). In this section, I will discuss some salient and critical points in my professoriate journey on the intersectionality railroad. This journey includes aboveground and underground experiences with administrators, faculty, and students where race and gender intersect, and how I compassed my own promised land through my faith in God.

critical stop #1

African American women continue to endure being sexualized, objectified, and mammy-fied in society. In places of higher learning all of this is manifested differently; it's sometimes packaged differently yet boils down to the same thing: oppression. One afternoon, a few years ago, I informed an administrator that I was pregnant. My husband and I were expecting our third child. I remember I was filled with a bit of trepidation as I approached the individual. As a faculty member with a leadership role, I was not sure how my news would translate. We had a strong and respectful working relationship inside of the workplace, with some kinship overtones. I believed the individual supported my work as a young scholar.

I entered the office asking for a moment of the individual's time. With an effusive greeting, I was welcomed to sit down and as the individual was flipping through a newspaper, I shared the news that I was expecting. The individual peered from the paper before placing it down.

"What? [pause] Are you a baby-maker?"

I was flabbergasted. In an instant I became a six-year-old girl in a great big chair, not knowing what to say, looking for her parents to bail her out. I clamored inside, but nothing exited my mouth. I was nervous and immobile.

"No… I'm not a baby-maker," I said, trying to recover. "This is a planned pregnancy and it's not like I'm trying to have a dozen children."

"Ah, yeah. I read an article in the *Times* that more middle- and upper-class African Americans are having more children these days as a status symbol of prosperity."

I nodded again, not knowing what to say. I informed the individual of my maternity leave date and said the customary end-of-meeting statements. This individual was an African American male, which made it especially difficult to digest. Who was this individual to render any commentary on my reproductive activity? Why did I feel I had to justify my pregnancy? I tried to unpack this exchange internally. I was and still am a happily married woman who was having another child. So what was wrong with this? The age of this individual had some bearing on the incident, too; he was old enough to be my father. If it had been a White male delivering the news that his wife is having another child, I surmise a cigar box would have been opened, coupled with high-fives and pats on the back.

With my head spinning, I headed to my car for my drive home. The entire exchange replayed in my mind and how it would certainly constitute a sexual harassment violation. I remember calling a close colleague and sharing the incident with her. She too was in disbelief. I still felt couched and wishing I would have stood up for myself.

On that winter afternoon, the intersection of race, gender, and class played out. The individual:

- Sexualized me by pigeonholing me into a stereotype and confusing my condition (being pregnant) with my whole identity and potential as a woman
- Objectified me by seeing me as an inanimate thing, a machine: a baby-making machine
- Classed me by assuming my socio-economic status and agenda on having children
- Raced me by knowing this was something that could not be said if I was a White woman (Insider/Outsider communication practices)

This *underground experience* situates me right in the center of intersectionality and multiple marginality. Racism and sexism are the two ubiquitous assailants in the assault of African American faculty in the academy. Racism and sexism usually work in concert against Black women (Logan Patitu & Hinton, 2003). This experience left me feeling inadequate and alienated and had the potential and potency to complicate the work environment and affect my productivity. To move forward, I dismissed the effrontery of this individual as ignorance. My faith in God was the fuel that propelled me to move beyond that day, and still be able to work with this individual. In this situation, I proclaimed "and the peace of God, which passeth all understanding, shall keep your hearts and minds through Christ Jesus" (Philippians 4:7).

critical stop #2

A few years ago, I experienced the hurt firsthand of when Black women turn on each other. It can be piercing because of our shared African American experience and history of oppression.

Tara and I were sister-colleagues. We planned our courses together, exchanged ideas, and mentored each other. Outside of work we shopped and dined together. In many respects, she had a front-seat view of my professional life and a good view of my personal life. Along with teaching at the university, I had an administrative role. She was privy to a lot of information working so closely with me. Tara was ambitious and wanted to climb the proverbial ladder of success. She grew more distant; although polite, there was less interaction. Initially, I dismissed it as us both being busy; however, Tara was plotting to undermine me. She wanted what I had worked for, in particular, the administrative position. And she declared war on me in one of the most treacherous ways laced with jealousy and deceit: Tara vehemently distorted information about me, attempted to tarnish my reputation, and launched her own self-promoting campaign to wiggle her way into an administrative role. She willfully violated the *sisterhood code* and manipulated a small number of colleagues—both White and Black—to turn against me.

Tara, being knowledgeable about the power of race, gender, and class, willingly subscribed to White-male dominant practices to advance her career.

> His [Scheurich, 1993] thesis suggests that for Black women to enjoy the rewards of tenure in the White male-dominated academy, their knowledge-production endeavors should mirror the behavior of White males. (Alfred, 2001, p. 115)

The legacy of slavery and higher education attainment for African Americans caused the dynamic intersection of race and gender for Tara and me. Tara fell victim to the plantation syndrome: there can only be one good house slave. And I thought we were both free, and committed to helping free others.

I was upset at myself for not seeing this coming. My intentions were always pure with Tara. I dealt honorably with her. The tension between us was palpable. A sine qua non to moving forward was forgiving this so-called sister. It was a battle within me; but through repetitious prayer, and long chats with family and friends, I was able to forgive and to heal. I had to "depart from evil, and do good; seek peace, and pursue it" (Psalms 34:14).

The sun comes out after a tumultuous storm. This ordeal catapulted me to mentor those coming behind me. I organized a project for African American and Latina female students to research, write, and present at professional conferences. Using biblical principles, I teach them that they never have to academically and spiritually prostitute themselves to achieve. Like Tubman, I want to be the conductor of prosperity and unity. The project has been successful in grooming students into becoming scholars as well as caring and considerate young women of promise. Carr (2013) in her song reminds me that the "shaking, breaking, beating, and the pressing" of this struggle, which was ordained by God, birthed one of my greatest purposes, that is, to help others.

PART 2. DENISE'S STORY: I AM BECAUSE WE ARE

I have been known to say on many an occasion that being a Black woman in academia is like dancing merengue in ruby-red six-inch heels; it looks really sexy and even easy and effortless at times, but it is in fact an everyday challenge that requires great skill, fortitude, and wisdom. Academia is indeed a strange and contradictory place. It is, on one hand, a place where powerful learning is possible, but it is also the place where, we can be "enticed away from ourselves" (Dillard, 2012). In my older age, I am less inclined to spend my words trying to make sense of all the things wrongheaded in and about academic spaces and am much more taken with sharing my strategies not only for surviving but also thriving within the despiritualized space of the academy, the place where circulating information seems far more important than engaging inspiration.

Many years ago, I read an essay by bell hooks (1992) titled "Revolutionary Black Women." In it, she talks about the importance of Black women making themselves subject and cultivating their wild, that is, moving against the status quo to name our realities. hooks went on to suggest that one way young Black women can cultivate a radical Black female subjectivity is by reading about the lives of revolutionary Black women. I heeded her advice and immersed myself in reading all the Black feminist work I could get my hands on—autobiography, biography, art, literature, theory, political analyses, and performance. It was in the midst of experiencing the lives lived and created by women such as

Mary Church Terrell, Anna Julia Cooper, Ida B. Wells, Assata Shakur, Angela Davis, bell hooks, Faith Ringgold, Anna Davere Smith, Katheryn Dunham, J. California Cooper, Ntozake Shange, and more recently Joy James, Cynthia Dillard, and Bernice McFadden, among others, that I began (re)member, to decolonize my own mind.

I was able to come into my own voice. It was the testimonies weaved into the context of their work that guided me, warned me, affirmed me, and fortified me in a place where there was no Black woman professor to mentor me in the ways that we work in the academy. Above all else, Black women's testimonies have inspired me; they have filled me with the spirit of Ubuntu—*I am because we are.*

Now I find myself weaving my own testimonies throughout my work as a way of paying forward, sustaining the spirit of Ubuntu. Now when I sit to write a paper or a performance, I always imagine my work as an opportunity to reach out and give someone a desperately needed hug, to let all of those young Black women and men struggling to find their voice, seeking the moment they can exhale—that it is possible to enter the complicated conversations on new terms.

PART 3. LISA'S STORY: A WELL-PLANTED SEED PRODUCES FRUIT

My journey in higher education began July 15, 1999. I had experienced a life-changing and meaningful journey during my doctoral studies at UW-Madison so I was confident employment in higher education would be *just like that!* Now 16 years later, I have been employed as a professor and held some type of administrative appointment/role at two predominately White institutions (PWIs) and two historically Black universities (HBUs) in the following order: PWI, HBU, PWI, and HBU.

For the maternal side of my family, I am third-generation college-educated and a third-generation teacher. My mother was a pioneer as an African American woman manager with South Central Bell, starting her career with that company in 1966. Additionally, she was the first African American woman in the state of Mississippi to hold an elected position on a county Board of Supervisors (the governing body of elected officials for the counties of Mississippi) and has held this role for approximately 23 years. I share these examples as I believe it's in my heritage and lineage to overcome obstacles.

To be honest and forthcoming, I have experienced more blatantly sexist and disparaging experiences in my professional career from members of my own race than I have racially negative experiences from others, and I am from Mississippi. I look at challenges as opportunities to reduce what I have perceived as negative-energy strongholds whether they are racial, class, or gendered.

STRATEGIES FOR EMPLOYMENT PERSISTENCE

I want to use the space in this chapter to focus on action, that is, what can be done to persist employment-wise when facing challenging situations based on race and/or gender from my perspectives as an African American and woman who lives intersectionality. Here, I provide perspectives on how an individual can endure because it sometimes takes time, resources, and legal action before institutions will change and/or correct situations. While one is waiting on the place of employment to take action or simply for deliverance, one must have strategies to survive, persist, and/or endure. This approach is consistent with the legacy of Harriet Tubman who was decisive and purposeful in traversing the Underground Railroad.

strategy 1: employ strategy, not emotion

My first suggestion is to reflect on, allow for, and understand one's own emotions in a given situation, in lieu of allowing emotions to dictate decisions. If possible, a person must be able to think critically in how to address a situation and document it. When faced with adverse situations, the individual should think through the experiences, ensure an accurate interpretation of them, and decide a course of action.

I prefer to be strategic and decisive so if/when I decide to respond, my response is measured, sculpted, and cultivated. I have noticed adult bullies, racists, or sexists want you to lose it or become overly emotional and want attention and/or a reaction. Sometimes, I will simply ignore the person and won't validate their responses with the privilege of getting a reaction from me or giving them the attention (in my opinion) they should have obtained from their caregivers as children and/or their respective spouses/significant others.

By giving an emotional reaction to those who want to see you discouraged and disparaged, you fulfill their dreams, not your own. I have purposefully chosen to refrain from being manipulated, but to intellectually and intelligently decide an effective response and whether or not to respond at all.

strategy 2: determine their role in your life

My second suggestion is to think about what the sexist, racist, misogynistic, other *-ist* or *-obic* (insert desired prefix; e.g., ageist) person means to you. Think *who are you to me? Are you important to me? Do I want/need your acceptance? Does your opinion of me really matter to me?*

Beyond those people who matter to me and whose opinions matter, I am comfortable preventing negatives from entering my spirit, as I do not care what some people think. I am open to feedback, but not disparagement. My mother always said to me, "no one can make you feel inferior without your permission."

Additionally, one Christian author, Ron Carpenter (2012), questions, "are there spoils to be gained through victory in this battle?" (p. 162). If you stand to gain nothing from an exchange, then there's no benefit in fighting. Rhetorically speaking, if the person means nothing to you, why engage and internalize their beliefs about and picayune and asinine comments to you?

strategy 3: know the organizational culture

My third suggestion is to critically think about a solution to address the situation based on assessment of the institutional culture. Unfortunately, the cultures in institutions change slowly and sometimes, stakeholders and power-wielders don't always address situations adequately, professionally, and/or expeditiously. With understanding the culture, this point is not to imply a person should not file a complaint, but one must know the culture enough to understand if the employer and employees will change and improve in order to persist.

As an example, I worked at one institution that was alleged to have made very minimal changes in the treatment of and equitable pay of female employees over decades. I have been informed that women were objectified and attempts were made to keep them from becoming tenured as a systematic and continued practice.

There are a number of ways to address an adverse situation, that is, file a complaint, obtain legal counsel, document the incidents, and/or present the issues to a supervisor. Depending on the culture of the institution, the issues may or may not be addressed. A person has to be able to persist and survive despite institutional actions or lack thereof. If my sanity, self-identity, and persistence had depended on employees of the two PWIs and two HBCUs I have worked at to address issues, I would not have completed 15 years of full-time employment in higher education. I work proactively to protect others and provide the information they need to be successful.

strategy 4: rest on the foundation of your identity

Lastly and most importantly, I rely on my faith as a strategy to persist. In my assessment, this piece resonates most prevalently with Harriet Tubman's legacy and identity as a woman of strong faith. I hold steadfast to biblical principles in how I relate to and treat others as well as how I remain uplifted and positive.

For every encounter I have had in my career, I can find a biblical principle that addresses the situation. I hold abidingly to these principles daily and they enable me to (a) help and encourage others, (b) make a positive difference in the organization where I serve, (c) remain in the situation until it improves or I obtain employment elsewhere, and (d) become a stronger person.

EVERY GOOD SEED WILL BEAR GOOD FRUIT

For every situation where I have experienced negatives, disparagement, and mistreatment in the workplace, I have eventually seen that person *reap the fruit of his or her actions*. There are universal laws governing life that actually work and are fulfilled. The seeds one plants, whether positive or negative, will grow and produce fruit when cultivated.

When you know the legacy you want to leave, this piece becomes your catalyst and focus. Ultimately, the seeds rest with and belong to you. Which ones will you plant, cultivate, and harvest?

CONCLUDING THOUGHTS

Given the paucity of African American women in higher education, we view our work as trailblazers. We view our work as sometimes challenging, but meaningful and necessary, similar to when a pioneer charts a new or previously unchartered course. Once you make it through the journey, it will be easier the next time because you have a road map to follow and share with others.

Our work in this chapter proposed to recognize the multiple subjectivities that coincide and contradict as the self-representations at the heart of our individual and collective narratives. To be true to the legacy of Harriet Tubman, we cannot allow adverse experiences to limit what we do and who/what we become. Understanding the beauty and value of our individual intersectionality can be a catalyst for the success of others.

REFERENCES

Alfred, M. V. (2001). Expanding theories of career development: Adding the voices of African American women in the White academy. *Adult Education Quarterly, 51*(2), 108–127.

Brah, A., & Phoenix, A. (2004). Aint I a woman? Revisiting intersectionality. *Journal of International Women's Studies, 5*(3), 75–86.

Carpenter, R. (2012). *The necessity of an enemy*. New York: Random House.

Carr, J. (2013). Greater is coming [Composed by Allen Carr]. On *Greater is coming* [CD]. Jackson, Mississippi: Lunjeal Music Group/Malaco Records.

Collins, P. H. (1991). *Black feminist thought: Knowledge, consciousness, and the politics of empowerment*. New York: Routledge.

Creswell, J. W. (2007). *Qualitative inquiry and research design: Choosing among five approaches* (2nd ed.). Thousand Oaks, CA: Sage.

Creswell, J. W. (2013). *Qualitative inquiry and research design: Choosing among five approaches* (3rd ed.). Thousand Oaks, CA: Sage.

Dillard, C. B. (2012). *On spiritual strivings: Transforming an African American woman's academic life.* New York, NY: State University of New York Press.

hooks, b. (1992). *Black looks: Race and representation.* Boston, MA: South End Press.

Ladson-Billings, G., & Tate, W. F. (1995). Toward a critical race theory of education. *Teachers College Record, 97*(1), 47–68.

Logan Patitu, C., & Hinton, K. G. (2003). The experiences of African American women faculty and administrators in higher education: Has anything changed? *New Directions for Student Services, 2003*(104), 79–93.

McCall, L. (2005). The complexity of intersectionality. *Journal of Women in Culture and Society, 30*(3), 1771–1800.

Scheurich, J. J. (1993). Toward a White discourse of White racism. *Educational Researcher, 22,* 5–10.

Tobin, J. L., & Dobard, R. G. (1999). *Hidden in plain view: A secret story of quilts and the Underground Railroad.* New York: Anchor Books.

Turner, C. S. V. (2002). Women of color in academe: Living with multiple marginality. *The Journal of Higher Education, 73*(1), 74–93.

CHAPTER FIVE

Eating from the Tree of Life

An Endarkened Feminist Revelation

KYRA T. SHAHID

INTRODUCTION

Cynthia Dillard's (2006) conceptualization of an endarkened feminist epistemology gave me the means to critique the violence perpetuated in the universal generalization of White male knowledge constructions of reality. Her work provides me with the language to voice a specialized knowledge positioned within my cultural, political, and historical identity as a Black woman so that I might reveal a different reality, a different epistemology, than what is traditionally recognized in academic research. Recognizing that non-White, non-male people think differently as opposed to deficiently flies in the face of positivistic and oppressive thinking that leads us to believe that one way of knowing is superior to others. Dillard (2006) acknowledges that her desire in articulating an endarkened feminist epistemology is not to substitute a dominating White male epistemology with a Black female one, but to reclaim and resituate research in the cultural origins from which they began. I share Dillard's desire and intend to use the framework she has conceptualized to identify the epistemic violence I encountered as a graduate student. This self-reflective process will shed light on the ways that an endarkened feminist epistemology supports the ability of a Black woman to respond, overcome, resist, avoid, and ultimately neutralize forceful displacements of knowledge and ways of knowing that maintain dominance over oppressed communities.

MY ENDARKENED EYES

I remember the exact moment that it all came crashing down. I was a master's student studying student affairs in higher education when I had my "spiritual crisis." I was sitting in a class participating in an intergroup dialogue on race. The practice of intergroup dialogue that I experienced asked for students of color to be rational concerning the irrational experiences that we were having and to be understanding of those who lack the epistemological capacity to dismantle the cognitive dissonance that plagues them. The process instituted in my graduate class was one that promoted conversations free of judgment and void of contentions. However well intentioned, this dialogue reinforced feelings of being dismissed and sustained the *epistemologies of ignorance* that protected many of my White and male counterparts from acknowledging my reality. The more I talked, the less they could hear me. It was as if their minds had been co-opted into perceiving everything that I said as "other"—as something distant and disconnected from their realities and therefore not as valid, important, or real as their own perceptions. Shannon Sullivan and Nancy Tuana (2007) explain that an epistemology of ignorance to issues of race and racism is not always an accidental oversight or gap in knowledge. Sullivan and Tuana write, "Especially in the case of racial oppression, a lack of knowledge or an unlearning of something previously known is often actively produced for purposes of domination and exploitation" (p. 1). As I sat in this dialogue, I witnessed the ways that this sort of ignorance protected the delusion of White racial superiority. It seemed as if it was perfectly rational for a White person to have no knowledge about the worlds of people of color. I, a Black woman, was not supposed to be upset by this strategic amnesia and cognitive dissonance. I remember that one of the White female students in the classroom began to cry as another Black student explained what racial micro-aggressions were and how she had been personally affected by them. The White woman's tears successfully seduced the conversation away from a critical turning point and held in place the dissonance of those who refused to believe that there was any validity to what was being said. Consequently, the Black female student, who was "responsible" for her tears, was silenced. That day was not the first time this happened. As these encounters continued, I began to think of it as the "White woman crying syndrome." This White woman crying syndrome was exactly what the name implies—a pattern reserved for White women. When women of color became emotional about something that was being said or something they themselves were sharing, their emotions were seen as bouts of rage and anger. Tears down black and brown cheeks meant that we were "taking things too seriously" or "taking it the wrong way." The presence of this dichotomy in the classroom reinforced the dynamics that we were trying to escape. Thus, students of color, including myself, became enraged with the idea that the dialogues we engaged in were indeed antiracist. It was in this moment that I realized that my voice was being silenced partly because I was attempting to speak through their voice. I had been convinced that my way of strategizing, theorizing, investigating, and understanding knowledge was not applicable in that space, and therefore I divorced my spiritual and intellectual self for the sake of appearing "smart."

The academy was so hostile to my spiritual self, my gendered self, my raced self. I entered that classroom not knowing that the experiences of confusion and uncertainty I was having were deliberately created. Although I knew that a sense of spirituality was a decreed lifeline of the African American community, it seemed that one had to conceal working from a spiritual center to be an academic. Sitting in that classroom, I heard God say to me, "It is not so. Your soul knows right well. Remember who you are." I was not completely sure what that meant for me as an emerging scholar. A few weeks later, a professor handed me a book titled *On Spiritual Strivings: Transforming an African American Woman's Academic Life* by Cynthia B. Dillard (2006). It was in reading this book that I began the process of what Dillard describes in her second book, *Learning to (Re) member the Things We've Learned to Forget* (2012). I understood that God was not asking me to simply remember as in recall my memory, but to (re)member by putting back together those things that had been severed and compartmentalized. This chapter takes readers on my journey of recognizing and embracing my endarkened feminist epistemology as a spiritual, intellectual, and political strategy that necessitates a response. I will use both personal and academic voice to articulate this strategy to demonstrate the plurality of the space from which my voice arises.

THE ART OF EPISTEMIC WARFARE

When I use the term *epistemic violence*, I am referring to behaviors that bring harm to one's understanding of knowledge or knowledge-making processes. Spivak (1988) first used this term to identify numerous projects in history, philosophy, and literature that endorsed claims to knowledge that identified colonized communities as "other." Teo (2008) builds on Spivak's use of the term by describing epistemic violence as a dangerous hermeneutic process that has negative consequences for the "other." According to Teo (2008), "The negative impact can range from misrepresentations and distortions, to a neglect of the voices of the 'Other,' to statements of inferiority, and to the recommendations of adverse practices or infringements concerning the 'Other'" (p. 58). Taliaferro-Baszile (2004) adapted the term *epistemic violence* to describe the actions by which the academy professes a commitment to critical thinking and social justice but continues to prescribe to standards, traditions, and ways of knowing that maintain hegemony. For me, epistemic violence encompasses all of these things. Epistemic violence is the forceful displacement of knowledge and ways of knowing in order to maintain dominance over oppressed communities.

As a graduate student, I encountered this violence on a daily basis. It was committed through language, when words like *spirit* and *faith* became unacceptable explanations within serious academic inquiries. Epistemic violence was waged through omission of scholars of color from the curricula of all my major classes and through the positioning of such work as "raced" and "gendered" work to be explored in ethnic and women's studies programs only. I experienced this violence when I encountered the epistemologies of ignorance that labeled me as the marginalized, oppressed "other" but did not label my White and male counterparts as *oppressors*. Epistemic violence placed implicit and explicit lacerations on my way of knowing, causing me to metaphorically bleed rage and frustration. It was in a radical return to myself during a "spiritual crisis" that I came to fully understand the necessity of Dillard's plea that we "cut to heal not to bleed" (2006). In those moments I recognized that my purpose in academe was not to arm myself with the same weapons that were intended for my demise. Audre Lorde (1984) had already cautioned that "the master's tools will never dismantle the master's house. They may allow us to temporarily beat him at his own game, but they will never enable us to bring about genuine change" (p. 3). With this in mind, I intentionally spent the remainder of my graduate school years reexamining the complexities of this violence and the countless attacks one encounters as a Black female navigating Western academic space. I did this not as an attempt to claim victimhood but to build a testament to the inherent wisdom I found in my spirit. Testimony, I argue, is not only epistemic but also transcendent, allowing me to escape the perils of present conditions to envision a curative and creative future. The next section of this chapter describes how an endarkened feminist epistemology enables me to stretch my intellect apart from traditional theoretical factions and embrace the spiritual and political originalities necessary for shifting hegemonic paradigms.

STUDY WAR NO MORE

An endarkened feminist epistemology carries with it six assumptions. These assumptions directly challenge ideologies that profess one unitary way of knowing. Dillard's (2006) first assumption states that self-definition forms one's participation and responsibility to one's community. Dillard explains in so many ways that knowing who you are guides your interactions with the world you live in. I had always known that this was true of myself. I often wondered why so many universities were located in remote locations, causing the Black scholars that chose to attend to be isolated from their communities. These Black scholars would then most often encounter research that depicted their communities through deficit models. By embracing an endarkened feminist epistemology, I have been able to counter these actions and (re)define my identity and that of the communities that my work is responsible to. I consider myself an emerging critical scholar with a research focus on race, spirituality, and leadership in higher education. As an educational researcher, I consider every research project as an opportunity to positively influence the Black community and ultimately the world. I agree with Dillard (2006) that educational researchers express a viewpoint that is personally and culturally rooted; this makes research a medium for expressing one's self-definition within a space that marginalizes that ability. Researchers, thus, have a responsibility to the communities from which those definitions arise. My spiritual crisis brought me to this understanding and helped me to recognize that my work in academe ought to reflect the spiritually salient African American Christian roots that anchor me. My spiritual walk is not separate from my intellectual journey in academe.

The spiritual crisis I experienced as a graduate student helped me to make meaning of this realization. I began to see academe like a metaphorical game of chess. Through my endarkened eyes, I understood that if I, as a Black woman scholar, chose to deny the cultural and spiritual communities from which my knowledge originates, I would be trading my position as a queen to become a pawn protecting their bishop. Thus, I understood more deeply what Dillard (2006) meant when she wrote:

> An endarkened feminist epistemology draws on a spiritual tradition, where the concern is not solely with the production of knowledge (an intellectual pursuit) but also with uncovering and constructing truth as the fabric of everyday life (a spiritual pursuit). (p. 20)

From that moment on, I have acknowledged my endarkened feminist epistemology as a demonstration of "stepping out on faith" and speaking a truth that is widely not expected to exist. Like the Negro spiritual states, I couldn't "study war no more." What this meant for me was that I could not let my mind "study" or dwell on the epistemic warfare that I had encountered. I felt that if I dwelled there, such practices would become acceptable to me, I'd become accustomed to epistemic violence and ultimately proficient in using the same tools toward others. Turning and returning to Dillard's conceptualization of an endarkened feminist epistemology, I sought to challenge the epistemologies or ways of thinking (not just the thoughts) that perpetuated the paradigms that labeled my culture and the knowledge within my culture marginal. Such a challenge would be more impactful than my bouts of rage expressed in the classroom could ever be. Collins (1990, as cited in Dillard, 2006) informed me that "much more threatening is the challenge that alternative epistemologies offer to the basic process used by the powerful to legitimate their knowledge claims" (p. 20). Causing an epistemological rupture in academe would leave us all bereft, however, if a healing steeped in radical love is not part of that process. Once again, my response and responsibility to this cause arises from my identity. As Dantley (2005) contends:

> much of Black life is a perpetual struggle against forms of oppression that would sap people's emotions and physical resources, drain their intellectual wherewithal, and could leave them bereft of any hope were it not for the spiritual dimension of their multifaceted lives. This spirituality becomes the foundation for the construction of the sacred self. (p. 657)

The notion of sacred is fundamental to an endarkened feminist epistemology. I often situate my understanding of sacred in the nexus of connectivity with others and the universe. Assumption three within an endarkened epistemology explains, "Only within the context of community does the individual appear (Palmer, 1983) and, through dialogue, continue to become" (Dillard, 2006, p. 22). The first time I read these words, my mind immediately recalled the Ubuntu proverb, "I am because we are." What I believe Dillard communicates through this assumption is that the process of dialogue does not begin or end with an individual; our existence and understanding of truth is in relationship to others. This understanding complicated my experience in that classroom dialogue because of the marginalizing standpoints that said that I was the distant "other" that warranted no authentic association. Reading Dillard's work gave me the language to articulate a belief that dialogue is a process of talking between two subjects and not one subject and an object. This implies that dialogue would require us to see one another as equally human and not as one person talking to or at a group of objects. Stated plainly, dialogue rejects domination and requires the presence of two equally existing voices. An endarkened feminist epistemology helped me bring about the evidence of an alternative, yet equally existing, voice.

An endarkened feminist's fourth assumption is that "Concrete experiences within everyday life form the criterion of meaning, the 'matrix of meaning making'" (Dillard, 2006, p. 23). Such an assumption makes it clear why these experiences, among others, during my graduate career are important moments for critical self-reflection. Under this assumption, the fine line between knowledge and wisdom is made clear. In my experiences, a learned wisdom accompanies the raced, gendered, classed identity that spirit occupies. That wisdom is therefore distinctive of me and others who share my experiences. This assumption within Dillard's work brings forth a level of meaning making that "book learning," as many older African Americans would say, cannot teach. Dillard suggests that as researchers, Black women consequently often seek to not only understand what the experiences of Black women and other people of color are, but also the meanings contained in those experiences. This is fundamental of an endarkened feminist epistemology. I must acknowledge that this is where I situate this framework as political strategy. Suggesting that positionality based on race, gender, class, and other identity markers delineates a knowledge base unique to its origins has within it an element of activism toward legitimizing these knowledge bases within the academy. This understanding will not only help to displace the power held within our so-called original canon of theories, but it will allow us to reshape the structure of academe to reflect these standpoint knowledges. Building on the work of previous scholar activists, we can loose programs such as Black studies from confined spaces and create programs such as psychology from an African American perspective in the main psychology department, or education in the Black experience within the school of education. Such an idea might be radical, but I believe that it is time that we completely displace the ideas, rules, and structures that marginalize standpoint knowledges and uphold dominant, Western epistemologies as normal. Re-conceptualizing academia could transform the future of our world to reflect a more inclusive history that accounts for the experiences of people from various communities in healing ways.

The fifth assumption of an endarkened feminist epistemology supports this assertion as it states that "Knowing and research are both historical (extending backward in time) and outward to the world: To approach them otherwise is to diminish their cultural and empirical meaningfulness" (Dillard, 2006, p. 24). This assumption explains why an endarkened feminist epistemology qualifies as intellectual activism (Hill Collins, 2013). Such a lens makes it possible to acknowledge a tradition and presence of Black feminist thought throughout time, while creatively advancing new understandings. Black feminist thought and Black spirituality are inherently creative, allowing one to "see those things that be not as though they were." This creativity is the personification of a God-consciousness through culturally constructed bodies to a spiritually connected human whole. I find this to be imperative to address the power relations that are the focus of the final assumption of an endarkened feminist epistemology. Dillard (2006) explains, "Power relations, manifest as racism, sexism, homophobia, and so on structure gender, race, and other identity relations within research" (p. 26). There is no doubt that these power structures were at play during my class discussion and continue to create a standard of who and what is normal, abnormal, acceptable, and unacceptable. Asymmetrical power relations are in essence the root of research that continually constitutes the "other" as problematic. As I have previously discussed, such projects are acts of epistemic violence. Countering in ways that causes our world to heal and not bleed demands an approach, endarkened or otherwise, that holds healing as its ultimate goal.

IN SEARCH OF HEALING

In sum, the theoretical assumptions of an endarkened feminist epistemology provided a lens for me to (re)member my identity as a scholar and discover my purpose in academe. I hold on to the memory of that dialogue in class not because of the anger and frustration of the moment, but because of the healing process that began on that day. My research in academe continues to forge that kind of healing and to proffer "words [that] help us to be with others in mutually beneficial and the loving ways" (Dillard, 2006, p. 106). My commitment is best expressed through the words of bell hooks (1993). It is a commitment to

> A profound unshaken belief in the spiritual power of black people to transform our world and live with integrity and oneness despite oppressive social realities. In that world, black folks collectively believed in "higher powers," knew that forces stronger than the will and intellect of humankind shaped and determined our existence, the way we lived.... They knew joy, that feeling that comes from using one's powers to the fullest. (p. 10)

This is my reality. Dillard and Okpalaoka (2011) write specifically about the importance of naming one's reality especially as it pertains to the healing process necessary for doing race work. Their use of endarkened feminist epistemology throughout their article allows them to articulate a definition of wisdom that acknowledges "that we must bring our whole selves—spirit, mind, and body—into the multiple contexts we occupy" (Dillard & Okpalaoka, 2011, p. 73). Such actions require an element of love that the authors explain moves us away from fear and helps us to engage in more authentic ways, consequently pushing us toward more authentic understandings of one another. This element of using an endarkened feminist epistemology helps Black women merge the "two-ness" and welcomes the presence of who we are as we see ourselves into spaces where we are commonly only acknowledged according to who others expect/believe we are or ought to be. Engaging in such a way also allows Black women to see how our experiences are influenced (positively or negatively) by our identity markers. There is a richness and vulnerability in spaces where such engagement is possible. It is with this understanding, orientation, and framework that I offer this reflection to the educators and educational leaders of academe.

REFERENCES

Dantley, M. E. (2005). African American spirituality and Cornel West's notions of prophetic pragmatism: Restructuring educational leadership in American urban schools. *Educational Administration Quarterly, 41*, 651–674.

Dillard, C. (2006). *On spiritual strivings: Transforming an African American woman's academic life.* Albany, NY: State University of New York Press.

Dillard, C. B. (2012). *Learning to (re)member the things we've learned to forget: Endarkened feminisms, spirituality, and the sacred nature of research and teaching. Black studies and critical thinking. Volume 18.* New York: Peter Lang.

Dillard, C. B., & Okpalaoka, C. (2011). The sacred and spiritual nature of endarkened transnational feminist praxis in qualitative research. *Handbook of qualitative research*, 147–162.

Hill Collins, P. (2013). *On intellectual activism*. Philadelphia. PA: Temple University Press.

hooks, b. (1993). A life in the spirit: Reflections on faith and politics. *Revision, 15*(3), 99.

hooks, b., & West, C. (1991). *Breaking bread: Insurgent Black intellectual life*. Boston, MA: South End Press.

Lorde, A. (1984). *Sister outsider: Essays and speeches*. Trumansburg, NY: Crossing Press.

Spivak, G.C. (1988). Can the subaltern speak? In C. Nelson & L. Grossberg (Eds.), Marxism and the interpretation of culture (pp. 271–313). Urbana: University of Illinois Press.

Sullivan, S., & Tuana, N. (2007). *Race and epistemologies of ignorance*. Albany: State University of New York Press.

Taliaferro-Baszile, D. M. (2004). "Who does she think she is?" Growing up nationalist and ending up teaching race in White space. In Darrell Cleveland (Ed.), In *A Long way to go: Conversations about race by African American faculty and graduate students* (pp. 158–170). New York: Peter Lang.

Teo, T. (2008). From speculation to epistemological violence in psychology: A critical-hermeneutic reconstruction. *Theory & Psychology, 18*(1), 47–67. doi:10.1177/0959354307086922

CHAPTER SIX

Colorist Dimensions of Black Feminist Knowledge

CARLA R. MONROE

Society owes a great debt to researchers who view traditional narratives as open to question and disagreement. The exemplary scholarship that has emerged from critical explorations of history (Anderson, 1988), curriculum studies (Alridge, 2006), sociocultural context (Hale-Benson, 1982), and other areas has enriched shallow representations of Black[1] schooling and, more importantly, challenged erroneous conclusions that are grounded by deficit thinking. Dillard's (2000) conceptualization of endarkened feminist epistemology accords with the best traditions of progressive research by situating streams of knowledge into a culturally relevant framework. Social scientists particularly benefit from the conceptual tools that Dillard (2006) provides to revamp feminist notions that have cast girls and women as an undifferentiated group for far too long. As she explains,

> in contrast with the common use of the term "enlightened" as a way of expressing the having of new and important feminist insights (arising historically from the well-established canon of White feminist thought), I use the term endarkened feminist epistemology to articulate how reality is known when based in the historical roots of Black feminist thought, embodying a distinguishable difference in cultural standpoint, located in the intersection/ overlap of the culturally constructed socializations of race, gender, and other identities and the historical and contemporary contexts of oppressions and resistance for African American women. (Dillard, 2000, p. 662)

Certainly ongoing attention to social forces, such as geographic and economic influences, cautions scholars against embracing essentialist myths (Morris & Monroe, 2009). Yet, while consequential factors such as social class, gender, and sexual orientation have gained traction in scholarly analyses, colorism does not receive comparable parity. Instead, discussions of race, to some degree, rest on a presumed racialized prototype of the Black female. When researchers fail to attend to social realities associated with the color complex, they, unfortunately, deprive themselves of crucial opportunities to examine how long-standing prejudices inform epistemologies through race, gender, and beauty politics.

In this chapter I deepen understanding of endarkened feminist knowledge by interrogating how and why colorism "naturalizes" social differences among African Americans in the United States and, subsequently, catalyzes alternative truths for Black females. More specifically, I situate gendered implications of colorism within historical and modern tendencies that have regularized intraracial inequities among African Americans. Based on prevailing patterns, I accent how color-focused investigations may carve pathways toward truths that are recognized within Dillard's (2000) vision.

CRAFTING DISTINCTION: COLORISM AND THE WHITE POWER STRUCTURE

Colorism is traditionally defined as discrimination and prejudice based on skin tone (Russell, Wilson, & Hall, 1992) although the concept is generally understood to include related phenotypic traits such as hair texture, eye color, nose shape, lip width, and body type (Monroe, 2013). The nation's legacy of racism, particularly concerning Blacks, and fascination with race has mediated troubling generalizations regarding skin color that are hardly insignificant. As historical accounts reveal,[2] White lineage and fair complexions, to some extent, have afforded light-skinned people of African ancestry relative advantages from slavery onward.

Economist Howard Bodenhorn (2002a), who has studied colorism during the antebellum period, documents how consequences of complexion difference tilted in favor of Black people with White ancestry and light complexions. His investigation of free Blacks in rural Virginia, for instance, suggests that light-skinned African Americans were probably raised in more "salubrious environments," that is, conditions that were favorable to good health (p. 31). Based on athropometric data, he draws plausible links between growth spurts, terminal height, and diet which support claims that light mulattoes likely had access to better nutrition than their dark peers. Likewise, census data reveal drastic differences in Black and White wealth in the urban South (Bodenhorn & Ruebeck, 2007). For example, according to the 1860 census, mulatto wealth was almost half of White wealth while the figure among free Blacks was only 20 percent.

Although free Blacks and mulattoes were a relatively small share of the nation's African American population, evidence among the enslaved population also suggests that mixed racial heritage contributed to stratification based on colorism. In fact, remembrances narrated by slaves themselves demonstrate that house servants, who were often light-complexioned, tended to receive a rudimentary education and be literate (Douglass, 1845/1988) as well as have access to better shelter, food, and clothing than field slaves (Brown, 1847; Jacobs, 1861/2000). Historical reports further show that skin color was a functionary in work assignments as light-complected slaves were often assigned to be butlers, maids, cooks, and trained as skilled workers (e.g., artisans) whose labor could be leased to generate additional income. Even when slave owners granted manumission, light-complexioned individuals were oftentimes the beneficiaries (Bodenhorn, 2002b; Bodenhorn & Ruebeck, 2007).

As outlined in other work (Monroe, 2013), physical variation among people with Black African heritage during the pre–Civil War era set the stage for deep and long-standing lines of intraracial stratification. Light-complexioned Blacks generally experienced Reconstruction from an "advantaged" standpoint as they tended to possess more wealth, such as land ownership, be more familiar with White norms as a result of closer interactions with slaveholding families, and possess marketable skills such as dressmaking and boot making. Well-regarded studies indicate that Blacks with mixed lineage were also well represented in newly established institutions of higher education and leadership positions (Frazier, 1957/1962). Although more investigations are needed to establish temporal links of continuity, contemporary findings underscore remarkable durability in color bias as light-skinned Blacks tend to outpace dark-skinned Blacks on several traditional measures of success such as income (Keith & Herring, 1991), employment and promotion decisions (Harrison & Thomas, 2009), and educational attainment (Allen, Telles, & Hunter, 2000).

Whereas material advantages for light-complexioned African Americans are reasonably well-documented, scholars have devoted fewer empirical efforts to querying reverse truisms. For example, some historians suggest that house slaves were somewhat distanced from the communal strength that flourished in slave quarters through camaraderie, spirituality, kinship families, and other institutions (Hine & Thompson, 1998). Contemporary theorists also posit that African Americans use colorism as a means of "redistributing" social power by marginalizing light-complexioned Blacks through charges of racial inauthenticity (Hunter, 2008).

COLORISM, POLITICS, AND ENDARKENED FEMINIST EPISTEMOLOGY

In explaining the fourth assumption of endarkened feminism, Dillard (2000) writes that "concrete experiences within everyday life form the criterion of meaning" (p. 675). Yet despite growth in research that focuses on the "everyday experiences" of Black girls and women, few authors elaborate on how the race-colorism calculus feeds social politics that, in turn, inform multiple truths. As evidenced by historical currents of identity and inclusion politics (Hochschild, 2006; Monroe, 2013), epistemologies among African American females reflect both cohesive and discordant elements of what it means to be Black and female in the United States.

Identity politics and struggles for liberation. A fair amount has been written about racial categorization for African Americans, much of which centers on definitions created by the White power structure (e.g., Census Bureau) (Hochschild & Weaver, 2007) and themes of relative advantage that correlate with light skin color (Bodenhorn, 2002a). Despite distinctions that were created and practiced by White society, however, historically racialized identity politics[3] tended to be remarkably consistent among people of Black heritage regardless of skin color. That is, people of African ancestry have regularly identified with Black communities and supported core struggles for liberation such as antislavery, literacy, and civil rights movements. As Hine and Thompson (1998) narrate, Black women confronted race and gender barriers whether they were free, enslaved, or manumitted, which set their experience apart from White women and Black men.

The cases of Harriet Tubman and Ellen Craft are instructive in illuminating how dynamics of racial identity and colorism may play out within the same collective storyline. Both women escaped from southern slavery, became respected figures in abolitionist circles, and achieved these ends by inverting White assumptions about skin color. Fair-skinned Craft, a quadroon in historical parlance, reached the northern territory by pretending to be a White male planter traveling with a male slave. In actuality, the man was Craft's husband. Iconic heroine Tubman's dark complexion, conversely, necessitated that she maneuver her way toward freedom by other means such as her well-chronicled ruse of pretending to read to avoid detection by a former master.

The Tubman and Craft examples illustrate how African Americans existed within the same overarching racial identity and chose to advance analogous goals, thus suggesting a shared understanding of racial oppression. Their unique backgrounds and specific resistance tactics, however, likely facilitated distinctive insights about Black women's involvement with racial justice struggles. How did both women assess their individual choices? What opinions did they hold of others' whose strategies differed from their own? And, what reactions did the two women receive in response to their actions? Investigating questions of this nature will help unravel how Black women understand divergent paths toward collective racial equity.

Politics of racial inclusion and exclusion. As previously discussed, conventional thrusts in research spotlight advantages that are afforded to light-complexioned Blacks. Considerably fewer voices analyze strands that challenge or expand long-standing perspectives. As a consequence, scholars have a relatively constrained understanding of colorism's varied iterations, save burgeoning conceptual work that offers provocative rhetorical insights. Hunter (2008), for instance, has published seminal work that expands ongoing dialogues to include intraracial tensions that question the understudied area of microaggressions directed against light-complected African Americans. Specifically, she narrows attention to how colorism may be used as a proxy for "racial authenticity" and a vehicle for redefining intraracial power relations. As she writes:

> The task of "proving" oneself to be a legitimate or authentic member of an ethnic community is a significant burden for the light-skinned in Latino, African American, and Asian American communities. For many people of color, authenticity is the vehicle through which darker-skinned people take back their power from lighter-skinned people.... One common way they regain their sense of power and pride is to accuse light-skinned Blacks of not being "Black enough"... Not being Black enough, or authentically ethnic enough, in any ethnic community, is a serious insult to many. It implies that they do not identify with their fellow co-ethnics, that they do not care about them, that they think they are better than their co-ethnics, or in extreme cases, that they wish they were White.
>
> ...light-skinned men and women are typically not regarded as legitimate members of the African American or Mexican American communities. They may be excluded from or made to feel unwelcome in community events and organizations. (pp. 70–72)

While anecdotal observations abound (e.g., Atkins, 2008), few social scientists systematically question how Hunter's (2008) assertions play out in empirical data.

Despite common epistemologies that may exist, researchers cannot foreclose on the notion that girls' and women's physical features invoke a myriad of truths that likely set forth contested versions of lived experiences. Endarkened feminists stand to play an important role in setting aside debates about whose stories are "authentic" or "more legitimate" than others by using the framework to document how and why narratives overlap with and/or detract from the prevailing record. What types of racialized encounters do Black females experience? How do girls and women square their experiences with their peers? Whose voices provide worthwhile counsel? Which voices are foregrounded and why? Case study, ethnographic, and life history methodologies are, perhaps, the most appropriate approaches for capturing novel insights to these types of questions. Absent such research, scholars will continue to have a distorted view of colorism as a social force in the United States as well as abroad.

CONCLUSION AND FUTURE DIRECTIONS

Race has fundamentally shaped Black women's experiences in the United States. Solely confining analyses to the construct, however, conceals intraracial differences and erroneously suggests that effects of racialization are uniform. Multipronged conceptual and empirical literature is necessary if scholars wish to relate more sophisticated stories. Future researchers should pursue strands of inquiry that target the core of Black females' lives such as how individuals are socialized as raced and gendered beings in different, but related, contexts such as within families, communities, schools, work settings, and the nation at large. Nuances regarding the types of support, challenges, methods of resistance, and modes of persistence that Black women and girls of different complexions engage are overdue in educational research.

How Black women are privileged or disenfranchised by beauty and racial identity politics in education domains is a fruitful avenue of study. Global tendencies to favor Whiteness and lightness on a mass scale (Hall, 1995) create spaces for light-complected African American women to benefit from complexion prejudice in predominately White environments. For instance, women of color who are lauded for their attractiveness are frequently light-skinned such as former Miss America Vanessa Williams, entertainer Lena Horne, model Tyra Banks, and actress Halle Berry. Empirical findings also evidence how marriage and dating choices are invested with colorist preferences (Hill, 2002; Hunter, 2008). Simultaneously, however, racial identity politics frequently position skin tone as the measure by which individuals are perceived and/or accepted as "legitimate" members of the Black race. Evidence of White ancestry vis-à-vis physical traits (e.g., complexion, eye color) is often seized as a wedge trait when individuals wish to demarcate lines of "authenticity," that is, to assert who is "really" Black. A high-profile example was the 2002 Newark mayoral race in New Jersey, a contest in which "It doesn't matter how White you are; it matters how right you are" became a catchphrase among some supporters of incumbent politician Sharpe James (Curry, 2005). Many observers interpreted the statement as a way to discredit the mayor's blue-eyed, fair-skinned opponent Cory Booker among Black voters. Other instances include controversies involving former spokeswoman and director of communications for the Democratic National Committee Karen Finney (Shapiro, 2013) and former Atlanta mayors William "Bill" Campbell and Maynard Jackson (Copeland, 1997).

Structuring educational work to unravel racial subtleties will uncover new insights that rightfully differentiate Black females' voices within their broader chorus. Endarkened feminist knowledge will benefit from scholarship that stimulates discussion about various forms of racial oppression and resistance that proceed from colorism. Researchers and theorists whose interests center on well-studied and conceptualized problems (e.g., the achievement gap, disciplinary disproportionality, tracking) should question how colorism influences trends among Black females. Such studies will help shatter imagined monoliths and, hopefully, spark novel insights regarding the cross-pressures of the race/gender/color nexus. Links are, of course, made more intricate by factors such as immigration, blended racial ancestry, and the complexities of cultural identification (e.g., individuals who self-identify with a racial group that differs from their socially-ascribed label).

Methodologies and procedures should be structured to gather information that facilitates connections between colorist notions and relevant research questions. Specifically, endarkened scholarship should be conceptualized and structured to account for conclusions that are informed by physical characteristics such as complexion. Other social science fields provide helpful research models such as Keith and Herring's (1991) use of the National Survey of Black Americans and Bodenhorn's (1999) application of historical anthropometry. Likewise, a sufficient body of work is available to inform tools such as interview protocols, field observations, and document sources. In spite of the clear need to view Black life through a colorist lens, empirical and conceptual responses from the educational community are sparse. What microaggressions do Black females confront? How do girls and women interpret their individual lives in light of prevailing narratives? And, what similarities and differences exist among diverse Black females? Given the traditional degree to which physical appearance mediates girls' and women's experiences (Wolf, 1991), color-focused studies conducted within the context of endarkened feminism represent a viable path toward answering these questions.

REFERENCES

Allen, W., Telles, E., & Hunter, M. (2000). Skin color, income and education: A comparison of African Americans and Mexican Americans. *National Journal of Sociology, 12*, 129–180.

Alridge, D. P. (2006). The limits of master narratives in history textbooks: An analysis of representations of Martin Luther King, Jr. *Teachers College Record, 108*, 662–686.

Anderson, J. D. (1988). *The education of Blacks in the south, 1860–1935*. Chapel Hill: University of North Carolina Press.

Atkins, E. (2008). Do light-skin Black people have an advantage? No. We face a different form of racism. *Ebony, 63*(4), 164

Bodenhorn, H. (1999). A troublesome caste: Height and nutrition of antebellum Virginia's rural free Blacks. *Journal of Economic History, 59*, 972–996.

Bodenhorn, H. (2002a). The Mulatto advantage: The biological consequences of complexion in rural antebellum Virginia. *Journal of Interdisciplinary History, 33*, 21–46.

Bodenhorn, H. (2002b). *The complexion gap: The economic consequences of color among free African Americans in the rural antebellum south* (Working paper 8957). Cambridge, MA: National Bureau of Economic Research.

Bodenhorn, H., & Ruebeck, C. S. (2007). Colourism and African-American wealth: Evidence from the nineteenth-century south. *Journal of Population Economics, 20,* 599–620.

Brown, W. W. (1847). *Narrative of William W. Brown, a fugitive slave.* Boston: The Anti-slavery Office.

Copeland, L. (1997, December 31). Atlanta gated community is enclave with a difference. *The Inquirer.* Retrieved from http://articles.philly.com/1997-12-31/news/25555293_1_gated-communities-gated-community-metal-gates

Curry, M. (Producer). (2005). *Street fight* [Motion picture documentary]. Brooklyn, NY: Marshall Curry Productions.

Dillard, C. B. (2000). The substance of things hoped for, the evidence of things not seen: Examining an endarkened feminist epistemology in educational research and leadership. *Qualitative Studies in Education, 13,* 661–681.

Dillard, C. B. (2006). *On spiritual strivings: Transforming an African American woman's academic life.* Albany: State University Press.

Douglass, F. (1988). *Narrative of the life of Frederick Douglass: An American slave.* Cambridge, MA: Belknap Press. (Original work published 1845)

Frazier, E. F. (1962). *Black bourgeoisie.* New York: Free Press. (Original work published 1957)

Hale-Benson, J. E. (1982). *Black children: Their roots, culture, and learning styles.* Baltimore: Johns Hopkins University Press.

Hall, R. E. (1995). The bleaching syndrome: African Americans' response to cultural domination vis-à-vis skin color. *Journal of Black Studies, 26,* 172–184.

Harrison, M. S., & Thomas, K. M. (2009). The hidden prejudice in selection: A research investigation on skin color bias. *Journal of Applied Social Psychology, 39,* 134–168.

Hill, M. E. (2002). Skin color and the perception of attractiveness among African Americans: Does gender make a difference? *Social Psychology Quarterly, 65,* 77–91.

Hine, D. C., & Thompson, K. (1998). *A shining thread of hope: The history of Black women in America.* New York: Broadway Books.

Hochschild, J. L. (2006). When do people not protest unfairness? The case of skin color discrimination. *Social Research, 73,* 473–498.

Hochschild, J. L., & Weaver, V. (2007). Policies of racial classification and the politics of racial inequality. In S. Mettler, J. Soss, & J. Hacker (Eds.), *Remaking America: Democracy and public policy in an age of inequality* (pp. 159–182). New York: Russell Sage Foundation.

Hunter, M. (2008). The cost of color: What we pay for being black and brown. In R. Hall (Ed.), *Racism in the 21st century: An empirical analysis of skin color* (pp. 63–76). New York: Springer Science.

Jacobs, H. (2000). *Incidents in the life of a slave girl.* New York: Signet. (Original work published 1861)

Keith, V. M., & Herring, C. (1991). Skin tone and stratification in the Black community. *American Journal of Sociology, 97,* 760–778.

Monroe, C. R. (2013). Colorizing educational research: African American life and schooling as an exemplar. *Educational Researcher, 42,* 9–19.

Morris, J. E., & Monroe, C. R. (2009). Why study the U.S. South? The nexus of race and place in investigating Black student achievement. *Educational Researcher, 38,* 21–36.

Russell, K., Wilson, M., & Hall, R. (1992). *The color complex: The politics of skin color among African Americans.* New York: Harcourt Brace.

Shapiro, R. (2013, March 3). Tim Graham's controversial tweet about Karen Finney provokes backlash. Retrieved from http://www.huffingtonpost.com/2013/04/03/tim-graham-karen-finney-tweet_n_3008849.html

Wolf, N. (1991). *The beauty myth: How images of beauty are used against women.* New York: William Morrow.

ENDNOTES

1. The terms "Black" and "African American" are used interchangeably to refer to U.S.-born populations of Black African ancestry. References to international groups are specifically noted where appropriate.
2. The historical summary emphasizes the U.S. South because most African Americans tended to live in the region, thus permitting examinations of distinct subgroups (e.g., Blacks who were enslaved, free, urban, rural).
3. Identity politics is often used as an umbrella term to describe a self-selected group.

CHAPTER SEVEN

(Her)story

The Evolution of a Dual Identity as an Emerging Black Female and Scholar

TUWANA T. WINGFIELD

As an emerging Black female scholar, I feel that it is important to reflect on how my identity evolved and what factors contributed to the woman that I have become. Cynthia Dillard's work on honoring the cultural ontological and epistemological research of people of color through the lens of Black feminism is essential to unpack how I view myself within the context of social, historical, and political oppressions that African Americans have experienced in this country (Dillard, 2000, 2008a, 2008b). Dillard (2000) introduces a new theoretical framework, called an endarkened feminist epistemology, to counter the hegemonic dominant research paradigms of White Europeans. Simply put, an endarkened feminist epistemology, rooted in Black feminism, is a way of honoring the historical and cultural contributions of African American women at the intersection of the construction of race/class/gender (Dillard, 2000). In this chapter, I will use the works of feminist writers such as Patricia Hill-Collins (1991), Cynthia Dillard (2000, 2008a, 2008b), bell hooks (2000), Deborah King (1988), Audre Lorde (1984), and Venus Evans-Winters (2011) to reflect on my lived experience and how those experiences shaped who I once was, who I am, and who I have yet to become (Dillard, 2008a). Telling my story will hopefully help other young African American women understand their lived experience and also contribute to the ongoing discussion of Black feminism and its use in educational research to explain the reality and improve the experiences of other young Black women in the academy.

W. E. B. Du Bois' conceptualization of a "double consciousness" (2011) provided the initial framework for understanding how my personal and professional dual identity evolved from childhood into adulthood. Du Bois explains that African Americans see themselves through the eyes of the other because we live behind the veil of American culture. The veil allows us to travel between two worlds, thus creating the "double consciousness" (Du Bois, 2011). Du Bois argues that this "double consciousness" can never be reconciled and tensions arise from balancing the demands of each identity; I believe these tensions within my dual identity drive my evolution, resulting in a more authentic self. DuBois' notion of a "double consciousness" supports the development of the dual identity framework presented in this chapter, which argues that as African Americans our personal and professional identities are shaped by lived experience behind the veil that informs our personal, cultural, and professional identity factors. Furthermore, as an African American female, I have another level of consciousness that I must reconcile if I am to become a more authentic self. This level of multiple consciousnesses (King, 1988) can best be explained by the intersectionality of my race, gender, and class. Dillard (2008a), referencing King (1988), notes Du Bois' conceptualization of "double consciousness" was based on the experiences of Black men and argues that Black women live in three worlds: African ascendant, American, and female. This intersection among race, culture, and gender informs my dual identity. This multiple reality (King, 1988) has influenced my own and others' perceptions of me as an emerging Black female scholar. Dillard (2008b) proposes that people of color move beyond Du Bois' limited definition of identity and embrace the notion of "(re)membering" to remember the things we learned to forget. Research should be conducted through a cultural lens that creates a relationship between the researcher and researched (Dillard, 2008a). An endarkened feminist epistemology creates this relationship through changing our "way of being (ontology) and knowing (epistemology)" (p. 90) and produces knowledge contrary to historical cannons of research and pedagogy (Dillard, 2000).

P. H. Collins (1991) explains that Black feminist thought evolved from critical social theory, which encompasses "bodies of knowledge and sets of institutional practices that actively grapple with the central questions facing U.S. Black women as a collective" (p. 9). In other words, Black feminist thought takes into consideration the social, cultural, and political experiences of women of color. An endarkened feminist epistemology is a hybrid of earlier works of other Black feminist scholars who refused to be silenced by White Eurocentric male canons of research or erased by white feminist paradigms. The works of Black feminists stress the importance of Black women's scholarship and activism. Their works allow women of color a voice in producing new forms of scholarship. Black feminist thought paved the way for Dillard to develop an endarkened feminist epistemology to (re)collect our intellectual contributions for the sake of future generations of Black females

(P. H. Collins, 1991; Dillard, 2000). Like the Sankofa Bird of Ghana, we must look back to re-collect the riches of our ancestors. As African American women, we have been shaped by the social construction and intersection of race, class, and gender within social, historical, and political contexts of racism and oppression throughout the world (Dillard, 2000). It is important for us, as Black women, to reclaim the coded wisdom (*Taking Root*, 2008) of our ancestors that was passed down from one generation to the next. We must remember who we are and where we come from to reclaim the contributions of our foremothers and forefathers if we want to see a more just and equitable society (Dillard, 2000).

Dillard's conceptualization of an endarkened feminist epistemology helped me find my voice, make meaning of my lived experience, and understand that there are as many other ways of knowing as there are intersections among race, culture, and gender. Using DuBois' "double consciousness" coupled with Dillard's endarkened feminist epistemology and her concept of the *life notes* (Dillard, 2000), I deconstruct the evolution of my dual identity, personal and professional, in this chapter.

ENDARKENED FEMINIST EPISTEMOLOGY (EFE) DUAL IDENTITY THEORETICAL FRAMEWORK

In this section, I deconstruct my lived experience and share an endarkened feminist epistemology (EFE) dual identity framework to unpack my identity as a Black female teacher and scholar. To begin, the EFE dual identity framework is composed of three concentric circles that represent the components of my constantly evolving identity; my lived experience; my identity factors, personal, cultural, and professional; and my dual identity, personal and professional. The largest concentric circle represents the messages received from my lived experience, childhood to the present, which include the following dichotomies:

You are a strong Black woman/you are weak.

You can trust/trust no one.

You don't matter/you do matter.

You are a natural leader/you are a follower.

You are professional/you are unprofessional.

You are competent/you are incompetent.

You are a hard worker/you do not work hard enough.

Know your place/step up.

Be independent/be dependent.

Black is beautiful/Black is a problem.

Education is the key to success and a better life/you are stupid and will fail.

Dillard (2008a) notes that these binaries are characteristic of Foucault's notion of subjectivity, which elucidates the fine line African American women walk in terms of "self-naming and being named by others" (p. 88). Hence, I must reconcile these dichotomies to develop a strong sense of individual agency to counter racism and sexism that I experience in my life.

The second largest concentric circle (see Figure 7.1) represented in the EFE framework represents the three sets of critical identity factors—personal, cultural, and professional—that informs my dual identity. The first identity factor, personal, is composed of attributes that make up my personal self. These include first-generation graduate, successful, racially and socially conscious, resilient, hard-working, independent, intelligent, and competent. Lee, Lomotey, and Shujaa (1990) assert that African American children who have an understanding of who they are and where they come from within the larger social and cultural contexts aids in protecting them from acculturating into the White supremacist culture. Although I did not attend an African-centered school, a school in which African American history and culture is centered and not marginalized (Lee, 1992), I had a strong sense of who I was as a Black child. I can attribute this strong sense of self to my family and the Black community in which I lived. Evans-Winters (2011) notes that the Black family and community serve as a buffer to counter racist and oppressive acts. My family, community, and school protected me from racism and oppression.

The second identity factor, cultural, is composed of cultural realities that inform how I see myself within African American culture. I am now a professional with credentials from a reputable institution and paid labor. At times, middle-class status is uncomfortable. For example, I lived in a housing project during childhood and was exposed to violence. My sister and I were raised by a single mother who taught us to be proud of where we came from. hooks (1990) defines cultural identity as the ability to move beyond narrow views of Black identity while still embracing this notion of Black liberation. Thus, just because I have obtained middle-class status, I am still a Black woman living in White supremacist America, and *yearn* (hooks, 1990) to continue to fight racism, sexism, and oppression.

The third identity factor, professional, is composed of professional roles that influence my professional identity: licensed clinical social worker (LCSW), educator, higher education administrator, graduate student, leader, and activist. The term *professionalism* is problematic because it is rooted in White Eurocentric knowledge and values of what is deemed appropriate behavior (Johnson, 2003).

Evans-Winters (2011), referencing Foucault (1984), explains how the student is a docile body that needs rules and regulations to control its actions. The same is true for paid labor; the education, training, and certifications that I have received were all designed to control how I would function as a professional.

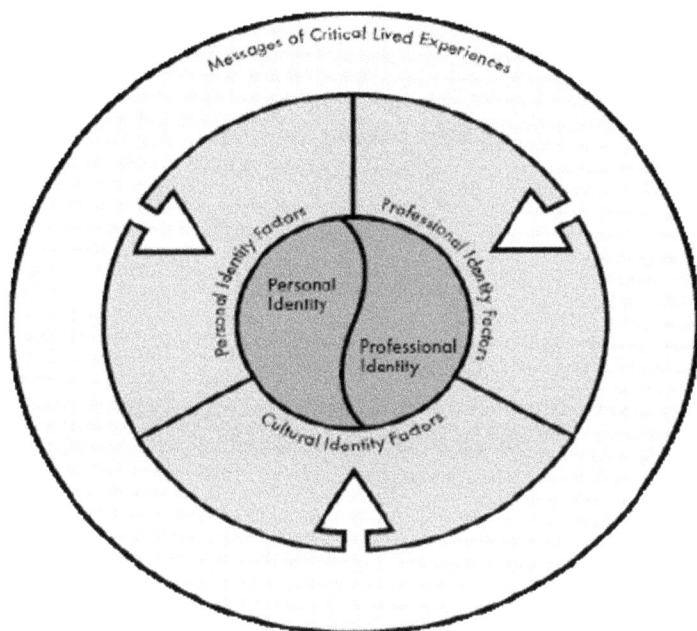

Figure 7.1. Endarkened feminist epistemology (EFE) dual identity framework

This limited view of professionalism does not take into consideration other ways of being and knowing. Basically, it can be viewed as another way of forcing African Americans to assimilate into the dominant hegemonic perception of the well-behaved and acceptable Black person (A. Davis, 1972; Evans-Winters, 2011; Johnson, 2003). All three critical identity factors contributed to the evolution of my dual identity.

The smallest concentric circle represents my dual identity, as both private and professional person. Identity has been defined as the foundation for how we view ourselves, our future prospects, and how we make meaning of lived experience (Swanson et al., 2012). Thus, the EFE dual identity framework delineates the process of identity development from lived experience to identity. The definition of identity is complicated by the intersection of race, culture, and gender. For example, racial identity is defined as the attitudes and perceptions a minority member has of her or his race in relation to the majority racial group (Swanson, Cunningham, Youngblood, & Beal Spencer, 2009). Thus, as a middle-class Black female, the development of my dual identity is influenced by my self-perception and the perceptions others have of me. Additionally, a dual identity is consistent with academic resilience within African American students to resist and buffer racism and patriarchy (Evans-Winters, 2011). The EFE dual identity framework represents how my identity developed and reveals the centrality of my racial identity. The framework is not static and will continue to evolve based on my continued lived experience as African ascendant, African American, and female scholar. Last, the EFE dual identity framework can provide new insights into the substantive differences Black women experience in comparison to White women in the conceptualization of racism and sexism (Dillard, 2000; King, 1988).

MY LIFE NOTES

I believe who we are as persons is the sum total of our lived experience and the meaning we make of that experience. What follows are stories that illustrate the messages received that formed my dual identity most profoundly. Although each story is embedded in a particular time, the messages have reverberated throughout my life.

lessons from mama

In my formative years, I received the first messages from my Mama that directly influenced how I saw myself and how others viewed Blacks. Today, I negotiate and reconcile those messages as a working, middle-class Black female. Mama taught me what it meant to be a strong Black woman. She worked long hours as a domestic worker, seven days a week with rarely any time off. I watched Mama navigate single parenthood, while working, to ensure that she could always take care of us. During the slave economy, Black women worked alongside Black men, never to be placed on a pedestal of purity and chasteness (A. Davis, 1972). King (1988) reminds us of the complexity of Black womanhood and the social, historical implications of racism and sexism. Labor, whether paid or unpaid, for Black women has always been a part of our role within the Black family and larger society (A. Davis, 1972; hooks, 2000).

Living in the "hood" shielded us from the realities of being Black in America and protected us from racism. The few times we did go outside of our "hood," Mama gave us explicit instructions on how we were to behave in public. During one of our trips, I learned for the first time how others viewed Black people. We went to a store in a predominately White neighborhood. While we were in the store a little White girl said, "Mommy look at the niggers." At the time I did not understand what *nigger* meant, but now I know the meaning and power of the word. The experience we had that day began my racial socialization, began my understanding of oppression and racism in America.

It was clear to me early on that I had to know who to trust and not trust to survive and thrive in this world as a Black woman. Living in an all-Black community taught me how to deal with racism and oppression. Evans-Winters (2011) asserts resilient African American girls have an adult or role model who helps them to understand race, class, and gender oppression and strategies to address it. Mama and other Black women in my school and community were my role models. My racial identity always would be a factor in the kind of life I could have. Hence, the early messages from Mama—be proud, be independent, be a hard worker, be a survivor, and trust no one—informed my personal, cultural, and professional identity factors.

lessons from school

I attended predominately Black schools until entering university. My teachers were successful African Americans who stressed that education was the key to success. Throughout my school years, I was considered smart, received high marks, and was respected by my teachers and the administrators. I wanted a successful career and the ability to take care of myself. I had watched Denise Huxtable go to college on the *Cosby Show* and I wanted the same experience. King (1988) notes that education is a significant factor in determining one's income level regardless of race and gender and the more education you have the more money you will make. However, the income level of Black women varied when comparing race/income level, income level/gender, race/education level, income level/education level (King, 1988). For example, in "Multiple Jeopardy Multiple Consciousness," King (1988) illustrates the complexity of race, class, and gender on socioeconomic status and income level. In a comparison of White men and women and Black men and women, the median income of White men was higher than White women and Black men and women, with Black women at the lowest socioeconomic level. In terms of educational level, White men had the most years of education. However, the level of education for both White men and women was higher than Black men and women. The role of gender is important to understand the socioeconomic status of Black women, but race is more relevant to understanding our educational attainment (King, 1988). In other words, the primary message I received during my school days was: "Education is the key to success and a better life."

My acceptance to college was a major accomplishment, but I was not prepared for the academics or for being the "token Black." I was often ignored in class and felt isolated and alone. I struggled academically because I did not know how to study and was uncomfortable asking for help. I had to learn to trust others and ask for help. Scholars note that the racial and ethnic bias African American students perceive while attending predominately White institutions contributes to feeling like they do not belong and may result in their early departure (Astin, 1993; Johnson, 2003; Tinto, 1975). Furthermore, these biases also reaffirm the threat of negative stereotypes that African American students believe others perceive of them (Steele, 1999). Claude Steele (1999) examined the concept of "stereotype threat" that minority students feel while attending predominately White institutions; higher education institutions with a predominately White student body. Stereotype threat is defined as the fear of being perceived negatively or doing something that supports or confirms the negative stereotype. Steele (1999) found that Black students did not perform as well as their White peers, even though both groups were statistically matched based on their academic ability. Thus, the chilly campus climate that I experienced coupled with stereotype threat negatively affected my ability to be academically successful as an undergraduate. As a result, I was placed on academic probation at the end of the fall semester of my sophomore year in college.

I met an academic advisor who was genuinely interested in my academic career. He became my first mentor because he understood the pressures I felt as a first-generation college student. I allowed myself to trust him and share my fears. The role of mentors or *muses* (Evans-Winters, 2011) serves as a protective barrier for African American students in the academy. Mentorship has been proven to positively influence African American student retention at predominately White institutions (D. J. Davis, 2010). Black students report feeling supported and understood by their mentor. My mentor was an African American male who shared with me his experiences with racism and oppression. Although the experiences of Black men and women differ in terms of how we experience racism and oppression (P. H. Collins, 1991; A. Davis, 1972; hooks, 2000; King, 1988), it was comforting to know that he understood what I was going through.

I graduated with semester honors and moved on to graduate school at a highly respected university. The primary messages from my college days were "you are a hard worker" and "you can trust others." These would reinforce my personal identity factors—resilient, hard-worker, intelligent, and independent—and set the foundation for my professional identity factors: activist, LCSW, administrator, and leader.

The little Black girl completed an undergraduate degree and had the audacity to begin earning a master's degree in social work. Although I had already accomplished so much, I felt like an imposter. My self-doubts coupled with the knowledge that the university had a history of barring Blacks contributed to my anxieties about being "good enough." My Black peers felt the same way and we formed an unspoken alliance. We knew our White counterparts thought we were admitted because of affirmative action. We were committed to disproving their assumptions. Class discussions often led to racist and insensitive comments made by our White peers. We spoke out to counter those racist messages. Talking back was not always viewed as an asset, especially for Black women, but as I matured and became more racially conscious, it became imperative to talk back, speak up, and speak out (hooks, 2000; Lorde, 1984).

In summary, the messages from this time were clear but contradictory: "you don't matter," "you are intelligent," "you are a hard worker," "Black is a problem," "Black is beautiful." My graduate experience strongly contributed to my cultural identity factor as a Black woman and to my personal identity factors as a successful and resilient person and to the early formation of professional identity factors: activist, leader, and scholar.

lessons from professional life

I embraced my life as a social worker practicing in agencies and in public schools. My experience taught me how powerful social work can be in the lives of underprivileged children. I grew to understand that social workers have the advantage of practicing at the intersection of the academic and social realities of their students' lives. I believed I could help more children by educating future social workers to act as agents of change and freedom. I accepted a position that included teaching responsibilities in a public university's school of social work as the director of recruitment and admissions.

During my first year of teaching, I felt disrespected by my students. I wanted to re-create the experience I had in my master's program and I had high expectations for my students' performance in my class. Sensing that there was something more going on, I asked for help. I solicited feedback from my students facilitated by another professor. I had no idea what would follow.

The students felt they were not treated equitably, I was too critical, and I would get defensive when faced with criticism. They even questioned my qualifications. I was blindsided, enraged, and unsure how to engage them. It took great restraint to unpack the racist overtones from the chat. Black female faculty report that they struggle to gain access and inclusion while teaching at PWIs (A. C. Collins, 2001; Jayakumar, Howard, Allen, & Han, 2009; Lorde, 1984). And I was no exception. I struggled to remain true to my lived experience without denying theirs. I knew I had to make it a teachable moment. I was not a teacher when I started, but by the end of that class I was well on my way to becoming one. My experience confirmed for me that I was learning to teach while teaching (Lorde, 1984).

The messages received as a professional shifted radically from "you don't matter," "you are incompetent," to "you do matter," "you are competent." My professional experiences reinforced my personal identity factors: competent, successful, and hardworking. The contributions from this period to my professional identity were the development of my roles as LCSW, educator, and higher education administrator.

THE CONTINUED JOURNEY FOR THIS BLACK FEMALE SCHOLAR

Since entering the academy, I gained new competencies, found my voice, and became unafraid to share my truth. As a result, I feel empowered to continue my journey. I envision applying my EFE dual identity framework in my work as an educator and as a scholar.

I have learned as an educator that teaching is a political act; the relationship between teacher and student mirrors societal tensions between oppressor and oppressed. In my work as an educator, I try to liberate my students' minds from conformity. I want them to think critically and question everything (Freire, 1993). Using this framework, I can critically evaluate the praxis and methodologies I use to educate my students. I will continue teaching from my own lived experience while honoring theirs.

The EFE dual identity framework can be used to engage in critical discussions about being culturally responsive to the changing needs of Black students in the academy. The framework coupled with Evans-Winters's (2011) research on protective factors and other Black feminist theories forces policymakers and educators to ask significant questions about the Black student experience, how their biases shape decisions made that affect a student's ability to survive and thrive in the academy (Evans-Winters, 2011; hooks, 1990). Additionally, the EFE dual identity framework bridges the gap between teacher-student, researcher-researched, object-subject to produce more culturally relevant theories and praxes to improve the educational experiences of Black women in the academy. This framework can help educators understand a student's raced, classed, and gendered experience (Evans-Winters, 2011) by unpacking their own experience through the personal/cultural/professional identity factors as referenced in Figure 7.1. By unpacking their own identity factors through a raced, classed, and gendered lens, educators (PreK–20) will become more aware of their biases and have a better understanding of their students' lived experiences.

I recognize that my lived experience is not the same as the lived experience of other sisters in the academy and to assume so would negate their lived experience and silence their voices (A. C. Collins, 2001; P. H. Collins, 1991; hooks, 2000; King, 1988; Lorde, 1984). Validating the realities of Black women and other people of color will ultimately lead to a more just and equitable society (Dillard, 2000). Last, only by telling our (her)stories can there be any real change to fight injustices from a social, political, historical, and economic standpoint (P. H. Collins, 1991; Dillard, 2000, 2008a, 2008b; Evans-Winters, 2011; hooks, 1990, 2000; Lorde, 1984).

REFERENCES

Astin, A. W. (1993). *Assessment for excellence: The philosophy and practice of assessment and evaluation in higher education.* New York: American Council on Education.

Collins, A. C. (2001). Black women in the academy: An historical overview. In R. O. Mabokela & A. L. Green (Eds.), *Sisters of the academy: Emergent Black women scholars in higher education* (pp. 29–42). Sterling, VA: Stylus.

Collins, P. H. (1991). *Black feminist thought: Knowledge, consciousness, and the politics of empowerment.* New York: Routledge.

Davis, A. (1972). Reflections on the Black woman's role in the community of slaves. *The Massachusetts Review, 13*(1/2), 81–100.

Davis, D. J. (2010). The academic influence of mentoring upon African American undergraduate aspirants to the professoriate. *The Urban Review, 42*, 143–158.

Dillard, C. B. (2000). The substance of things hoped for, the evidence of things not seen: Examining an endarkened feminist epistemology in educational research and leadership. *Qualitative Studies in Education, 13*(6), 661–681.

Dillard, C. B. (2008a). Re-membering culture: Bearing witness to the spirit of identity in research. *Race, Ethnicity, and Education, 11*(1), 87–93.

Dillard, C. B. (2008b). *Learning to (re)member the things we've learned to forget.* New York: Peter Lang.

Du Bois, W. E. B. (2011). The sociological souls of black folk. In R. A. Wortham (Ed.), *Essays by W. E. B. Du Bois* (pp. vii–207). Lanham, MD: Lexington.

Evans-Winters, V. E. (2011). *Teaching Black girls: Resilience in urban classrooms.* New York: Peter Lang.

Foucault, M. (1984). The subject and power. In P. Rabinow (Ed.), *The Foucault reader* (pp. 208–226). New York: Random House.

Freire, P. (1993). *Pedagogy of the oppressed.* New York: Continuum.

hooks, b. (1990). *Yearning: Race, gender, and cultural politics.* Boston, MA: South End Press.

hooks, b. (2000). *Feminist theory: From margin to center.* Cambridge, MA: South End Press.

Jayakumar, U. M., Howard, T. C., Allen, W. R., & Han, J. C. (2009). Racial privilege in the professoriate; an explanation of campus climate, retention, and satisfaction. *Journal of Higher Education, 80*(5), 538–563.

Johnson, C. (2003). The mask: A survival tool. In A. L. Green & L. V. Scott (Eds.), *Journey to the Ph.D. How to navigate the process as African Americans* (pp. 168–194). Sterling, VA: Stylus.

King, D. K. (1988). Multiple jeopardy, multiple consciousness: The context of a black ideology. *Signs, 14*(1), 42–72.

Lee, C., Lomotey, K., & Shujaa, M. (1990). How shall we sing our sacred song in a strange land? The dilemma of double consciousness and the complexities of an African-centered pedagogy. *Journal of Education, 172*, 45–61.

Lee, C. D. (1992). Profile of an independent Black institution: African-centered education at work. *The Journal of Negro Education, 61*(2), 160–177.

Lorde, A. (1984). *Sister outsider: Essays and speeches by Audre Lorde.* Berkeley, California: Crossing Press.

Steele, C. (1999). Thin ice: Stereotype threat and Black college students. *The Atlantic,* 08. Retrieved from http://www.theatlantic.com/magazine/archive/1999/08/thin-ice-stereotype-threat-and-black-college-students/304663/

Swanson, D. P., Cunningham, B., Spencer, M., Dell'Angelo, T., Harpalani, V., & Spencer, T. T. (2002). Identity processes and the positive youth development of African Americans: An explanatory framework. *New Directions for Youth Development, 2002*(95), 73–99.

Swanson, D. P., Cunningham, M., Youngblood, J., & Beal Spencer, M. (2009). Racial identity development during childhood. In H. A. Neville, B. M. Tynes, & S. O. Utsey (Eds.), *Handbook of African American psychology* (pp. 269–281). Thousand Oaks, CA: Sage.

Taking root: The vision of wangari maathai. (2008). L. Merton (Producer) & A. Dater (Director). DVD. Available from http://takingrootfilm.com/production-team.htm

Tinto, V. (1975). Dropout from higher education: A theoretical synthesis of recent research. *Review of Educational Research, 45*(1), 89–125.

CHAPTER EIGHT

Having Our Say in Higher Education

African American Women's Stories of "Doing Science" Through Spiritual Capital

EZELLA MCPHERSON

African American women are one of the fastest growing populations in higher education, yet they remain underrepresented in science, technology, engineering, and mathematical (STEM) fields. In 2010, African American women represented 14,858 (15%) of the 100,000 undergraduate women STEM recipients (National Science Foundation, 2013). Research also shows that spirituality affects college students' academic achievement, engagement, persistence, and retention (Bowman & Small, 2012; Donahoo & Caffey, 2010; Gilford & Reynolds, 2011; Strayhorn, 2011). A growing body of scholarship confirms that African American women rely on faith and prayer to navigate college and/or graduate school (Agosto & Karanxha, 2011/2012; Patton & McClure, 2009). The reliance on the Lord through prayer, faith, and church are important components of spiritual capital (Chaney, 2008a; Friedli, 2001; Wortham, 2007). Yet, there has been little research that examines the connection between spirituality and African American women's retention and persistence in STEM fields (Jordan, 2006; McPherson, 2012; Warren, 2000). Even fewer studies have explored African American women's challenges in science majors (Agosto & Karanxha, 2011/2012; Jordan, 2006; Warren, 2000) and the role of spiritual capital in their college student persistence.

To fill these gaps, the purpose of this study is to investigate African American women's experiences in STEM fields and persisting in the face of adversity. The chapter begins with a review of the literature on church and spirituality in higher education, followed by a discussion of the spiritual capital and Black feminist thought frameworks. The sections that follow help us to understand African American women's experiences in the culture of science and how spiritual capital accounted for their college persistence.

OUR LEGACIES: THE CHURCH AND SPIRITUALITY

Historically, African Americans have relied heavily on the church for spiritual guidance and biblical teachings through religious denominations, such as the Baptist, Lutheran, Catholic, and Pentecostal (Giles, 2010; Hill, 2003). Additionally, African Americans are involved in churches for a variety of reasons, including fellowship, hope, prayer, love, community involvement, and hearing the spoken word (Chaney, 2008b). A limited number of studies have examined spirituality in the context of higher education for African American women (Abar, Carter, & Winsler, 2009; Dennis, Hicks, Priya, & Dennis, 2005; Patton & McClure, 2009; Strayhorn, 2011; Watt, 2003).

Abar et al. (2009) and Donahoo and Caffey's (2010) research found a positive correlation between religion and academic performance in college. Additionally, engagement in church and choirs gave African American female students a sense of belonging to a church family and home, which aided in their persistence and resilience in college, especially at predominately White institutions (PWIs) (Donahoo & Caffey, 2010; Strayhorn, 2011). Ceglie (2013) also found that African American women from religious families attributed their continuance in science majors in college to their spirituality and religious beliefs. To conclude, the literature review above reflects what we know about spirituality and religion in higher education. The abbreviated review also shows some research gaps through the omission of the two frameworks, spiritual capital and Black feminist thought.

CONCEPTS FOR GUIDING OUR STORIES

This chapter combines spiritual capital with Black feminist thought to create a unified framework for understanding African American women's experiences of *doing science*. Spiritual capital involves a connection to God through prayer, church attendance (Chaney, 2008a), and involvement in religious organizations (Wortham, 2007). Verter (2003) shares three additional criteria to describe spiritual capital, including the embodied state (e.g., knowledge about religion), objectified state (e.g., texts, scriptures), and the institutionalized state (e.g., church). Spiritual capital builds a buffer that enables people to be resilient (Friedli, 2001).

This form of capital helps people by promoting positive mental health, well-being, and a *good life* (Friedli, 2001; Wortham, 2007).

Similarly, Black feminist thought has the potential to advocate for the positive health of Black women by exposing their everyday lived experiences with interlocking forms of oppression, including racism, sexism, and classism (Collins, 2000; hooks, 2000). It also privileges Black women's knowledge through everyday lived experiences with multiple identities (e.g., race, class, gender, sexuality, nationality), which can account for their experiences with discrimination (Collins, 2000; Feagin & Yanick, 1998). These experiences include "being the only one" in employment or educational settings, and health issues (Collins, 2000; hooks, 2000; McPherson, 2012). By merging spiritual capital with Black feminist thought we can better understand African American women's stories of risk and resilience in STEM majors.

SETTING THE STAGE TO TELL OUR SCIENCE STORIES AT A PWI

The purpose of this original study is to investigate African American women's experiences in STEM fields and persisting in the face of adversity. The study answers the question: How does spiritual capital influence African American women's persistence in science majors? The sections below describe the data collection and analysis methods.

Multiple Case Study. For this multiple case research study, the participants were six African American women who initially majored in biology, engineering, and math at Town University, which is a PWI. Each participant also engaged in interviews and completed journal reflections. This multiple case study methodology is an appropriate methodology to compare and contrast findings between experiments (Yin, 2009).

Data Analysis. The electronically recorded interviews were transcribed verbatim. The interviews and journal entries were then coded to develop patterns consistent with qualitative research data analysis (Lofland & Lofland, 1995). The qualitative research results demonstrate that meaningful patterns and trends can be found in the data, which are presented in the next section.

THE SPOKEN WORD: OUR STORIES OF RISK AND RESILIENCE IN SCIENCE

African American women participants encountered barriers while *doing science* at PWIs, due to their multiple identities of race, class, and gender. However, making use of spiritual capital accounted for the persistence of the women in their respective fields. Below are some narratives that reveal these women's lived experiences in STEM majors at Town University from the Black feminist thought epistemology.

Speaking Up About Teaching and Learning in STEM. From a Black feminist thought perspective, one challenge that undergraduate African American women endured due to their race and gender were White male professors who promoted course failure through their teaching styles and course workloads in the culture of science at Town University. The culture of science revolves around teaching and learning within STEM fields using a Western mode of thought that is dominated by White and male perspectives (Harding, 2006; Seiler & Gonsalves, 2010). The narratives below revealed that White male professors' teaching styles and course workloads were *ill-fits* for African American women's learning styles. When asked about the teaching style of White male professors in Town University's Department of Biology classes, health science graduate Danielle responded:

> [In biology classes]... I don't think I need to know all that information. I don't think anyone does. They push it all on you and it kind of forces people out of the major a little bit. They put those [weed-out] classes up front.

Similarly, an engineering graduate, Simone, spoke about the structure of engineering classes that made her want to leave college in the senior year.

> Every Thursday when I am doing homework. I would say the worst time [was when] I had moved off campus my junior year. I moved kind of far off campus. I was tired of engineering. The way that engineering works [is that] we have a lot of classes before we get to our core [classes].... So, the classes that I am interested in are in the 400 level.

These excerpts confirmed that the teaching styles in STEM courses forced some African American women to drop courses and/or to change their majors to obtain their degrees from Town University. All participants mentioned that there were no African American female faculty members in their respective programs to help them fully understand the culture of science at Town University.

Speaking Out About the Academic Rigor in STEM. From a Black feminist thought perspective, another obstacle that African American women faced was a rigorous curriculum that weeded out students based on race, class, and gender. A lower-middle-class social science graduate, Carmen, disclosed her experiences:

> My first semester, *I failed two, four-hour courses*.... It was a biology class and I had a BioChem class. I think that I may have had a *D*. It was so crazy, I had those two that I did horrible on. Then I had three other classes that I got two B's and an A in. So, it was like night and day.... Then, someone was like they are weed out classes.... I am just glad that is over. Cause my first year sucked. *I was crying every day.*

Additionally, Town University's Department of Biology culture made African American women such as low-income health science graduate Amber consider dropping out of college. "I probably feel like I kind of want to... because *I kept failing the exams....* Is this really for me? Is this really what *God* wants me to do with my life?"

Despite these risks for failure in the biology major, due to race, class, and gender and the culture of science at Town University, a low-income, African American woman, Briana, earned her bachelor's degree in biology. She provided some recommendations for changing the Department of Biology's culture. She states:

> I know that the departments are not in control of the grading scale[s] for exams and the curve. I had a really difficult class last semester. They did not care who, their goal was pretty much for everyone, and [well about] 50% of the class to get a "C" or below and they definitely achieved that. So maybe, like I said, try not *to weed out students so much*.

The above narratives illustrated that the culture of science leads to feelings of self-doubt and a defeatist attitude, which confirms prior research on students of colors' experiences in STEM majors (Espinosa, 2011; McGee & Martin, 2011; Ong, Wright, Espinosa, & Orfield, 2011).

Experiences with White Male Peers. In college classrooms, the Black feminist thought perspective showed that African American women experienced adversity working with White male peers due to their race, class, and gender. Below, a low-income biology graduate, Ashley, describes her experiences in a physics class while working on a group project:

> I was the only Black student in class, which I am used to, but in this group, I was the only female. I was the *only Black person, Black female*. There were three White guys and a lot of times, I definitely couldn't get a word in or if I had an idea about something it would be wrong, at least they thought that it was wrong, even though it was probably right.

A low-income chemistry graduate, Kayla, described similar difficulties in terms of comfort levels in working with peers for physics, biology, and chemistry classes. She states:

> [I am] pretty much [comfortable with] African American males and females [in classes]. But I can also be comfortable around any other gender and culture, like Caucasian males, Indian males, as long as they're willing to communicate with me and don't make things awkward.... It gets easier as the semester progresses, because we're a little more comfortable with each other.

From these narratives, the Black feminist thought epistemology enabled us to gain a greater understanding of African American women's adversity in STEM majors due to their multiple identities and the culture of science at Town University.

The section that follows describes how spiritual capital accounted for their college persistence.

Spiritual Capital and Persistence. African American women in the study who persisted in science majors drew on spiritual capital. For example, when undergraduate African American women contemplated departing from their respective majors, they attributed their persistence to the Lord keeping them in their majors.

> I had moved off campus my junior year.... I was tired of engineering... I talked to my parents about it.... They basically told me that they will support the decision that I made and to *pray* about it and get back to them. That is what I did. (Simone, engineering graduate)

> Freshman year, I still do sometimes. *My parents just pray for me....* Everybody *prays* for me.... Then they will *pray* for me. So, just having that support on my side with my parents. (Danielle, health science graduate)

> I have never had an issue with science except for math until I got here.... *A lot of prayer*, because at the moment that it was going down I was so ashamed and scared that I didn't tell anybody until it was all done with.... Lots of church. Lots of *prayer*; lots of fasting, [and] lots of Bible reading. (Carmen, social science graduate)

> Spirituality was a very big part.... At [one] point I [questioned myself], is this a sign from God [that] I shouldn't be doing it? At the same time in the Bible, he talks about he will give you desires of your heart and that's something I really want to do then it's going to happen. *I'm going to be able to make a way* so health science was the best way with the *least amount of stress*. I can probably finish biology and do well and be okay at it.... I don't want to be mediocre. *Mediocrity is not my policy*; excellence is [my policy]. So, I want to [be] excellent and great at something. I'm going to do what's going to make me excellent. (Amber, health science graduate)

The above reflections illustrate how spiritual capital kept these African American women engaged in science despite obstacles during their journeys. These findings are consistent with research on spiritual capital (Chaney, 2008a) and spirituality (Patton & McClure, 2009), which confirms that spirituality served as a buffer to help African American women cope with challenges in college. In this study, it is also apparent that spiritual capital kept African American women pursuing science majors in the face of constant adversity.

REFLECTING BACK AND MOVING FORWARD: AFRICAN AMERICAN WOMEN IN STEM IN THE 21ST CENTURY

In sum, from a Black feminist thought standpoint African American women *doing science* endured hardships, including teaching style in STEM courses, academic rigor, and working with White male peers. In the culture of science at

Town University, African American women were in a White and male-dominated environment. They also had few African American females as classmates, and there were no African American female faculty members in their respective programs. This finding is similar to previous scholarship that revealed the absence of African American female faculty in the academy (Patton, 2009) who are needed to mentor younger scholars in STEM fields (Jordan, 2006; Warren, 2000). Despite these barriers, spiritual capital helped to explain how African American women persisted in science majors at Town University. By highlighting spirituality and religion, this research has implications regarding the use of spiritual capital as a factor that can help explain the persistence, retention, and graduation of African American women in undergraduate STEM majors.

This scholarship adds to our knowledge on Black feminist thought and spiritual capital, in this case *doing science* on the part of the silenced population of African American women in STEM fields. Their narratives will in turn help future African American female science scholars to better understand their current or future experiences in science fields and how spiritual capital is one source of support. This research also has implications for higher education policies. Two-year and four-year institutions should consider providing spiritual support by distributing information on faith-based student organizations, academic coaches, and local churches that can encourage more African American women's continuance in science majors.

REFERENCES

Abar, B., Carter, K. L., & Winsler, A. (2009). The effects of maternal parenting style and religious commitment on self-regulation, academic achievement, and risk behavior among African-American parochial college students. *Journal of Adolescence, 32*(2), 259–273.

Agosto, V., & Karanxha, Z. (2011/2012). Resistance meets spirituality in academia: "I prayed on it!" *Negro Educational Review, 62/63*(1–4), 41–66.

Bowman, N. A., & Small, J. L. (2012). Exploring a hidden form of minority status: College students' religious affiliation and well-being. *Journal of College Student Development, 53*(4), 491–509.

Ceglie, R. (2013). Religion as a support factor for women of color pursuing science degrees: Implications for science teacher educators. *Journal of Science Teacher Education, 24*, 37–65.

Chaney, C. (2008a). Religiosity and spirituality among members of an African American church community: A qualitative analysis. *Journal of Religion & Spirituality in Social Work: Social Thought, 27*(3), 201–234.

Chaney, C. (2008b). The benefits of church involvement for African-Americans: The perspectives of congregants, church staff, and the church pastor. *Journal of Religion and Society, 10*, 1–23.

Collins, P. H. (2000). *Black feminist thought: Knowledge, consciousness, and the politics of empowerment*. New York: Routledge.

Dennis, D. L., Hicks, T., Priya, B., & Dennis, B. G. (2005). Spirituality among a predominately African American college student population. *American Journal of Health Studies, 20*(3/4), 135–142.

Donahoo, S., & Caffey, R. A. (2010). A sense of home: The impact of church participation on African American college students. *Journal of Research on Christian Education, 19*, 79–104.

Espinosa, L. L. (2011). Pipelines and pathways: Women of color in undergraduate STEM majors and the college experiences that contribute to persistence. *Harvard Education Review, 81*(2), 209–240.

Feagin, J., & Yanick, S. J. (1998). *Double burden: Black women and everyday racism.* Armonk: M.E. Sharpe.

Friedli, L. (2001). Social and spiritual capital: Building "emotional resilience" in communities and individuals. *Political Theology, 2*(4), 55–64.

Giles, M. S. (2010). Howard Thurman, Black spirituality, and critical race theory in higher education. *The Journal of Negro Education, 79*(3), 354–365.

Gilford, T. T., & Reynolds, A. (2011). My mother's keeper: The effects of parentification on Black female college students. *Journal of Black Psychology, 37*(1), 55–77.

Harding, S. (2006). *Science and social inequality: Feminist and poststructural issues.* Urbana: University of Illinois Press.

Hill, R. (2003). *The strengths of black families.* Lanham, MD: University Press of America.

hooks, b. (2000). *Feminist theory: From margin to center.* Cambridge, MA: South End.

Jordan, D. (2006). *Sisters in science: Conversations with Black women scientists on race, gender, and their passion for science.* West Lafayette, IN: Purdue University.

Lofland, J., & Lofland, L. H. (1995). *Analyzing social settings: A guide to qualitative observation and analysis.* Belmont, CA: Wadsworth.

McGee, E. O., & Martin, D. B. (2011). "You would not believe what I have to go through to prove my intellectual value!": Stereotype management among academically successful Black mathematics and engineering students. *American Educational Research Journal, 48*(6), 1347–1389. doi:10.3102/0002831211423972

McPherson, E. (2012). *Undergraduate African American women's narratives on persistence in science majors at a PWI* (Unpublished doctoral dissertation). Urbana: University of Illinois.

National Science Foundation. (2013). *Minorities, women, and persons with disabilities in Science and Engineering: 2013.* Retrieved from www.nsf.gov

Ong, M., Wright, C., Espinosa, L. L., & Orfield, G. (2011). Inside the double bind: A synthesis of empirical research on undergraduate and graduate women of color in science, technology, engineering, and mathematics. *Harvard Educational Review, 81*(2), 172–208.

Patton, L. (2009). My sister's keeper: A qualitative examination of mentoring experiences among African American women in graduate and professional schools. *The Journal of Higher Education, 5*, 510–537.

Patton, L., & McClure, M. L. (2009). Strength in the spirit: African American college women and spiritual coping mechanisms. *Journal of Negro Education, 78*(1), 42–54.

Seiler, G., & Gonsalves, A. (2010). Student-powered science: Science education for and by African American students. *Equity & Excellence in Education, 43*, 88–105.

Strayhorn, T. L. (2011). Singing in a foreign land: An exploratory study of gospel choir participation among African American undergraduates at a predominantly White institution. *Journal of College Student Development, 52*(2), 137–153.

Verter, B. (2003). Spiritual capital: Theorizing religion with Bourdieu against Bourdieu. *Sociological Theory, 21*(2), 150–174.

Warren, W. (2000). *Black women scientists in the United States.* Bloomington: Indiana University Press.

Watt, S. K. (2003). Come to the river: Using spirituality to cope, resist, and develop identity. *New Directions for Student Services, 104,* 29–40.

Wortham, R. A. (2007). Spiritual capital and the "good life." *Sociological Spectrum, 27,* 439–452.

Yin, R. K. (2009). How to do better case studies (with illustrations from 20 exemplary case studies). In L. Bickman & D. J. Rog (Eds.), *The Sage handbook of applied social research methods* (pp. 254–282). Los Angeles: Sage.

CHAPTER NINE

Truly Professin' Hip-Hop—The Rewind (1996)

Makin' Black Girls Embodied Musical Play the Teacher

KYRA D. GAUNT

In this chapter, I, the author, present a series of personal reflections in third-person narrative. Narrating memories from my earliest year of professing hip-hop as music to a diverse group of male and female students as an ethnomusicologist teaching Black popular music at the predominately White University of Virginia in the fall of 1996 and the spring of 1997. Teaching undergraduate students to understand hip-hop as music through the games Black girls play was a radical act back in 1996 and perhaps still is. My intention was to embody both the intersectionality of Black girls—hidden musicians with their embodied beats and rhymes from handclapping games and double-dutch—and the non-gendered beats of hip-hop's sound, which was dominated by a masculine misogyny in the name of gangsta rap. Teaching back then was an experiment as a new professor and ideas for my pedagogy were a sort of musical revolution in departments that generally restricted themselves to jazz and classical music.

As I rewind back to the academic year of 1996–1997, three significant events took place during her first year, narrated in third person. One event dealt with mass-mediated images of Black women just before she arrived. The second involved rap music's place in popular culture and her thinking through its politics as a scholar of gender relations. The third was public debate about Black English that brought an unexpected and paradoxical index of the tensions we now live in when anyone claims we live in a "postracial" time. So she begins with recorded cassettes and images of Black women on the silver screen.

Mary J Blige's platinum single "Not Gon' Cry" was the summer jam of 1996 after the successful December 1995 film release of *Waiting to Exhale*, a romantic drama that was the "prequel" to reality TV's *Real Housewives of Atlanta* and directed by Forest Whitaker. It was based on the 1992 novel of the same name by Terry McMillan. The film struck a chord with lower- and middle-class Black women who vicariously watched Angela Bassett perform "Bernadine's rage" after her husband of 11 years left her for a White woman. She attended the film against the backdrop of a feud incited by artists and fans played about in popular discourse between East Coast and West Coast rap.

The feud involved on-stage battles and off-stage beefs—real and imagined—between Bad Boy Records in New York and Death Row Records in California, or "Cali" as we came to call it after the LL Cool J single. Students entered her classroom having debated whether Biggie or sometimes Nas was better than Tupac. The feud came to a dead stop with a drive-by shooting death. Tupac was shot on September 13, 1996, just two weeks into her first semester of teaching. Notorious B.I.G. would be shot six months later on March 9, 1997. Far too many non–hip-hop fans assumed these hyper-masculine lyrics were exclusively autobiographical as if metaphor is not available in Black English or in a world where masculinity seems to bounded and hard. The brute force of the stigma of being Black and male left no room for the artfulness that continually was born against various dreamscapes of bleak urban nihilism born from rappers' discourse at least for Black and White youth in 1996.

As wagons circled around rap lyrics and the murder of a famous rapper-actor, a national controversy erupted on December 18, 1996, over *Ebonics*. The Oakland, California, school board attempted to pass a resolution acknowledging *African American Vernacular English* (AAVE) as a distinct language. Rap, she thought, was surely evoked in the minds of non-Blacks who were being virtually assaulted by the soul sonic forces and "criminal" rhyme syndicates known as gangsta rap. Media pundits and opponents including Reverend Jesse Jackson and New York Governor Mario Cuomo panicked. Critics assumed the school board was sanctioning and thereby mandating that Black English be *taught*. Actually, the authors of the resolution were proposing that the historical origins of AAVE be used as a pedagogical tool in an English as a second language context, which she dug. It would help students whose *native tongue* differed from the "Standard English" or business/public vernacular found in children's textbooks. Unfortunately, the school board actually called it a "genetic-based" origin before revising it to historical origins in West and Niger-Congo languages. Things got twisted and the initiative was no more. She wasn't surprised.

All these events were happening front and center in the public sphere, but the classroom was the backdrop as she attempted to use Black girls' body-musicking to shift and disrupt the hegemonic anchor of patriarchy and Black masculinity in hip-hop as well as the anchors of literacy and White superiority that privileged speech and Her pedagogy had been inspired by the writings of third-world diva girl bell hooks' definitions of patriarchy (hooks, n.d.) thought in even historically Black classrooms of higher learning back in 1996. She would have never imagined the current commercial soundscape where hip-hop music is dominated by Cash Money Records artists such as Lil' Wayne, Drake, and Nicki Minaj revealing a critical insight that sociologist Margaret Hunter (2011) aptly describes: "Rap sells more than just sex, drugs and politics" (p. 15), it sells "a lifestyle" of consumption versus the early patterns of creating a more consciously political hip-hop. She'd be sure to teach "The Message" by Grandmaster Flash and the Furious Five (1982).

She wanted to write a kind of experimental auto-ethnography with retrospection on the small number of Black feminist scholars teaching hip-hop in 1996 but she opted to tell a more simple story of her transition from doctoral student to faculty member. Storytelling in the third person is retrospective and speculative in mood. She liked that. The purpose of her chapter: to highlight early attempts at inventing a new way of knowing and doing hip-hop study that included gender. She explored two main memories: first, driving to the University of Virginia and the embodied pedagogical tool she created based on girls' musical play; and second, recollections of her first encounters with the historically charged landscape of slavery at the University of Virginia during the moment of Tupac's death in 1996.

This is her praisesong to embodied ways of knowing Black girls in hip-hop, to embodied ways of being hip-hop through Black girls' ears and mouths and bodies. It is also her praisesong to the endarkened feminist praxis of Cynthia Dillard honored in this edited volume.

Her story began three years before Joan Morgan's *When Chickenheads Come Home to Roost*. Morgan's words would be the first to release her from a certain kind of silencing and self-censoring when it arrived in 1999. Just once, she didn't want to have to talk about "the brothers," "male domination," or "patriarchy." She wanted a feminism that would allow the author to explore who we are as women—not how we'd been victimized by beats and rhymes settling for the rhythms that occupied our own play (Morgan, 1999, p. 56).

"READY OR NOT (HERE I COME)": A BLACK FEMINIST'S DRIVE TO TEACH HIP-HOP

It's the end of the weekend and the end of the summer in 1996. August was the time of year when old and new professors had to go back to school. At 9 a.m. the Monday morning, she would begin new faculty orientation at the University of Virginia. She was A.B.D., as they say, at the University of Michigan. That meant she was a candidate who had finished "all but the dissertation" to complete her Ph.D. That summer she was selected as a *multicultural postdoctoral teaching fellow* to offer a course on Black popular music at Tufts University, just outside Boston. Right after her summer session she had an idea about creating a sort of handgame to teach Black musical ideals and to privilege embodied thinking about musical Blackness and being.

She was supposed to leave for Virginia at 9 a.m. that Sunday but C.P. time got the best of her plan to leave Boston early for the eight- to nine-hour drive from Boston to Charlottesville. C.P. time stands for Colored People's Time— "an inside reference within the black community on the tendency of black folk to show up late for just about anything. Other ethnic groups have their own versions" (Baratunde Hurston, 2010). Clearly, her now faded memory of falling asleep at the wheel and surviving a near-miss, head-on collision 10 years earlier wasn't making a difference. She also didn't recall that back then she also knew how dangerous it was to drive alone late at night. She had survived wrecking the axle on a new car when she fell asleep at the wheel at 21.

While she left Tufts at 9 p.m., she tried to reason with herself that *it was gonna be alright*. She used the artful dodge the same way women and men lie about the power of rap music. You know the one where we say *I don't listen to the lyrics, it's the beat*.

Cruising onto the highway in her '88 Dodge Dart with a trunk and car full of personal belongings, her fear tried to claim the convenient and partial truth that was native to the tongues of various hip-hop generations in 1996—*it's all good*. She'd be fine with her favorite *Low End Theory* cassette tape on deck. The rhymes of Phife and Q-tip and the phat, jazzy beats of Ali Shaheed Muhammad would keep her company. This would turn into another lie. Psychologists and folks interested in logic call this kind of thinking "cognitive bias." We are susceptible to it when it's late, when we're tired like she was after eight hours of packing, loading her car, and cleaning a dorm room she had occupied since late May. She was "anchoring"—a form of cognitive bias involving a tendency to rely too heavily on one piece of information when making decisions. Logic itself is always so evasive around things you are convinced are right. All her logic that night rested upon that Tribe Called Quest cassette. Yeah, she was truly buggin' out!

Of course, she had ignored the fact that the cassette deck in her Dodge Dart, passed down to her when her granddaddy passed, was by then repeatedly trying to eat the thin, brown magnetic-coated tape inside one out of three cassettes she loaded each week. The signal came when a cassette went silent. The remedy was to quickly eject and slowly pull all the tape out of the mechanism. In each of these cases, the plastic, polymer tape would droop all wrinkled and creased about six inches outside its container. The hack was to stick a pencil or a pen neatly into one of two holes of the cassette. It was always just the right size to catch the teeth for the sprocket that would pull or supply the magnetic tape during playback, fast forward, and reverse. Ordinarily, she would pop that bad boy right back in the system without skipping a beat. The trauma left could be heard in a garbled word or bass line but any passenger with a cassette tape deck recognized the traces of the hack and mindlessly omitted any distortion. The strange became familiar to us all. The hack was routine. The normal functioning of the deck was a vague and unessential memory. Like *when we were queens* respected as women or some shit like that, right? Raaaiight. LOL.

OK. So she rolled onto the ramp to I-95 South heading toward Providence and New York. It's probably 9:30 or 9:45 p.m. when she popped *Low End Theory* into the deck. And you know what happened. THE. DAMN. TAPE. GOT. STUCK!!! But she had no choice. She had to be in Charlottesville by sun-up, do or… *DAMMMN!!!* This was one of those moments where she still wouldn't wake up to the cost of C.P. time.

The first hour of the drive she mindlessly tried to get that tape out of the deck that was inside the dashboard right below the radio. We try to anthropomorphize technology. Trick it while it's not paying attention, some dumb shit. Only this would explain why you keep trying to make something happen when nothing is changing. She kept pushing eject mindlessly with her eyes on the road. Looking at the damn tape deck wasn't helping. The thing just wouldn't pop out. It just *clicked-clicked-clicked-clicked* an endlessly clicking loop in a steady beat of stuckness and silence. Stuckness. Silence. Stuckness. Silence. That was the A side, the first hour's soundtrack. The hidden track of the tape was that there would be *no* radio to replace Quest. With no soundtrack to carry her back to ol' Virginny, no Q-Tip or Phife-Dawg, no "Check the Rhime," there was virtually nobody to keep her on track, or more importantly, awake.

NOT GON' CRY (WAITING TO EXHALE): MAKIN' TRACKS DOWN I–95

So what does as a budding Black feminist ethnomusicologist who was first an R&B fan and then a classical singer do in this predicament while heading to her first tenure-track job? What does anybody who teaches musical Blackness with "sampled" beats from girls' handclapping, foot-stomping, and jump rope do? She makes beats on the steering wheel. She chants rhymes and sings hooks as if the click track of stuckness and silence was a distorted boom-bap, a rhythm section. She sang her favorite R&B songs by Chaka Khan to the click track. She shifted into classical music repertoire from bygone days as a lyric soprano. She sang "Musetta's Waltz" from Puccini's *La Bohème*, the "Silver aria" from *The Ballad of Baby Doe* by Douglas Moore, a few American and English art songs, a few chansons (French art songs), and a lied or two (German art songs). She never dared play with the classical beats. No remix allowed for Puccini and for Baby Doe. You don't mess with the classical shit: *You can't touch this!* None of her college professors, hell not even she might have guessed, that after 12 years of learning to sing Western classical music from Bach to Barber, she would define her career by teaching Black vernacular music and hip-hop.

Back in 1996, hip-hop was the antithesis of "music" and was conventionally regarded with disdain and even horror in academic circles as well as within the professional circles of Black jazz musicians and White pop musicians. That year Delfeayo Marsalis of the famed New Orleans jazz family published a critique of rap. It was formed as a question: "The Art of Rap?" It appeared in the first issue of the hip-hop magazine titled *Elementary*. (Her friend Joe Schloss, a remarkable hip-hop scholar, introduced her to the piece.) Marsalis argued that rap could not enhance one's knowledge of music theory or musical education, that it was merely for enjoyment and "boodie-shaking," nothing else. He went on to say it was primarily a vulgar, explicit use of slang and obscenities. Then he asked, how does vulgarity fit into creating art?

Those early years she gave the article as an assignment in analyzing reactions to hip-hop. Her male and female students, Black, White, Asian, and international, would push back with examples from great literature. Her personal favorite from their responses highlighted the presence of vulgar language in the English literature of Chaucer's *Canterbury Tales*, which became a standard in the American curriculum since long before the 20th century and remained in high school curricula into the 21st. Marsalis argued that rap sacrificed the tradition of Negro greatness in America by perpetuating stereotypes and coon images, that the evidence that rap was not a *true* art form was that it had no geniuses. Only a commercialized history of music needs to authorize geniuses for a consuming public, she thought.

After four hours on the road, she was struggling. Fighting fatigue in the middle of her drive to Charlottesville, without the music that anchored her logic, she tried her damnedest to stay awake to the sound of her own singing. Driving near slumber with a long stretch of highway before her, she was fiending for something that might rob the time ahead.

The car swerved a few times as she caught herself nodding, slipping into darkness in a war with time. She searched her mind: *What do I need do to wake this trip up?* Long after midnight it came to her. She started re-composing elements of practice she had begun to create in the classroom the previous week.

As she drove 60–80 mph farther and farther down I-95 South, the tempo of the click track had too often been limiting. Stuck with a monotonous click at 42 bpm (hip-hop DJs usually spin at about 80–110 beats per minute), she decided to take the slow tempo to string a pattern of embodied beats together in her mind, substituting the steering wheel for the thigh claps and her chest cavity or the dashboard for foot-stomps, to create two or three distinct timbres required for drum-dance continuum in African states, the African diaspora, Black girls' games, and hip-hop's boom-bap.

She built the game's embodied beats from the essential features of handclapping, thigh-slapping, body-patting, and foot-stomping that define practice in playing hand-clapping games or doing cheers. All this accompanied a set of rhymed chants and songs that told stories about gender, ethnicity, and youth. The lyrics of this invented tool would be simplified given the probability that non-Black students would dominate her classrooms. They needed some help back in 1996 as hip-hop hadn't fully taken hold of their embodied practices. With four beats per line and accents on beats two and four, she'd hang deeper meanings on four simple phrases in time and later her students could intuitively unpack or analyze the mnemonic meanings on their own.

> *Check One (clap) Get Two-the-floor (clap)*
> *Get Free (c) Sync-it off Four (clap)* [accenting the off-beats with the last two syllables]
> *Check One (clap) Get Two the floor (clap)*
> *Get Free (c) Sync-it off Four (clap)*
> *Check One (clap) Get Two the floor (clap)*
> *Get Free (c) Sync-it off Four (clap)*
> *Check One (clap) Get Two the floor (clap)*
> *Get Free!* [insert a tacit break at the end of 16 bars of the pattern]
>
> Repeat from the top.

She created a system within the game to embody the multi-limbed-ness of the rhythms as best she could. To shake up the monotony of the click track that still lulled her deceptively into a rut of slumber, she would tap the gas pedal, giving just enough juice to inch the car forward as if it was stressing the downbeats. You know the feeling of nodding your head to the beat. The good nodding, in this case, not the bad. That nodding effect told the reticular activating system in her brain to remain wide awake; we're dancing.

Over about 35–40 minutes of time and distance, she had worked out the structure, played with the assonance, and switched some of the end rhymes, trying to capture the right flow. Simple yet clearly signifying the idea of individuality within collectivity and mic-checking (*Check One*), the social imperative that there is not music without dance (*Get Two-the-floor*), leaving room for explanations of the art of *signifyin'* and the legacy of sociolinguistics and African retentions on our tongues (*Get Free* vs. Get Three) allowing the word "three" to be pronounced "free" like the "tree" black Caribbean folk use for the third number, and an element that both emulates and signifies on the embodied tension and sonic aspects of syncopation (*Sync-it off/four*) distinctly articulating the final –*f* and the initial *f*– of the last two words of the four-bar groove that measured up to 16 bars total.

The practice purposefully played with aspects of Ebonics and with the phonics and symbolic meaning of being musically and socially "free." *Get free* called attention to Black girls and hip-hop emcees' play with words as well as the interplay within and retention of non-dominant accents. Black English was stigmatized compared to, say, a French or German accent. The general public is up in arms over Ebonics but most people find it appealing when a Frenchman who has lived in the United States his whole life says "Ze door is open" or "Zat is not correct." When Black people say "dis" or "dat" or "tree" instead of "three," high-brow folks

White and non-White wanna catch a heartache. When you teach students that Black people are non-literate vs. illiterate, their fixed mindset about Black people shifts. It helped that *Check One* was a game, that it embodied movement and music that shifted the brain. If you can perform Blackness and still be White, if you could decenter Whiteness and allow musical Blackness and Ebonics to be all right, then maybe it could really be *all good* after all.

The lesson of this part of the oral-kinetic etudé, the play around the notion of *free*, also symbolizes how sounds *make* difference, not rational or literate sense. It forces students to learn how musical improvisation works; how it symbolizes black ways of being and knowing. It helps them get free not only on the dance floor of some kinetic aesthetic in musical Blackness, but free from the mental slavery of race and gender. Expressions like "turn it loose," "funk it up," "get down," "I wanna be down," or "get into it/get involved," "gettin' jiggy with it" or "freak out" all refer to this notion of freeing one's self from the constrictions of our nation's past and political ideology. It brought enough of an improvisational sensibility to verbal and embodied performance, to individual and group expression, to music and to the dance that students can start to really think through the social body, not just their personal reasoning about race, gender, and the body.

She had invented a little game; a little sumpin sumpin. *Check One* became the lab for a particular claim in her dissertation—Black girls' games were the earliest formation of a Black popular musical style that was a precursor to rhythm and blues, soul and hip-hop. She wanted and needed the tool to be playful to confront the emotional and psychological stressors that talking about race and gender usually presented. She wanted to emulate the games collected from African American girls and women whose childhood play captured the snatches of song and dance found in their later interactions with commercialized Black popular music whether they grew up in Baltimore and D.C., Detroit and Chicago, Los Angeles and Oakland, or Shreveport, Louisiana, and Memphis, Tennessee, to name a few of the places represented in her sample.

Girls' play, like hip-hop, was a trans-local phenomenon of musical Blackness defined by girls rather than boys, by vernacular culture only rather than steered primarily away from its vernacular roots by commercial and mass culture. Girls' local and regional musical play linked Black youth—female as well as male as younger boys were "forced" to listen in and play along with girls' dominant practices at a younger age. It also linked Black youth culture around the country creating a pool of resources occasionally accessed later by adult male producers, songwriters, rap artists, and emcees to influence Black popular taste in a highly competitive commercial market demanding sales rather than creativity or equity.

The creation of *Check One* evolved from a distinct approach in her dissertation: to analyze game-songs through close readings, to linguistically and musically unpack what it sounded and felt like to be musically Black through a female-gendered practice linked to more public, commercial, and masculinized forms of music-making. This she distilled further in her book *The Games Black Girls Play: Learning the Ropes from Double-Dutch to Hip-Hop* (Gaunt, 2006).

The idea as it was articulated in her dissertation came from her thoughts about the somatic historiography of Black girls' musical play conceiving of each musical game as an *oral-kinetic etude* in Black musical style. Each game in this repertoire represented a mnemonic device for learning, sharing, and transmitting social and musical ideals of sound, movement, and social interaction first among girls and by extension among the boys who went on to make beats and spit rhymes as a profession. *Check One* was a sociological practice as well as a musicological one that involved negotiating oral and kinetic idea technology or culture. *Check One* was meant to emulate the word-of-mouth, word-of-body practices that define Black networks of musical culture.

Using Black girls' musical games as the center of her pedagogical approach reflected an embodied "social media" that forged Black vernacular tastes or social sensibilities in sound and movement generation after generation while these games were popular before digital culture led girls inside to play. She didn't call it "social media" back in 1996 but our 21st-century use of the term is a great way of thinking about the necessary and alternative network segregated communities offered and maintained that influenced African American social cohesion. Out of Jim Crow remains a segregation defined by fear and ignorance; from social myths and stereotypes about one drop of blood, thick noses or asses, and nappy hair. These beliefs were kept in place with more formal discriminatory laws and practices.

Figure 8.1. The Mason-Dixon Line symbolized a cultural boundary between the North and the South (Dixie). It was a line of demarcation for the legality of slavery often recalled by elders in her family from Maryland.

After crossing the infamous Mason-Dixon Line, a border she had heard about since childhood as a southerner, she was dead tired. There were a couple times during the middle of the trip after too many swerves and not enough trip that she had to stop and take a 15-minute "power nap." But she made it to Virginia, to Charlottesville, to her new job and her new home just two hours from where she was raised in the D.C. area. The work of that early-morning drive involved staying awake without any company, without any accompaniment. The reward of that working ride was her embodied meditation on a kind of new jack pedagogy: *Check One.*

HOW DO YOU WANT IT: TEACHING IN THE WAKE OF A SLAVE PAST AND TUPAC'S DEATH

In the middle of June, months before her trip down I-95, she visited Charlottesville to both see UVa's campus and find a place to live in Charlottesville. During the short visit, she met a brother named Yaz Cooper. He was a student earning summer money driving the campus bus from the visitor parking lot to *The Lawn*. The Lawn referred to the original grounds designed by Thomas Jefferson dating back to 1895 after his 1815 plans to build an *academical village* known as the University of Virginia. The place was all about history but never slavery.

Seniors vied for 50 rooms on the Lawn that came with a rocking chair and a fireplace but no running water nor a bathroom or shower. Essentially, students on the Lawn had *outhouses*. Black students rarely applied to occupy these prestigious residential spaces. One Black student told me he refused to sleep where our ancestors were once slaves. Ghosts. The memory of their torture might haunt his sleep.

In 1996, Virginia ranked as the number one public university in the nation according to *U.S. News and World Report*. Blacks represented 12% of the student population and the university could proudly boast that Black and White students graduated at a comparable rate over four to five years. Around 89%, she recalled.

The undergraduate student population at UVa was generally conservative. Khaki pants and ties. White blouses, heels, and bow ribbons. That was on formal days. Years later, a White, female music major who played jazz bass one night for a frat party described a roomful of frat boys as a "sea of khaki," which made her bust out laughing. Or should I say "burst."

ASK THE DJ, TELL THE DJ

Yaz was a DJ from New York City. He was excited to learn that she would teach a class that included hip-hop and became the catalyst for spreading the word among the Black student population. The administration had left her course off the schedule until the last minute, so Black students were the only ones who knew it was coming. On the first day of class 80 Black students showed up. There were 90 slots available. Having 80 Black students in a music course was quite an anomaly not only in UVa's music department but probably at any predominately White institution.

That day, Yaz shared that most of the Black students at UVa were from what was called NOVA, referring to the Northern Virginia area that included D.C. and Maryland where Go-go music was their hip-hop. So he said he could never play Nas or Biggie. They wanted Chuck Brown and Trouble Funk. She knew the music. She graduated high school in Rockville, Maryland, in 1979 when Trouble Funk was riding on the coattails of Chuck Brown and the Soul Searchers' legacy. Her single mom had danced to Chuck Brown in downtown D.C. parties and events. Go-go's mix of syncopated beats between the bass, snare, and high-hat drums along with conga drums, timbales, and hand-held cowbells in a funk-style of jamming was quite distinct from the highly sampled tracks in Nas or even the party jams of Bad Boy in the early 1990s. Yaz was excited to hear about the course and he eventually spread the word through his routes as a campus bus driver, a black undergrad, and as a DJ. If you want to get the word out on campus, tell a DJ.

THE ARCHITECTURE OF *THE LAWN*

Lunch involved getting to know her new department chair, a composer of primarily classical instrumental music who was White and Jewish; a liberal like many of Virginia's faculty. She and the composer walked from Old Cabell Hall, which housed the music department at one end of The Lawn, past the Rotunda at the other end. They grabbed a bite at *The Corner*, not the kind with brothers hanging out singing doo-wop or busking for a dollar. The Corner referred to a shopping and restaurant district primarily serving faculty, staff, and students.

After lunch, as they walked back to the department, the composer gave her a descriptive tour of *The Lawn*. She shared history about the student residences without bathrooms and other conventional history but nothing about slaves. They had to have help. All she could think about as they stopped to look into one of the student rooms was *Where did they keep the slaves? Where were the slave quarters?* This was colonial history preserved in quaint material ways but she was experiencing culture shock. The slave past was so close she could see it. Her dumbfoundedness gave way and with some trepidation she said (*cuz' lawd knows White folks can't talk about slavery*):

Her: "This campus looks like a plantation."
The composer: "Oh no! (She took a beat to add) It's Italianate architecture."
All she could think was, I'm fucked! When did Italians live here??!!!??!

Almost in silence the two colleagues—one African-American recalling her past, one Jewish translating the present—walked back to Old Cabell Hall offering only innocuous chit-chat after that.

SHE DONE GON' BALD-HEADED: HAIR AND HOW BLACK UVA GIRLS DEFINE FEMINISTS

Soon after her first semester of teaching began, she noticed that most, if not all, of the Black female undergraduates wore their hair long past the shoulders in a press and curl or a perm. A number had assimilated to the Abercrombie & Fitch fashion sense by wrapping their pressed ponytail back up in a white ribbon striped with UVa's colors of orange and blue. One of these young Black women boldly asked once if she considered herself a "radical feminist." "Femi-nazi" was whispered behind her back simply because she wore a natural. Damn! She was practically bald-headed.

They didn't know that she had accidentally cut all of her own hair off attempting to give herself a trim without any prior skill in cutting natural hair. She'd only gone natural during grad school. Not one of the few Black beauty salons in Charlottesville cut natural hair. It was perms all the way. She had never been to a barbershop, a male space, before and had avoided it, preferring the possible disaster to venturing into the lion's den. Meanwhile, she'd listen to all manner of misogynist hip-hop until she couldn't take it no more.

At her first music faculty dinner, being the only Black in the department, none of her colleagues commented or complimented her on the new 'do she was sporting since the interview six months earlier. At the time she thought no one could believe a woman would cut all of her hair off willingly. Later, she realized that her colleagues thought that the unmentionable c-word—*cancer*—had happened. For her Black female students, it was the f-word—*feminism*—and this kind of discourse deviance they had to challenge. She remembers one Black female student, staying late after class to correct her use of syllabuses. "It's syllabi, not syllabuses," she offered. Confronted in her new position of authority as a budding hip-hop professor, she freestyled an etymological truth from thin air. "Well, if you look it up in the dictionary you'll find that one is Latinate and the other is Anglicized." "Oh!" said the student, who was surely triggered by the professor's liberal use of Black English during the second lecture. Returning to her office, her well-worn *American Heritage Collegiate Dictionary* corroborated her articulate guesswork.

HATE ON ME, HATER: EBONICS AND THE POLITICS OF A WHITE SOUTHERN ALUMNUS

In January 1997, just before the spring semester began, she went to pick up her faculty mail and found a letter. It was addressed to her on the envelope but when she opened the letter the salutation read: "Dear Ms. Afro." It was postmarked from Hampton Roads, Virginia. It had been composed on a mechanical typewriter and signed in pen, "J.S. Berkovich" in legible cursive. Berkovich wrote:

> Dear Ms. Afro,
>
> Please excuse me for not hypernating [sic] the name of your cursed race with American. You Afro Twit. You should be teaching at an Afro university not a White university. [#YCMTSU]

It was hate mail. The letter went on in the same vein. It suggested she would not succeed. She believed it was signed with a fake name. Someone suggested that older alums strongly attached to the past were likely to reside in Hampton Roads.

Much later, she learned that Hampton Roads, specifically Portsmouth, Virginia, was the same area from which her great, great grandfather Sheridan Ford had escaped. It was five years after the Slave Fugitive Act of 1850 was enacted as part of the Great Compromise that ended Reconstruction and led to the institution of Jim Crow. Evidence of his escape on the Underground Railroad was documented in a letter written in his own hand to a friend back in Portsmouth, Virginia, part of the Hampton Roads region. From Boston on February 15, 1855, he wrote: "i love my freedom." She was learning that having academic freedom and citizenship didn't stop hate and couldn't fix the discriminatory practices in education that led to disparities in her classroom and with the number of Black Ph.D.s in academe. Then it was less than 1%. By 2014, it had reached 3%.

She *was* the only Black faculty in the music department in 1996–1997. After opening the letter and reading its content, she laughed at first. She thought that one of her old Michigan buddies was playing tricks on her as the Ebonics debate had grown comical and because every time she had shared that she was heading to her new job at Virginia, someone from the North always made some prejudicial joke about the South, which she actually missed. When it set in that it was real, *real* hate mail, she admitted to herself that it wasn't expected, but it wasn't a surprise. Being Black and female in America was more and more political the more social status you acquired.

Even in 1997 there was talk about race being over, that it didn't exist anymore.

When students challenged her discussions of Blackness, she pushed back by pulling the letter out of its file. She'd read it aloud when White students accused her of favoring the Black students when the quotient got too high; too many Black students, not enough White students getting her attention.

That drive to reach Virginia, and the oral-kinetic lesson she invented while makin' beats on her steering wheel, launched her into a mode of intellectual play in her classroom. Her first lecture was spoken-word referencing The Lawn and the students' participation along with her new P-H-and-D. After leaving UVa, she would add one-minute talks on the first and last day of class from every student. They answered "What is hip-hop?" in one minute or less. She would frame their freestyled responses with a collective embodied beat like one based on "Computer Love" by Roger Troutman that a Black male student taught an earlier class. It served as musical transition between each student's response. It was a kind of collective call-and-response revealing what each individual thought at the beginning and after all we learned at the end.

CONCLUSION

Check One was a gift to her and her students. Students rarely forgot it. The embodied lesson was taught orally though the body without any handwritten notes or music notation. It was learned on the job as a social practice that became harder and harder to facilitate as the Black student enrollment dwindled with the usual politics of enrollment for underrepresented students.

During that school year, she strategically changed the course title *Black Popular Music* to *African American Popular Music*. The non-Black students couldn't wrap their head around anything but race-as-skin-color while they tried to dismiss the politics of Blackness and hold on to the privileged location of Whiteness in a classroom at UVa, which she jokingly referred to as Uncle Tom's Plantation in private. It was a useful environment in which to play with identity, music, and hegemony.

These stories as praisesong, "located in the intersection/overlap of the culturally constructed socializations of race, gender, and other identities" (Dillard, 2000, p. 661), were a useful way of re-membering multiple pasts—slavery, stucknesses and silences, the hair politics of difference, embodied politics of race. Since leaving UVa, she never taught in such a historically politicized political space. Nor has she had 80 Black students in any other class. That was never repeated. But writing from retrospection through story called Foucault (1982) to her mind with his emphasis on the body as technology and on power and the subject. He always aimed at shining a light on power relations not through rationalization but through actual resistance to power. Rather than analyzing the internal rationality of patriarchy leaving so much room for lies and cognitive bias, Foucault asserted that it was far better to analyze power through the antagonism of strategies. The study of hip-hop through girls' musical and embodied practice might be considered by others an artificial antagonism designed as an intellectual exercise, an abstraction in an ivory tower. But the classroom is the only space where we can play with antagonizing discourse of gender, race, and the body without it leading to drive-by shootings, the exploitations of women and children, or imprisonment. It's a place where we can learn to play with getting free from our realities even for 16 measures.

REFERENCES

Dillard, C. B. (2000). The substance of things hoped for, the evidence of things not seen: Examining an endarkened feminist epistemology in educational research and leadership. *Qualitative Studies in Education*, *13*(6), 661–681.

Foucault. M. (1982). The subject and power. *Critical Inquiry*, *8*(4), 777–795.

Gaunt, K. D. (2006). *The games Black girls play: Learning the ropes from double-dutch to hip-hop*. New York: New York University Press.

Thurston, B. (2010, April 25). Black History Month: An Explanation of CP Time by Your Very Delayed Guest Book Editor. Huffington Post. Retrieved March 30, 2015, from http://www.huffingtonpost.com/baratunde-thurston/black-history-month-an-ex_b_472959.html.

Grandmaster Flash and the Furious Five. (1982). The Message (record album). Sugarhill Records.

hooks, b. (n.d.). Understanding patriarchy. *Imagine no borders*. Louisville Anarchist Federation. Accessed at http://imaginenoborders.org/pdf/zines/UnderstandingPatriarchy.pdf

Hunter, M. (2011). Shake it, baby, shake it: Consumption and the new gender relation in hip-hop. *Sociological Perspectives*, *54*(1), 15–36.

Marsalis, D. (1996). The art of rap? *Elementary*, *1*(1), 38–40.

Morgan, J. *When chickenheads come home to roost: A hip-hop feminist breaks it down*. New York: Simon & Schuster, 1999.

SECTION II

Black Feminism in Educational Research

CHAPTER TEN

If You Listen, You Will Hear

Race, Place, Gender, and the Trauma of Witnessing Through Listening in Research Contexts

ROBERTA P. GARDNER

Sometimes in the context of conducting qualitative research, participants will share stories that researchers are not ready to hear—stories that open up wounds and cause us to remember things that we have purposefully learned to forget (Dillard, 2012). That's what happened to me when I entered into the field to gather data for my research *Reading Race in a Community Space* (Gardner, 2013). My inquiry was focused on exploring how racialized epistemologies and lived experiences appeared to influence literacies and how literacies in turn shaped perceptions of race (Ladson-Billings, 2003). Using African American children's literature as hermeneutic prompts, I facilitated focus groups with Black mothers and children who lived in a low-income apartment community in the South, and together we read race as a phenomenon of our lived experience. Although I foregrounded race as a primary text, I also recognized gender, class, and geographic location as mutually constitutive elements of our literacies (Street, 1993). As such, many of the embodied, racialized, gendered, and spatialized ontologies of my participants (as well as my own) were brought to bear. Essentially, through stories, my participants allowed me to witness their lives. However, in listening to their stories, I soon realized that I wasn't prepared for the degree to which I would also have to be a witness to myself.

One day prior to one of our reading sessions, several women began discussing the gang rape of a "loose neighborhood chick."

You heard about ol' girl getting gang raped?
Yeah, it was like five or six dudes.
They know they were wrong.
But come on, she should've known better than to be around them. What do you expect?
One of the women glanced my way.
You know, she's a loose neighborhood chick.
Around here, that's what happens when you loose and stupid.
What happened to the guys that did it?
Nothing.
They still around. (interview, June 13, 2012)

The comments and collective narration of this tragic rape catapulted me into a deep personal, political, emotional, ethical, and spiritual quandary. As Caruth (1995) described, it opened a "speaking wound—a trauma borne by another that speaks to the wounds of the hearer" (p. 8). It was an insidious trauma or what Maria Root (1992) referred to as a trauma to the soul. The rape occurred earlier in the week, and like far too many acts of sexual terrorism that take place in poor and working-class Black communities (Miller, 2008), the men were not punished. Instead, they existed in the community with impunity, privilege, and power. Conversely, women navigated the neighborhood using various forms of risk avoidance cloaked in the mantle of silence.

As I sat in the midst of the story, I remained silent while I screamed. I was well versed in the cosmologies of Black female discourse, and the response to the harsh realities of neighborhood life was not a complete shock to me. They were much like the response to similar traumas in the all-Black working-class neighborhood where I had grown up. As Richardson (2009) described, we "were marked for violation" (p. 763) as such, and being "street wise" and "knowing better" was our best defense. The quick glance and "you know what I mean" reference to the "loose neighborhood chick" was an indication that I was expected to understand the young woman as culpable and responsible for her own rape, and be complicit in the sexist discourse. It also meant being willing to adhere to the code of silence.

Silence and victim blaming are patriarchal societal responses to rape that stigmatize and diminish the value of all women, and like Miller (2008) I am not arguing that rape attribution is directly correlative to race, but rather to the structural inequalities of racial oppression. Socially constructed racialized gender hierarchies that have historically pathologized Black female bodies and suppressed our experiences of trauma influenced the women's assertion that females who are considered stupid, less pure, or "anti-virgin" are somehow less deserving of empathy, support, and action. The realities of the gender structure in their neighborhood deeply pained me. It was an intimate pain, because I had lived it, and when my sister was raped by two men in a city park, people said that she should've known better too—and that she just should've never gone to that park.

CAN I GET A WITNESS?

Listening in teaching and research contexts is "fraught with emotional landmines" (Boler, 1997, p. 255), and in this chapter, I use theories in endarkened feminism (Dillard, 2006, 2012) and feminist trauma studies (Griffiths, 2009) to address the tension of telling a story that I knew needed to be told, while simultaneously *not* knowing how to tell it. Rather than discussing the traumatic incident of rape, I address the traumatic effects (Eyerman, 2002) of being a vicarious witness to this particular story, as well as a witness to my own painful and personal cultural memories. I narrate what it was like to (re)discover my spiritual consciousness, how (re)membering served as a catalyst for clarifying and unifying my academic inquiry, as well as the desires of my spirit. I address the messy, emotional, relational, and spiritual tensions of a research endeavor that challenged and transformed my humanity as a Black mother/daughter/sister/researcher/educator, and how ultimately enacting a methodology of surrender (Dillard, 2006) provided a cathartic opportunity for me to *listen and hear* my spirit so that I could stop wearing the mask of a strong Black girl from the hood (Beauboeuf-Lafontant, 2009) and become an effective silence breaker within my teaching, research, and writing.

In order to put back together what is severed when a trauma occurs, we must have a witness...

Knowing what to do with a traumatic story is important, because as listeners we are challenged to be both a witness to the trauma and a witness to ourselves (Felman & Laub, 1994, p. 58). Jennifer Griffiths (2009) noted that the landscape of our memories arises from our cultural and racialized gender contexts that are situated in public and private spheres across space and time. Similar to Felman and Laub, Griffiths argued that traumatic stories "exposes the vulnerability of listeners... [causing us] to face [our] limitations, [and our] morality, through the story of another's trauma"(p. 2). In short, when we become a witness we are challenged to become more fully human (Freire, 1970).

Drawing from Freire (1970), Dillard (2006, 2012) asserted that an endarkened feminist approach in teaching and research allows us to be fully human because we engage and enact "all that we are" intellectually, emotionally, and spiritually. This engagement includes addressing our cultural memories and the "evidence of our lives that is unseen, spiritual, cultural, and embodied" (Dillard, 2012, p. 17). In her in-depth synopsis of cultural memories, Dillard argued that memory matters and that it is an absent and lingering presence within research contexts that complexifies our inquiry. She asserted that researchers must interrogate the joyous and painful memories of oppression that arise from historical and contemporary contexts—and that we must also confront the memories that "break our hearts" (p. 11). In some respect, we are all wounded witnesses (Dutro, 2011), and the traumatic narrative that was folded into the fray of my participants' casual discourse evoked a traumatic personal memory, and produced a host of emotional transgressive data (St. Pierre, 1997), spiritual discontent, and methodological dissonance.

St. Pierre (1997) described emotional transgressive data as "messy, uncodable" (p. 179), disruptive data that are often unready to hand. These data are tethered to our cultural memories, which are inherently raced, classed, and gendered. As Dillard (2012) described, cultural memories are connections to the landscapes of our lives, "they are alive and present within us" (p. 4). As an outsider within this community (Collins, 2000), the cultural memories and emotional data that I accumulated over the course of my research were at times stifling. Although I grew up in the Midwest, and my study took place in the South, across space and time, many of my own Black girlhood experiences (positive and negative) mirrored those of my participants' neighborhood life: the games of freeze tag and hide and seek between parked cars in the street, the ice cream man who sold popsicles and drugs, and the imperative to be street smart in the midst of the ubiquitous and unpredictable violence. Addressing the ways in which my reflexivities of discomfort (see Pillow, 2003) were influencing this research, as well as who I was and who I was becoming in the face of their stories, was not only unavoidable, it was critical.

A traumatic memory is defined as an embodied experience that bears a psychic resemblance to an original experience (Griffiths, 2009). It is a socially produced trauma, and as the rape narrative was shared, painful memories from my past came rushing forth; parts of my spirit that "until that moment had been asleep within [me]" were aroused (Dillard, 2012, p. 3). The response and conversational tone of the women was reminiscent of those I overheard on the back of school buses, in the girl's restroom, at the beauty shop, or on my neighborhood street corner.

> That's what happens when you loose… stupid. What do you expect? She should've known better… she should've never gone to that park.

Voices from the past were interspersed with those of my participants, and at times, I also heard my own. It was one string of the same story—the nameless, faceless young woman who was raped in the community, other victims of sexual assault, and my sister. They were one, and their story was the same. *They should've known better*. Growing up, these stories of Little Red in the hood served as cautionary tales. They were passed down so that the rest of us would learn how to navigate the wolves on neighborhood streets. We were instructed about how to dress, how to talk back, and when to be silent. We also learned to develop a thick skin, and how to wear the mask of a strong Black girl. We performed hard girl cool posing personas to thwart the ways that we were assailed, judged, or verbally raped by the cat-calling language of the street. We pretended not to care, or to be too hurt by the drama and trauma of our world. This was much like the response of the women in my study. Such responses to gender oppression are agentive acts and forms of psychological preservation. However, they often diminish our ability to love, respect, protect, and demonstrate compassion for all of us. It was ironic that one of our readings that afternoon was the following instructive poem by Lucille Clifton (1970).

> Listen children...
> keep this in the place
> you have for keeping
> always
> keep it all ways...
> we have been ashamed
> hopeless tired mad
> but always
> all ways
> we loved us
> pass it on...

Although we discussed the poem, I didn't feel like any of us were actually listening. I certainly wasn't, because on my way home, when the painful memories came rushing forth again, I drowned them out with the radio. But, as Dillard (2012) argued, memory always makes a demand on the present, and although I tried, I couldn't suppress whatever it was their story was demanding from me.

WALKING IN THE SPIRIT

> I hurt with the hurt of my people. I mourn and am overcome with grief. —*Jeremiah 8:21*

The next day, I rescheduled our reading session. I needed to determine where the study was going and how to tame my emotions, which were suddenly spilling over in supremely unproductive ways. That evening, when I attempted to transcribe data, simply listening to the voices of my participants caused me a significant amount of tension, and when I attempted to write through my wounds, the sentiments refused to flow. I decided to go for a walk on a path in a park in my neighborhood. It was a place of solace for me, the same park where my youngest son who was now in high school used to chase squirrels and collect leaves. The southern sun was heavy as were the swarms of bugs that hovered in the thickness of the air. I was anxious to get back to "more productive work," so I began walking with an aggressive pace and an elongated gait. As I moved deeper within the canopy of the trees, a vexing sadness erupted from out of nowhere. Soon, a bevy of hot tears were streaming down my face. I vigorously wiped my eyes and attempted to keep walking—then, I simply stopped, stood there, and prayed. Everything within me was calling me to, and something in my heart told me that there was no better place to do it.

I am not a religious person, but I am faithful, and at that moment I became aware that to make it through this research I needed to *allow my spirit to strive* (Dillard, 2006). There was nothing else. I could no longer submerge the emotions that I clearly needed to reconcile. Moreover, rendering some of my cultural memories as uncomfortable, painful, and uncontainable was a significant part of this research process. As I listened to what my spirit was telling me, I understood that my inquiry into reading race was inextricably connected to my desire to use stories of our past and present to heal *myself* and to also heal the collective wounds of the Black women and children who participated in my study. In researching their racialized, gendered, classed, and spatialized literacies, as Dillard argued, I was also researching my own.

Dillard emphasized that our cultural memories are a pathway "toward (re)membering our spiritual identities" (p. 13). As such, "remembering what we learned to forget" (Dillard, 2012) and giving voice to oppression and injustice through reading, writing, speaking, and teaching is "a radical response to our individual and collective fragmentation at the cultural, spiritual, and material levels" (Dillard, 2006, p. 17). It is how we heal and counter the muting isolation (Griffiths, 2009) and false divisions created between mind, body, and spirit when we attempt to "live over" traumatic realities. Vickroy (2002) argued that racist and sexist discourses attempt to silence, regulate, and deny traces of trauma on Black female bodies. This denial creates a violent silence that fractures the individual and collective psyche of all Black women. We must therefore listen to the ways in which we are complicit with patriarchal discourses and recognize that the discourse of strength is a "half-told tale" that diminishes our humanity (Beauboeuf-Lafontant, 2009, p. 1).

I learned to push the painful wounds of my sister's rape within the bowels of my being, and so did she. We have rarely discussed what the rape did to her or to the rest of *us*. My sister and I, like all Black women, have so much left to unsilence. That day, after I prayed within the fold of the trees, I realized that I didn't want what I witnessed within my research to get buried deep inside of me and to become a lingering pain. I had already been there and done that. It will probably take a lifetime for me to unearth everything that I buried, and perhaps much of it will die with me. I had already worn the mask of the strong Black girl from the 'hood, and I didn't want to do it anymore.

> Wounds never stop speaking, seeking out listeners who will hear them or, if such a thing is possible, heal them. —*(Oliver, 2011)*

We are all positioned and challenged by our wounds (Dutro, 2008) and as researchers and educators working within our own communities, this presents a unique challenge, because as Dillard (2012) argued, we must embrace all that we are (especially our wounds) for the good of all of us. A methodology of surrender is a radical subjectivity stance that allows us to embark on the path toward healing ourselves and others. It includes love, compassion, reciprocity, and ritual. This reflexive methodological process provides an opportunity to unify our spiritual epistemologies and academic lives. Although I was midway into collecting data, when I stopped resisting and began listening to my spirit, once I discovered a methodology of surrender, I was able to more effectively meditate the emotional complexities that I faced as a sistah outsider-within (Lorde, 1984). Walking, surrendering, praying, and *then writing* became a mandatory and integral part of my research process. As Pillow (2003) argued, I didn't "seek a comfortable, transcendent end-point," in this research endeavor; however, this methodological commitment helped me to navigate "the uncomfortable realities of doing engaged qualitative research" (p. 193) as an outsider within. It allowed me to thwart the violence of silence and the rape of the spirit that occurs when we attempt to foreground the work of the mind over the needs of our spirit. It also provided an opportunity for me to understand that we must purposefully touch our past and why we must *listen* and *hear* our spirit, particularly when we are in places and spaces of contradiction.

REFERENCES

Beauboeuf-Lafontant, T. (2009). *Behind the mask of the strong Black woman voice and the embodiment of a costly performance*. Philadelphia: Temple University Press.

Boler, M. (1997). The risks of empathy: Interrogating multiculturalism's gaze. *Cultural Studies, 11*(2), 253–273.

Caruth, C. (1995). *Trauma: Explorations in memory*. Baltimore: Johns Hopkins University Press.

Clifton, L. (1970). Listen children. In B. Rochelle (Ed.), *Words with wings: A treasury of African American poetry and art*. New York: HarperCollins.

Collins, P. H. (2000). *Black feminist thought: Knowledge, consciousness, and the politics of empowerment* (2nd Ed.). New York: Routledge.

Dillard, C. B. (2006). *On spiritual strivings transforming an African American woman's academic life*. Albany: State University of New York Press.

Dillard, C. B. (2012). *Learning to (re)member the things we've learned to forget: Endarkened feminisms, spirituality, and the sacred nature of (re)search and teaching*. New York: Peter Lang.

Dutro, E. (2008). "That's why I was crying on this book": Trauma as testimony in children's responses to literature. *Changing English, 15*, 423–434.

Dutro, E. (2011). Writing wounded: Trauma, testimony, and critical witness in literacy classrooms. *English Education, 43*(2), 193–211.

Eyerman, Ron. (2002). *Cultural Trauma: Slavery and the Formation of African-American Identity.* Cambridge: Cambridge University Press.

Felman, S., & Laub, D. (1994). *Testimony: Crisis of witnessing in literature, psychoanalysis, and history.* New York: Routledge.

Freire, P. (1970). *Pedagogy of the oppressed.* New York: Continuum.

Gardner, R. (2013). *Reading race in a community space: A narrative phenomenological exploration.* (Unpublished doctoral dissertation). University of Georgia, Athens.

Griffiths, J. L. (2009). *Traumatic possessions: The body and memory in African American women's writing and performance.* Charlottesville: University of Virginia Press.

Ladson-Billings, G. (2003). Forward. In S. Greene & D. Abt-Perkins (Eds.), *Making race visible: Literacy research for cultural understanding* (pp. vii–xi). New York: Teachers College Press.

Lorde, A. (1984). *Sister outsider: Essays and speeches.* Trumansburg, NY: Crossing Press.

Miller, J. (2008). *Getting played: African American girls, urban inequality, and gendered violence.* New York: New York University Press.

Oliver, S. (2011). Bearing witness to the witness: Some thoughts on hearing wounds talk. Retrieved from http://talkingwound.wordpress.com/2011/05/

Pillow, W. (2003). Confession, catharsis, or cure? Rethinking the uses of reflexivity as methodological power in qualitative research. *Qualitative Studies in Education, 16*(2), 175–196.

Richardson, E. (2009). My ill literacy narrative: Growing up Black, po and a girl, in the hood. *Gender and Education, 21*(6), 753–767.

Root, M. (1992). Reconstructing the impact of trauma on personality. In L. S. Brown (Ed.), *Personality and psychopathology feminist reappraisals* (pp. 229–267). New York: Guilford Press.

St. Pierre, E. A. (1997). Methodology in the Fold and the Irruption of Transgressive Data. *International Journal Of Qualitative Studies In Education, 10*(2), 175–89.

Street, B. (1993). *Cross-cultural approaches to literacy.* New York: Cambridge University Press.

Vickroy, L. (2002). *Trauma and survival in contemporary fiction.* Charlottesville: University of Virginia Press.

CHAPTER ELEVEN

Black Feminism in Qualitative Education Research

A Mosaic for Interpreting Race, Class, and Gender in Education

VENUS E. EVANS-WINTERS

> Only a few black women have rekindled the spirit of feminist struggle that stirred the hearts and minds of our nineteenth century sisters. We, black women who advocate feminist ideology, are pioneers. We are clearing a path for ourselves and our sisters. We hope that as long as they see us reach our goal—no longer victimized, no longer unrecognized, no longer afraid—they will take courage and follow. —*bell hooks, Ain't I a Woman*
>
> No could wish for a more advantageous heritage than that bequeathed to the black writer in the South: a compassion for the earth, a trust in humanity beyond our knowledge of evil, and an abiding love of justice. We inherit a great responsibility as well, for we must give voice to centuries not only of silent bitterness and hate but also of neighborly kindness and sustaining love. —*Alice Walker, In Search of Our Mothers' Gardens: Womanist Prose*

In the above opening quote by Black feminist author Alice Walker (1983), she poetically describes the inherited knowledge and ethos that Black writers possess, by virtue of having to make and sustain life in often hostile environmental and social conditions. As Walker explains throughout her writings, it was through familial love, the support of the Black community, and an appreciation for what the earth yields that Black people learned to sustain their own life and that of others. Consequently, when inscribing the social world, Black women bring forth critical perspectives about vulnerability and struggle, resilience and resistance, and love and justice.

Acknowledging the unique experiences of Black women in the United States and across the diaspora, it is essential that women of African ancestry, and other women of color, carve out theoretical and methodological spaces of our own. As intellectuals, researchers interested in the lives of Black women have much herstorical, theoretical, and practical knowledge to contribute to contemporary educational challenges and discourse. Considering recent demographic shifts in the United States and abroad, it is imperative that those committed to social justice paradigms give more attention to how non-White women understand contemporary and historical patterns in education. Moreover, it is equally important for us to consider the ways in which Black women seek to question, understand, and challenge, via the formal inquiry process, contemporary educational problems, such as the imposition of deficit-thinking models, White supremacy, and gender bias in schooling as well as the research process itself.

In the past, qualitative research has been metaphorically described as a bricolage, a montage, quilt-making, and musical improvisation (Denzin & Lincoln, 2000). In this chapter, I would like to describe Black feminism, and specifically its possibilities to qualitative research in education, as a mosaic. Mosaic as an art form is the process of creating images with an assortment of small pieces of colored glass, stone, or other objects put together to create a pattern or picture. In most instances, the mosaic has cultural and spiritual significance. Black feminist scholars bring a wealth of knowledge, skills, talents, and experiences into the research process. These bits of experiences mold together to construct our multiple identities. And from these multiple identities yields a creative, distinctly mosaic worldview. Using the metaphor of a mosaic, a piece of artwork composed of a combination of diverse elements, patterns, and forms, I propose a gender- and race-based approach to qualitative research in education. Black women scholars have a long tradition of facilitating knowledge of the connection between culture and educational politics.

As educators, caregivers, community workers, and subaltern citizens Black women offer insight into the relationship between race and education. Throughout the text, I put forth the stance that due to continually navigating the contours of racism, classism, and sexism by virtue of existing in the confines of a White patriarchal society, women of African ancestry offer unique perspectives on the ways in which inequality persists within and across cultural contexts and institutions. In the following discussion, the tenets and methodology of Black feminism/womanism are explained in relation to qualitative research methods in education. Also discussed is the usefulness of Black feminism to expose and trouble educational disenfranchisement in the U.S. educational system. It is argued that a researcher's embracement of a Black feminist consciousness shapes (1) the questions raised about education and schooling, (2) how one interacts with subjects throughout the research process, (3) one's understanding of the context where the study takes place, (4) the body of literature reviewed, and (5) interpretation and analysis of data.

Although more recently there has been an increase in research conducted with or about women and girls of African descent, this body of research still receives less attention in educational change efforts, in particular when looking at how the research is applied to recent school reform efforts and classroom practices. To echo Ladson-Billings (2000), "The process of developing a worldview that differs from the dominant worldview requires active intellectual work on the part of the knower, because schools, society, and the structure and production of knowledge are designed to create individuals who internalize the dominant worldview and knowledge production and acquisition process" (p. 258). The mosaic of Black feminism brings forth an aesthetically distinct alternative to widely accepted notions of how knowledge production and acquisition should transpire in educational research.

THE MOSAIC OF BLACK FEMINIST THOUGHT

Black feminism or womanism (a term coined by Alice Walker [1983] to address the concerns of Black women about the history of racism in the feminist movement) was borne out of Black women's experiences and struggles against slavery, American apartheid, and their ongoing political involvement in the Black and women's liberation movements. In the post–civil rights era, a Black feminist consciousness is developed from hearing family members share stories of struggles and triumphs against race and oppression, participation in de facto segregated spaces, experiences with hyper-surveillance in urban schools and neighborhoods (e.g., racial profiling, metal detectors in schools, drug testing of students, etc.), witnessing symbolic lynchings (e.g., Don Imus referring to a group of educated Black female athletes as "nappy headed hoes," and watching intently the Anita Hill and Clarence Thomas hearings on public television), militarized public schools (e.g., zero tolerance policies), and being allowed in White spaces for the sole intent of "speaking for the race" at a time when affirmative action initiatives are being rolled back in education and employment; leaving many Black women lonely, vulnerable, and absent of community.

Black feminist thought is a reflection of multiple theoretical traditions, including African-centered thought, feminist theory, Marxism, sociology of knowledge, critical social theory, and postmodern theory (Collins, 2000). Black feminism as it is known today is "a continuation of intellectual and activist traditions" (Guy-Sheftall, 1995, p. 1) as well as African and African American values, beliefs, and traditions. Black feminist scholar Guy-Sheftall (1995) points out that Black feminism is not a monolithic static ideology; however, there are consistent axioms consistent throughout Black feminist thought, including the belief that:

1. Black women experience a special kind of oppression, due to their racial and gender identity, and access to limited resources in a racist, sexist, classist

society. Guy-Sheftall (1995) refers to the interlocking systems of race, class, and gender oppression Black women confront as a triple jeopardy.
2. The political, social, and intellectual needs of Black women are characteristically different from that of Black men and White women; therefore, strategies of resistance might also differ. Black women must fight for racial and gender equality simultaneously, and because of this verity they cannot afford to privilege one group's struggle over the other, for Black liberation will not eradicate gender oppression and the elimination of gender domination will not automatically eradicate White racial domination.
3. Black women's commitment to challenging racism and sexism is rooted in their lived experience as Black and woman.

Black feminism as theory and praxis is useful to qualitative researchers. In fact, I will argue that Black feminism as a tradition of Black female intellectual thought is underutilized and theorized in educational research and practice. Oversight of Black women's insight into educational challenges can be attributed to educational researchers' lack of knowledge of Black women's intellectual contributions and a tradition of racial and gender exclusion in academe. Unfortunately, both of the aforementioned reasons can lead to qualitative researchers overlooking the possibilities of Black women's contributions to educational research and discourse. Black feminism is a critical social theory born out of the lived experiences and struggles of Black women living at the intersections of race, class, and gender oppression.

Black women's cemented status at the bottom of the social hierarchy enkindles a unique vantage point for understanding sexist socialization and racist oppression in relation to education and schooling. "There is much evidence substantiating the reality that race and class identity creates differences in quality of life, social status, and lifestyle that take precedence over the common experience women share—differences that are rarely transcended," posits Black feminist theorist bell hooks (2000, p. 4) in *Feminist Theory: From Margins to Center*. Black women as researchers, and the researched, bring our lived experiences into the research process. The charge of the qualitative researcher, then, is to add to the body of evidence that already exists about different groups of women and the genders; to descriptively capture and illustrate the nuanced differences between groups of women's social and material conditions; and to bring forth alternative analyses for referencing gender and racial oppression.

CRAFTING RACE, CLASS, AND GENDER INTO EDUCATIONAL RESEARCH

Black feminism is a theoretical, methodological, and political discourse (and tradition) that gives voice to Black women's sociopolitical struggles in a White patriarchal society that privileges whiteness, maleness, and wealth. Black feminism has a concern for addressing the needs of non-White women and the poor. As a theoretical lens, Black feminism provides a conceptual model for understanding how racism, sexism, and classism intersect to constrain women's bodies and psyches. Moreover, Black feminism as a standpoint theory also offers original suppositions into how Black women are able to confront the social world order, while being simultaneously vulnerable and resilient in the face of systematic inequality, including marginalization in the academy. Anthropologist Leith Mullings (1997) states in her book, *On Our Own Terms: Race, Class, and Gender in the Lives of African American Women*, "To only focus on the strengths, accomplishments, and victories does not give sufficient attention to the system of domination. Yet to emphasize too heavily the structure of oppression underplays the creative energy of a people" (p. xii).

Mullings's (1997) musings remind those committed to writing women's lives that we should responsibly set out to interweave into our observations and theoretical understandings stories of systematic racism and sexism, alongside stories of individual and collective struggle and victories. Such an interweaving creates a mosaicism of possibility as opposed to defeat, which can serve as a theoretical and heuristic guide for researchers interested in educational reform. Methodologically, Black feminism offers researchers, non-White women especially, alternative methods of studying and interpreting African Americans' and women of African ancestry's culture and histories. Black feminism offers a political interruption of traditional academic discourse. For instance, a major modus operandi of Black feminism is the intellectual practice of claiming the margins. Black feminist scholar Patricia Hill-Collins (2000) explains:

> When in the 1970s and 1980s Black women and other similarly situated groups broke long-standing silences about their oppression, they spoke from the margins of power. Moreover, by claiming historically marginalized experiences, they effectively challenged false universal knowledge that historically defended hierarchical power relations. Marginality operated as an important site of resistance for decentering unjust power relations. (pp. 43–44)

Black feminist researchers center Black women's ways of knowing and being, thus concomitantly disrupting hegemony and in counteracting distortions about African American women and African Americans, in general. Collins coined the phrase *oppositional knowledge* to describe Black women's scholarly commitment to claiming and redefining their "place" in society, not as a place of victimization and powerlessness, but as a claimed space of collective power that yields intellectual creativity.

In brief, Black feminist thought (1) puts forth a social critique of traditional research and interpretations of social relationships; (2) fosters dialogue for understanding power and privilege, and (3) strategically agitates the status quo. "Science, including social science, is practiced in the context of society; it is influenced by the power relationships of a given society, and knowledge (or what passes for knowledge) may be used as an instrument for subjugation or liberation," reminds Mullings (1997, p. 77). With this verity in mind, in relation to education, Black feminism offers the opportunity to expose and challenge relationships between science and schooling, and narratives produced and proliferated by mainstream knowledge (or what Payne [1984] refers to as everyday folklore and myths), in reproducing social inequality.

Contemporary topics of relevance to researchers that adopt a Black feminist stance might include research on Black girls' schooling experiences (Evans-Winters, 2011); African American female educators (Dixson & Dingus, 2008); single-sex education; Black women's experiences in higher education (Mabokela & Green, 2001); teacher educators' experience with teaching race/racism; girls' educational and social development across the African diaspora; Black parental engagement in schools; Black female preKindergarten–12 administrators; community activism for educational reform; gender and the school-to-prison pipeline (Winn, 2011); Black women's preparation for the postindustrial marketplace; Black women in STEM careers; Black women's work and participation in alternative learning communities; literacy programs (hooks, 2000) and gender and culturally relevant curriculum and pedagogy (Evans-Winters & Ivie, 2009; Evans-Winters & Esposito, 2010); Black female peer relationships; representations of Black girls and women in popular culture; gender and educational law, theology, and educational theory; the education of female athletes; and gender and race socialization in schools.

Civil rights activist and historian Bernice Johnson Reagon (1993) writes,

> A lot of us do not understand what it really would take to make our work available to the next generation—not only for those who follow us to read about what we believed and valued and tried to do with our living, but also to receive our stories as models and the base from which our children may move in the world they struggle to shape. The idea that the world you live in is one you should work to shape moves across time only if it is a part of the cultural environment you create and put in motion. (p. 207)

Although the number of Black women entering into social science fields has increased over the last decade, there are still not enough educational researchers who hold the privilege of (re)shaping others' perceptions of African Americans, women, and the poor. Even more importantly, interpreting Reagon's (1993) words from a Black feminist scholar's perspective, there is an urgent need for budding and seasoned researchers in education with a concern for getting the story right for the next generation of scholars, practitioners, students, and policymakers. When researching education from a race and gender-based perspective, qualitative researchers provide the opportunity to simultaneously re-construct and co-construct those values and worldviews that have helped to sustain our culture, while combating intellectually, spiritually, and corporally White supremacy and patriarchy. Below I outline major themes of Black feminism that are in alignment with qualitative research in education.

BLACK WOMEN AS KNOWERS

Black women's experiences are at the center of the research process, as the researcher and the researcher. In Black feminist research, the researcher often begins with reflection on her lived experiences and brings those insights into the research process. Although she may not be an expert on a particular research topic or subject, she does view her observations of the social world just as significant to the research process as that of other (usually White) researchers and participants in the research process. Unlike traditional research paradigms, Black feminist researchers question the notion that research is or needs to be completely objective, and instead believes that all research is subjective. Black women historically have served as objects of so-called science and as scientific commentary; therefore, Black women know for sure that science is not always objective in its purposes or consequences (e.g., the U.S.-led Eugenics movement, sterilization projects, and the 1965 Moynihan report; for a thorough discussion of science experimentation and Black women abuse and exploitation see Roberts, 1998). In agreement with Angrosino and Mays de Perez (2003)

> Whatever else may be said about the postmodern turn in contemporary studies of society and culture, its critique of assumptions about the objectivity of science and its presumed authoritative voice has raised issues that all qualitative researchers need to address. Earlier criticism might have been directed at particular researchers, with the question being whether they had lived up to the expected standards of objective scholarship. In the postmodern milieu, by contrast, the criticism is directed at the standards themselves. In effect, it is now possible to question whether observational objectivity is either desirable or feasible as a goal. (p. 109)

Arguably, Black feminist methodology preceded postmodern leanings. Women and non-Whites have long questioned the objectivity of science, scientists, and the scientific process itself. Furthermore, Black feminists have always proclaimed, for personal and political reasons, that objectivity in the critique of society is neither desirable nor feasible in ongoing efforts to employ systematic investigation methods in combating White supremacy and male domination. Black feminism maintains that research with women and racial/ethnic minorities at the center of analysis is necessarily subjective, with the intent of promoting social change, self-knowledge and empowerment, or community uplift. A questioning of the objectivity of science and the purpose of science coincides with critical qualitative research paradigms.

DIALOGICAL VOICE(S)

In the pursuit of self-determination, Black women have relied on creative and alternative ways of producing and validating knowledge and of naming and identifying our experiences. Taking on a dialogical voice in the design and pursuit of knowledge is a result of Black women's experiences in communal and civic spaces (Collins, 2009). Consequently, it is common for those who take on a Black feminist stance to use personal narratives, to share personal conversations or symbols and metaphors as a way to convey information or to question the validity of knowledge claims (Dillard, 2000). Sojourner Truth and Maria Stewart are two public pioneers who brought the usefulness of Black women's expressiveness to the forefront of race and gender liberation discussions (Davis, 1983; Giddings, 1996; hooks, 1999).

As pointed out by Lee (2005) in King (2005), *Black Education: A Transformative Research and Action Agenda for the New Century*, African Americans "have a highly embedded appreciation of language play, a love of playing with language as an aesthetic end in itself, as opposed to a strict utilitarian tool of communication. Use of rhythm, alliteration, metaphor, irony, and satire are routine in the language practices of this speech community (p. 83). This assertion is noteworthy, because King (2005) lays out a progressive agenda for the improvement of Black education. Therefore, it is significant to note that language and literacy is a worthwhile topic of discussion in research and practice. Speech, in the African and African American tradition, in written or oral form is regarded as a creative and divine act. Speech, which includes the skill of listening, is used to pass down tradition and preserve the culture (Carruthers, 1999). Once more, nor is speech to be taken lightly or as apolitical.

Therefore, in the African and African American tradition, a dialogical voice (the act of listening, writing, and conversing and grounded in one's cultural point of reference) is preferred in Black feminist methodology as opposed to the use of stale scientific language. Scientific jargon can be exclusionary, while privileging formally educated, middle-class, and Eurocentric styles and patterns of speech. Similarly, narration in the form of storytelling, metaphors, and analogies is more relational in nature, and thus inherently dialogical. There is an attempt at mutuality in questioning, observing, theorizing, and contemplating one's interactions with the social world. Stated differently, "The narrative approach entails a distinct type of research, but over and above that it comprises a clear vision of the social world and the way we think, feel and conduct ourselves in it" (Spector-Mersel, 2010, p. 209). The narrative approach is not simply a qualitative research technique but a research strategy. Accordingly, narrative voice in all of its multifacetedness (i.e., oral history, storytelling, biography, etc.) sets out to paint a picture of Black women's perceptions of the social world order and how they might choose to respond to such (dis)order. It is at the intersection of discussions of vulnerability and agency that race-, class-, and gender-conscious theory manifests.

Hence, one objective of the dialogical approach in Black feminist research is coming to some mutual understanding of a social problem, with the ultimate goal of collectively imagining how to solve the identified problem. Another objective of the use of narratives in Black feminist writing is to provide counter-stories to racist and patriarchal portrayals of women and non-Whites, especially those stories that have been detrimental to Black women. With the recent rise in popularity and embracement of critical race theory and critical race feminism, there is also more awareness of the utility of counter-narratives in countering racial and gender oppression in law (see Wing, 1997, for an overview of critical race feminism in the legal field) and in educational research (Ladson-Billings & Tate, 1995; Taylor, Gilborn, & Ladson-Billings, 2009).

Lastly, a narrative voice allows for the acceptance of emotion in knowledge attainment and claims. An ethics of caring and empathy is important in the knowledge validation process and in assessing the validity of an argument, for many African Americans, according to Collins (2000). The dichotomy between rationality and emotionality is blurred. If the messenger is absent of emotion or fails to capture and keep the attention of the receiver of the message, the message itself might be loss or the messenger may be dismissed as less than credible. Black feminist scholars have embraced this intellectual challenge (born out of grassroots activism and community engagement), and so can qualitative researchers in education.

Issues of credibility and validity are an ongoing point of contention for qualitative researchers in education. Wright (2006) claims:

> Recent developments within qualitative research itself and even more recent developments outside qualitative research have produced a situation in which a new (or revived) tension exists between foundationalism, positivism and postpositivism in educational research on the one hand and post-foundationalism, critical and postmodernist and poststructuralist work on the other. Thus a period that was supposed to have ended in the 1980s has re-emerged in the present (2000–). In fact it could be argued that the Paradigm War never really ended, that the widely held assumption of an end following the period of détente was a collective overly optimistic (mis)reading of a simmering situation that is now threatening to boil over once again into open hostilities. (p. 797)

Black feminist methodological approaches emerge at the liminal space of these paradigmatic wars. The crisis of legitimacy (Denzin & Lincoln, 2000) in qualitative educational research is between positivist thinkers and postmodernist/poststructuralist. However, Black feminist researchers must be concerned with being true to ourselves, so to speak, and the populations we serve. Black women's lived experiences, and reflections of these socially constructed experiences, are legitimate subjects of research and analysis.

As I have asserted elsewhere (Evans-Winters, 2011), Black women's experiences are always shifting between the modern and postmodern; therefore, to get entangled in the philosophical wars described above by Wright (2006) is a distraction to a Black feminist agenda in education. At any given moment in history, positivist or postpositive methodologies may benefit a Black feminist perspective. A good example of Black feminist research in education shifting between positivist (or modern) and postpositivist (or postmodern) approaches, or what I will refer to here as the "objective" alongside the "subjective," is Muhummad and Dixson's (2008) use of educational longitudinal survey data in conjunction with qualitative and narrative themes of Black female students' schooling experiences. The researchers contemporaneously draw from quantitative data, tenets of critical race feminism, literary accounts, ethnographic description, and other research by Black feminists. In their analysis, not one methodological model is privileged over the other. In essence, each form of "data" holds its own merit, yet all are used to corroborate or legitimate the claims of the other. Muhummad and Dixson (2008) seemingly shift between the modern and postmodern in their analysis and interpretations of Black girls' experiences in educational contexts, thus offering readers an example of a nonsynchronous parallel (Evans-Winters, 2011) approach to studying the complexities of Black girls' experiences in schools.

TEXTUAL MULTIPLICITY

Black feminism is concerned with theory and practice that is accessible and consumable to diverse audiences, with a special objective of including undereducated women and men in the struggle against White supremacy and male domination. bell hooks (2000) poignantly states, "If feminist writing and scholars aim to promote and advance feminist movement, then matters of style must be considered in conjunction with political intent. There will be no feminist movement as long as feminist ideas are understood only by an educated few" (p. 113). One of the most effective means for conveying a feminist agenda to both those a part of and outside of formal educational institutions, as well as those turned off from theory, is by integrating nontraditional texts or a multiplicity of texts into feminist writings.

In the tradition of Black feminist critique, textual analysis involves a multiplicity of texts. The idea of what is considered text itself is scrutinized. Does a piece of literary work make a meaningful contribution to interpretations of Black women's existence? Does a film portray deep-seated stereotypes of Black women, the family, or community? How do musical lyrics contribute to misogyny and sexism, or poor relationships between Black women and men? How can popular culture be used as a vehicle for educating the masses on interlocking systems of oppression and mobilize the public? What is the role of the White corporate media elite in sustaining White supremacy and patriarchy? Because mainstream knowledge has traditionally excluded Black women from participating in knowledge construction or constructed narrow images of women and non-Whites, often for Black and female scholars it is necessary to turn outside of academic knowledge and turn to other sources for examining interlocking systems of oppression.

Moreover, simply because something or someone has not been legitimated by academe does not mean that person, idea, or text is not worthwhile to involve in knowledge construction. For instance, even the human body can serve as text. Collins (2005), for example, in *Black Sexual Politics: African Americans, Gender and the New Racism*, provides a historical overview of White Europeans' objectification of the Black woman's body, especially the rear end, for scientific exploitation and commodification. In the analysis process, Collins connected historical patterns of conquest and control to present-day media images and exploitation of Black women's body parts to illustrate how sound bites distort images of Black women for others' consumption and material gains. The media have traditionally served as a technology of the state. At any rate, everyday images, symbols, artifacts, gestures, and languages are reflections of human behavior and relationships, and thus can inform social scientists about the state of affairs. Existing at the intersections of race, class, and gender, Black women bring multiple perspectives to the research process; therefore, Black women's tools of analysis and objects of analysis will also be varied.

Visual art, fiction, drama, poetry, music, and storytelling are creative and consumable ways of sharing Black women's experiences. Ntozake Shange, Queen Latifah, Alice Walker, and Toni Morrison are just a few creative artists who have presented in alternative textual forms the daily struggles Black women endure from a Black feminist perspective. Adopting a Black feminist lens, qualitative researchers have the opportunity to share research findings with a broader audience. Because educational disenfranchisement is spilling over into all sectors of education (e.g., early childhood education, community education programs, and higher education), it is an important time for qualitative researchers to be even more concerned with educating the masses about the challenges confronting educational attainment. Even more important, it's an opportune time for qualitative researchers to use ideas and knowledge acquired from our research to mobilize the masses against educational exclusion and tyranny.

THEORY AND PRAXIS

In past writings, I have admitted that a White woman told me what a feminist was, but it was my grandmother who showed me how a feminist lives. This revelation exposes my devotion to both the development of my theoretical sensibilities and putting words into action. A concern for ideas and action is not uncommon for those with Black feminist leanings. It is not enough to point out the social conditions challenging Black people and women in the United States and abroad. In addition to observing and naming those conditions, there also must be efforts toward self-definition and self-empowerment. Agency is an important spoke of Black feminist thought. Black feminists have a long-standing commitment to bridging the gap between theory and practice. hooks (2000) reminds us that,

> By dismissing theory and privileging organization work, some women of color are able to see themselves as more politically engaged where it really counts. Yet by buying into this dichotomy between theory and practice, we place ourselves always on the side of the experiential, and in so doing support the notion (too often fostered by white women) that their role is to do the "brain" work, developing ideas, theories, etc., while our role is to do either the dirty work or to contribute the experience to validate and document their analysis. (p. 115)

There is a need in qualitative research to ensure that educational theory moves beyond the confines of the ivory tower and provokes change at the micro- and macro-level. It is important for students of qualitative research to engage theory; however, it is just as important for educational scholars to discover the ways in which their findings might be used for improving pedagogy, curriculum change, or policy formation. Even more important, as indicated above by hooks (2000), Black women and other non-White women must recognize that they have the knowledge base and skill set to "do theory."

Also, consistent with Black feminism as praxis, is Black women's historical legacy of connecting educational reform to consciousness-raising about the conditions affecting the Black community and women. Such consciousness-raising can take place in different forums, such as classrooms, prisons, and print and visual media. More recently, social media is playing a greater role in disseminating information and sharing Black feminist intellectual work. All of these alternative spaces may be outlets for the qualitative researchers' findings and recommendations for educational reform.

CONCLUSION

If "analyzing and creating imaginative responses to injustice characterize the core of Black feminist thought" (Collins, 2000, p. 12), then how researchers respond to present-day inequity in education can characterize the future of Black feminist educational research and reform. Conversely, how Black feminists respond to educational inequity might inform future directions in educational research. Black feminism as a conceptual framework is a useful and timely rejoinder to calls for more critical, relevant, action-oriented methodologies in educational research.

Furthermore, Black feminist thought is a useful lens for studying and analyzing racism and sexism in schooling and the role of schooling in the formation and continual perpetuation of institutional and structural inequality, while simultaneously seeking to understand how formal and informal education has been used to buffer systematic oppression.

Black feminism inherently poses an obstruction to ideological segregation and bastardization that exists in the intellectual community. Such a covenant is achieved by including Black women as active participants in educational research, drawing on and referencing Black women theorists (something I have attempted to show here) in scholarly ponderings, mentoring the next generation of Black feminist scholars, and taking up Black women's concerns about education as topics worthy of exploration. The adoption or continuation of Black feminism in qualitative education research can foster critical understandings of how women and non-Whites creatively piece together personal experiences into educational research and spaces, innovatively mold educational research and practice to raise critical consciousness, and critically imagine educational transformation.

REFERENCES

Angrosino, M., & Mays de Perez, A. (2003). Rethinking observation: From method to context. In N. Denzin & Y. Lincoln (Eds.), *Collecting and Interpreting Qualitative Materials* (2nd ed.). Thousand Oaks: Sage.

Carruthers, J. H. (1999). *Intellectual warfare*. Chicago, IL: Third World Press.

Collins, P. H. (2000). *Black feminist thought: Knowledge, consciousness, and the politics of empowerment* (2nd ed.). New York: Routledge.

Collins, P. H. (2005). *Black sexual politics: African Americans, gender and the new racism*. New York: Routledge.

Davis, A. (1983). *Women, race, and gender*. New York: Vintage.

Denzin, N., & Lincoln, Y. (2000). *Handbook of qualitative research* (2nd ed.). Thousand Oaks: Sage.

Dillard, C. B. (2000). The substance of things hoped for, the evidence of things not seen: Examining an endarkened feminist epistemology in educational research and leadership. *International Journal of Qualitative Research in Education*, *13*(6), 661–681.

Dixson, A., & Dingus, J. E. (2008). In search of our mother's gardens: Black women teachers and professional socialization. *Teachers College Record*, *100*(4), 805–837.

Evans-Winters, V. E. (2011). *Teaching Black girls: Resiliency in urban classrooms* (2nd ed.). New York: Peter Lang.

Evans-Winters, V. E., & Esposito, J. (2010). Other people's daughters: Critical race feminism and Black girls' education. *Educational Foundations*, *24*(1–2), 11–24.

Evans-Winters, V. E., & Ivie, C. (2009). *Lost in the shuffle: Re-calling critical pedagogy for urban girls*. New York: Peter Lang.

Giddings, P. (1996). *When and where I enter: The impact of Black women on race and sex in America*. New York: HarperCollins.

Guy-Sheftall, B. (1995). *Words of fire: An anthology of African-American feminist thought*. New York: New Press.

hooks, b. (1999). *Ain't I a woman: Black women and feminism*. Cambridge, MA: South End.

hooks, b. (2000). *Feminist theory: From margin to center*. Cambridge, MA: South End.

King, J. (2005). *Black education: A transformative research agenda and action agenda for the new century*. Mahwah, NJ: Erlbaum.

Ladson-Billings, G. (2000). Racialized discourses and ethnic epistemologies. In N. Denzin, & Y. Lincoln (Eds.), *Handbook of qualitative research* (pp. 257–277). Thousand Oaks: Sage.

Ladson-Billings, G., & Tate, W. (1995). Toward a critical race theory in education. *Teachers College Record, 97*(1), 47–68.

Lee, C. (2005). The state of knowledge about the education of African Americans. In J. King (Ed.), *Black education: A transformative research agenda and action agenda for the new century* (pp. 73–114). Mahwah, NJ: Erlbaum.

Mabokela, R. O., & Green, A. (2001). *Sisters of the academy: Emergent Black women scholars in higher education*. Sterling, VA: Stylus.

Muhummad, C. G., & Dixson, A. D. (2008). Black females in high school: A statistical educational profile. *The Negro Educational Review, 59*(3–4), 163–180.

Mullings, L. (1997). *On our own terms: Race, class and gender in the lives of African-American women*. New York: Routledge.

Payne, C. (1984). *Getting what we ask for: The ambiguity of success and failure in urban education*. Westport, CT: Greenwood Press.

Reagon, B. J. (1993). Women as culture carriers in the civil rights movement: Fannie Lou Hamer. In V. Crawford, J. A. Rouse, & B. Woods (Eds.), *Trailblazers and torchbearers: 1941–1965*. Bloomington, IN: Indiana University.

Roberts, D. E. (1998). *Killing the Black body: Race, reproduction, and the meaning of liberty*. New York: First Vintage.

Spector-Mersel, G. (2010). Narrative research: Time for a paradigm. *Narrative Inquiry, 20*(1), 204–224.

Taylor, E., Gilborn, D., & Ladson-Billings, G. (2009). *Foundations of critical race theory in education*. New York: Routledge.

Walker, A. (1983). *In search of our mother's garden: Womanist prose*. San Diego: Harcourt.

Wing, A. (1997). *Critical race feminism: A reader*. New York: New York University Press.

Winn, M. (2011). *Girl time: Literacy, justice, and school-to-prison pipeline*. New York: Teacher College Press.

Wright, H. K. (2006). Are we (t)here yet? Qualitative research in education's profuse and contested present. *International Journal of Qualitative Studies in Education, 19*(6), 793–802.

CHAPTER TWELVE

Me, Myself, and I

Exploring African American Girlhood Through an Endarkened (Photographic) Lens

KARLA MANNING, ADRIENNE DUKE, AND PHILIP BOSTIC

INTRODUCTION AND BACKGROUND

There are many ideas, opinions, and questions about the construction and representation of adolescents, particularly in visual contexts. Media representations are often problematized by a single narrative based on sociocultural notions of race, gender, and sexuality (Wissman, 2008). This single narrative of adolescence comes from pseudo-scientific, racialized, and sexualized theories about the construction of mankind that can view adolescents as problematic, in a crisis, trouble-some, and "in need of attention" (Lesko, 2012). Similar views are promoted about African American females and disturbingly shift to degrading images concerning identity. African American females are placed within historical fabrications of "self" (specifically originating during slavery and Reconstruction eras) such as the Mammy, the Jezebel, or Hottentot Venus (Smith-McKoy, 2011). These images often re-present Black females as subservient to the White social order by providing sexual, familial, or economic benefits to others (Willis & Williams, 2002). Problematically, these images continue to persist and depict Black females as "nappy-headed hos," Aunt Jemimas, who continue to be seen on pancake boxes, or as the hyper-sexualized sassy supermama (Dunn, 2008; Ladson-Billings, 2009). As Cobb (2010) convincingly suggests, these stereotypes "serve to justify not only individual prejudices, but also oppressive power relationships" (p. 210). Such discourses create boundaries and fixtures of the "normal," which subsequently positions Black females as marginalized, liminal, and an "outsider" (Jordan-Zachery, 2009; Tesfagiorgis, 2001).

Although there are many problematic representations of African American females in mass media, this study sought to interrupt the voices of outsiders and examine how media created by an African American female could define her own identity. Self-definition allows space for the "recovering" of one's own body (Bennett & Dickerson, 2001). Although much of the research concerning images of African American females focuses on adult women, the purpose of this chapter is to understand and examine how African American adolescent girls think about their identities in relationship to their socially constructed selves and standards of culture, bodily aesthetics, and spiritual ways of being. This chapter contends that African American adolescent girls can do this through the use of photographically constructed life notes. Life notes are reflections of one's life (Bell-Scott, 1995) and are predicated on the understanding that girls of color are the owners and producers of their adolescent epistemologies and socially constructed identities. We propose that with digital media, African American girls are fostering new ways of learning, are deeply reflecting on their various identities, and can potentially see their identities that lie outside of the Westernized, oppressive structures, within a liberatory and spiritual consciousness (Pleasants, 2008). This chapter is guided by the following questions:

- In what visual and aesthetic ways do African American girls build upon their cultural and spiritual beliefs to articulate their inner desires, voices, identities, representations, and beliefs of self?
- How can the production and discussion of photographic life notes serve as spaces for remembering and healing cultural and spiritual knowledge, memories, interests, experiences, and histories of African American girls?

We chose to use the voices of African American girls to defy the illusions that knowledge from youth of color is not legit, welcomed, "good" enough, and/or not existing. The authors of this chapter reject all mythic, inferiorizing, myopic, and oppressive views, representations, and images of Black girls. Instead, we suggest that African American girls are spiritual beings who embody a significant amount of resiliency and agency, thus possessing the capacity to use it to foster their learning processes (Evans-Winters, 2005).

THEORETICAL DISCUSSION OF ENDARKENED FEMINIST EPISTEMOLOGY

This study draws on the scholarly framework of Dillard's (2000, 2012) endarkened feminist epistemology. This framework promotes indigenous and culturally organic ways of knowing, while also drawing attention to the ideological and epistemological rift between the construction of teaching and knowledge (Manning & Bostic, 2013). Endarkened feminist epistemology uses language to unveil oppressive cultural constructions to responsibly situate women of color's ways of knowing within culturally appropriate origins and roots. In contrast to "en-*lightened*" knowledge that relates to Eurocentric and modernist approaches to knowledge construction, en*darkened* feminist epistemology articulates how realities are known when located in Black feminist thought (Collins, 2000; King, 1988). According to Dillard (2000), endarkened feminist epistemology consists of epistemological and methodological assumptions that seek to highlight the dynamic historic, cultural, and spiritual constructions of knowledge by women of color. These assumptions are (1) self-definition forms one's participation and responsibility within a given communal space; (2) research is both a spiritual and intellectual pursuit that is filled with a purpose; (3) the individual appears through a dialogic and communal context; (4) one's experiences form the criterion of meaning-making; (5) the knowledge constructions from women of color are (and should be) acknowledged as ontologically and epistemologically viable within the academy and society at large; (6) there is a desire to understand the interwoven complexities and identities of women of color, which are often linked to power relations such as race, gender, and class.

This study focuses on the second theoretical assumption, "research is both a spiritual and intellectual pursuit, a pursuit of purpose." Through interrogating the dominant constructions and narratives about identity, both intellectual and spiritual understandings of identity can be expressed.

LITERATURE REVIEW: CULTURAL AND PSYCHOLOGICAL DEVELOPMENT OF AFRICAN AMERICAN GIRLS

One of the primary tasks of adolescence is to engage in identity work. Identity work at the individual level refers to the range of activities individuals engage in to create, present, and sustain personal identities that are congruent and supportive of their self-concept (Sears, 2010). By framing identity as work and not exploration, it is seen as a "production which is never complete, always in process, and always constituted within, not outside, representation" (Hall, 1990, p. 222). This is particularly important for Black girls. Stevens (2002) found that negative racialized and gendered experiences early on caused girls to engage in identity exploration and identity work earlier than their White counterparts. Therefore, although Pipher (1994), found that in adolescence, the gap between girls' true selves and the cultural prescriptions for what is properly female creates a decline in self-esteem, a risk for decrease in mental health, suicide, and low academic achievement, research shows that this does not occur to the same extent for African American adolescent girls (Greene & Way, 2005).

In a study done by Greene and Way (2005), self-esteem trajectories of adolescents were measured. According to this study, Black girls were able to retain higher levels of self-esteem through adolescence than their White and Latina counterparts. Belgrave (2009) further suggests that positive attributes of the self among African American girls are likely due to the socialization within the family, extended family, communities, and church or other religious institutions. She states:

> A girl's sense of self is determined by how others see her and what others expect from her. If significant others provide her with information that she is a person of value and worth, her beliefs about herself will be positive. If significant others provide her with information that she is not valued then her beliefs about herself may be negative. (p. 12)

Along with supportive environments, positive identity can be linked to the idea of self-complexity and resistance. Self-complexity is defined as the extent to which one perceives herself of having several dimensions to one's life (Lineville, 1985). According to Belgrave (2009), having self-complexity includes seeing oneself as a daughter, a student, a member of a particular organization, or a good friend. High levels of self-complexity allow multiple aspects of self to be present. Therefore, if individuals are failing in one domain, they are less likely to experience extreme negative emotions if they do well in other domains that are important to them (Belgrave, 2009; Lineville, 1985).

Along with self-complexity, resistance in the form of self-definition is also important as African American girls develop their identities. Resistance in this context is defined as, "the refusal to accept the relevance of certain knowledge of oneself" (Pitt, 1997, p. 129). In accordance with this definition, Ward (2000) found that resistance strategies were important in girls' development because it is central to girls' dismissal of hegemonic images concerning their identities. Therefore, exploring the ways that African American girls define themselves outside of mainstream images becomes an important developmental inquiry.

RESEARCH BACKGROUND AND METHODOLOGY

This study used case study methodology and photovoice methods to understand the ways one adolescent girl, Candace, utilized digital photography to explore her identity. Robert K. Yin (1993) defines the case study as an empirical inquiry designed to bring out the details from the viewpoint of the participants by using multiple sources of data, as well as a multi-perspective analysis. Within this method a particular individual, program, or event is studied in depth for a defined period of time (Yin, 1993). In this study, Candace and her photovoice project are the case under analysis.

Various scholars contend that photovoice is a participatory action research approach infusing photography along with participants' perspectives and analyses of the photographs (Dreyfous, 2005; Wilson et al., 2007). Photovoice was helpful in gaining perspective on Candace's life experiences because it allows for participants to expound on photographs that they've taken, which represent their worlds, identities, and experiences (Wang, 2006).

Photography was chosen as a medium of examination because it is a potent tool used in the sociocultural construction of identity with people of color (hooks, 1995). Photography allowed us to examine ways that identity and knowledge constructions in Africa American girls occur within visually designed epistemic media. Researchers have recognized the power of images, over oral interviews, to generate deeper conversations about the community, memories, and self-identity (Guerrero & Tinkler, 2011; Meo, 2010).

DISCUSSION OF IMAGES

photographic interpretations

This study borrows inspiration from deep learning theory (Tochon, 2010). In her photographic interpretations Candace was asked to go further into her reflection about her identities and representations. This deep learning framework advocates for reflexivity, adaptability, and self-determination. Deep learning includes the capacity for the student to draw on a repertory of knowledge, which allows for problems and assuring a coherent progression. These aspects require participants to reflect on their initial narratives about their identity and use repertory knowledge from their responses that produces space for new and multiple knowledge(s) to be created about self. Through her use of photography and making meaning of the visual signs and symbols in her photographs, she was able to explore her identity. Thematic analysis of her identity perspectives is also interwoven in her descriptions.

our collaborator

In this study we choose to use the term *collaborator* instead of participant to recognize her contributions to this project and linguistically assert her as an agent and not a passive object of inquiry. Our collaborator, Candace, was chosen through purposefully sampling. Due the spiritual focus of our project, Candace's involvement in a religious institution fit our requirements. We received consent from her mother to allow her to participate in the project. A list of prompts were sent to Candace to keep in mind as she was taking pictures. Two examples were: Are you doing something in the photograph and what do these actions mean? And What meaning do your clothes and appearance have to you? She subsequently sent her pictures via email, which included a narrative that explained how they related to her identity. Correspondence throughout the project was done through email and at the end, through a phone interview within a six-month time frame.

candace

Candace is a 16-year-old African American female who lives in a Midwestern suburban town. By doing a thematic analysis of her initial reflection and images, we were able to infer that the most salient aspects of her identity included (a) a thinker; (b) a "fashionista"; (c) a Christian. At some points in her life, Candace is more of a thinker—in which she pontificates on phenomena occurring in her life, school, church, or future events. For example, in her first picture, she is posing with a modest yet firm gaze to the viewer (see Figure 12.1). Her neatly decorated right wrist is positioned under her chin—an image that she suggests portrays her "thinking pose." She claims that taking the time to think in life is important because it allows for reflection and analysis of her past, present, and future. We quote her here:

> Loving myself means taking care of my body both spiritually and physically while also treating it as a prized possession. Demonstrating confidence to me means being comfortable with the way I am and understanding that I can't please everyone. Also being able to justify who I am through myself and God and not by what others believe I am. (K. Manning, personal conversation, October 11, 2012).

Figure 12.1. ("Thinking Pose") Copyright permissions belong to Malika Monger-Evanco © 2012

Figure 12.2. ("Praise Dancing") Copyright permissions belong to Malika Monger-Evanco © 2012

In this sense, Candace is using photography as a digital medium that affords her the opportunity to produce a narrative of herself, which involves using imagination and generative notions of self (Mills, 2011). As Dillard (2000) reminds us, one element of salience to the endarkened feminist epistemology theories is the pursuit of intellectual and spiritual productions of knowledge. To illustrate her spiritual identity, Candace provides us with a photograph of her and a group of other young Black girls in a church setting preparing for a praise ministry show (see Figure 12.2). In a follow-up narrative interview, Candace indicated "dancing is a huge part of my identity because it is one of the ways that I express myself when I don't have the words to say." She also connects this to her belief in God, thus embodying a significant part of her identity. This method is consistent with multiple researchers which describe how semiotic and digitized photographs are used to produce self-constructing identity narratives (Wissman, 2008).

FINAL THOUGHTS

This chapter sought to explore ways that photography can be used as a tool to explore identities. We found that when youth are approached about identity and photography, they become increasingly aware of their presence in society, how their experiences affect their self-image, and the role that they play in constructing that identity regardless of the medium or circumstance (Guzzetti, 2009). This chapter emphasizes that youth can and should construct their own identities and representations according to their values, standards, and personal assumptions. A viable medium in which to do this is through photography.

We have attempted to argue that the theorizing of the Black female body can potentially serve as a meaning-making opportunity to validate and centralize her knowledge, experiences, and subjectivities. The purpose of this article was to "critically study" the Black female body in an effort to examine the visual discourses and representations of the Black adolescent body in relationship to pedagogies, power, and politics (Giroux, 2002). To this end, the authors offer a possible framework in which educational researchers and teachers might consider how the body can be positioned as a possibility of literacy that is "rooted in conceptions of knowledge, identity, and being" (Street, 2003, p. 78).

This positioning is aligned with what the cultural theorist bell hooks (1995) calls a "visual politics," which seeks to "imagine new ways to think and write about visual art," which can lead to "a process of cultural transformation that will ultimately create a revolution in vision" (p. xvi). These visualities of the Black female body can then be seen as a potential of resistance and possibly transcend the historically oppressive discourses and visual representations (Willis & Williams, 2002). We insist that this work engenders the possibility to continue to inform and authenticate paradigms for ourselves, paradigms that allow us to emerge from the boundaries and norms that transgress against the whole being of African American females, hence leading to the ultimate goal to create and search for multiple ways of being and knowing that leads to a healing of the mind, body, and spirit (Dillard, 2012).

REFERENCES

Belgrave, F. Z. (2009). *African American girls: Reframing perceptions and changing experiences*. New York: Springer.

Bell-Scott, P. (Ed.). (1995). *Life notes: Personal writings by contemporary Black women*. New York: Norton.

Bennett, M., & Dickerson, V. D. (Eds.). (2001). *Recovering the Black female body: Self-representations by African American women*. New Brunswick, NJ: Rutgers University Press.

Cobb, W. J. (2010). The hoodrat theory. In D. Willis (Ed.), *Black Venus 2010: They called her "Hottentot"* (pp. 210–212). Philadelphia: Temple University Press.

Collins, P. H. (2000). *Black feminist thought: Knowledge, consciousness, and the politics of empowerment* (2nd ed.). New York: Routledge.

Dillard, C. B. (2000). The substance of things hoped for, the evidence of things not seen: Examining an endarkened feminist epistemology in educational research and leadership. *The International Journal of Qualitative Studies in Education, 13*, 661–681.

Dillard, C. (2012). *Learning to (re)member the things we've learned to forget: Endarkened feminisms, spirituality, and the sacred nature of research and teaching*. New York: Peter Lang.

Dreyfous, G.W. (Executive Producer), & Kauffman, R. & Briski, Z. (Directors). (2005). *Born into brothels* [Documentary]. USA: HBO/Cinemax Documentary Films.

Dunn, S. (2008). *"Baad bitches" and sassy supermamas: Black power action films*. Urbana, IL: University of Illinois Press.

Evans-Winters, V. (2005). *Teaching black girls: Resiliency in urban classrooms*. New York: Peter Lang.

Giroux, H. (2002). Body politics and the pedagogy of display: Youth under siege. In. S. Shapiro & S. Shapiro (Eds.), *Body movements: Pedagogy, politics and social change* (pp. 45–74). New York: Hampton Press.

Greene, M. L., & Way, N. (2005). Self-esteem trajectories among ethnic minority adolescents: A growth curve analysis of the patterns and predicators of change. *Journal of Research on Adolescence*, *15*(2), 151–178.

Guerrero, A., & Tinkler, T. (2011). Refugee and displaced youth negotiating imagined and lived identities in a photography-based educational project in the United States and Colombia. *Anthropology & Education Quarterly*, *41*(1), 55–74.

Guzzetti, B. (2009). Adolescents' explorations with do-it-yourself media: Authoring identity in out-of-school settings. In M. Hagood (Ed.), *New literacies practices: Designing literacy learning* (pp. 41–59). New York: Peter Lang.

Hall, S. (1990). Cultural identity and diaspora. In J. Rutherford (Ed.), *Identity: Community, culture, difference* (pp. 222–237). New York: Lawrence and Wishart.

hooks, b. (1995). *Art on my mind: Visual politics*. New York: New Press.

Jordan-Zachery, J. (2009). *Black women, cultural images, and social policy*. New York: Routledge.

King, D. K. (1988). Multiple jeopardy, multiple consciousness: The context of a black feminist ideology. *Signs*, *14*(1), 42–72.

Ladson-Billings, G. (2009). "Who you callin' nappy headed?" A critical race theory look at the construction of Black women. *Race Ethnicity and Education*, *12*(1), 87–99.

Lesko, N. (2012). *Act your age!: A cultural construction of adolescence*. New York: Routledge.

Lineville, P. W. (1985). Self-complexity and affective extremity: Don't put all eggs in one cognitive basket. *Social Cognition*, *3*, 94–120.

Manning, K., & Bostic, P. (2013). A review essay: Learning to (re)member the things we've learned to forget: Endarkened feminisms, spirituality, and the sacred nature of research & teaching. *International Journal of Qualitative Studies in Education*. doi: 10.1080/09518398.2013.834391

Meo, A. I. (2010). Picturing students' habitus: The advantages and limitations of photo-elicitation interviewing in a qualitative study in the city of Buenos Aires. *International Journal of Qualitative Methods*, *9*(2), 149–171.

Mills, K. (2011). "I'm making it different to the book": Transmediation in young children's multimodal and digital texts. *Australasian Journal of Early Childhood*, *36*(3), 56–65.

Pipher, M. (1994). *Reviving Ophelia: Saving the selves of adolescent girls*. New York: Ballantine.

Pitt, A. (1997). Reading resistance analytically: On making the self in women's studies. In L. Roman & L. Eyre (Eds.), *Dangerous territories: Struggles for difference and equality in education* (pp. 127–142). New York: Routledge.

Pleasants, H. (2008). Negotiating identity projects: Exploring the digital storytelling experiences of three African American girls. In M. Lamont-Hill & L. Vasudevan (Eds.), *Media, learning, and sites of possibility* (pp. 205–234). New York: Peter Lang.

Sears, S. D. (2010). *Imagining Black womanhood: The negotiation of power and identity within the girls' empowerment project*. New York: SUNY Press.

Smith-McKoy, S. (2011). Placing and replacing "The Venus Hottentot": An archaeology of pornography, race, and power. In N. Gordon-Chipembere (Ed.), *Representation and Black womanhood: The legacy of Sarah Baartman* (pp. 85–97). New York: Palgrave Macmillan.

Street, B. (2003). What's "new" in new literacy studies? Critical approaches to literacy theory and practice. *Current Issues in Comparative Education*, *5*(2), 77–91.

Tesfagiorgis, F. H. W. (2001). In search of a discourse and critique/s that center the art of Black women artists. In J. Bobo (Ed.), *Black feminist cultural criticism* (pp. 146–172). Malden, MA: Blackwell.

Tochon, F. (2010). Deep education. *Journal for Educators, Teachers and Trainers*, *1*, 1–12.

Wang, C. (2006). Youth participation in photovoice as a strategy for community change. *Journal of Community Practice, 14*(1–2), 147–161.

Ward, J. V. (2000). *The skin we're in: Teaching our children to be emotionally strong, socially smart, spiritually connected.* New York: Free Press.

Willis, D., & Williams, C. (2002). *The Black female body.* Philadelphia: Temple University Press.

Wilson, N., Dasho, S., Martin, A., Wallerstein, N., Wang, C., & Minkler, M. (2007). Engaging young adolescents in social action through photovoice: The youth empowerment strategies (YES!) project. *Journal of Early Adolescence, 27*(2), 241–261.

Wissman, K. (2008). "This is what I see": (Re)envisioning photography as a social practice. In M. Lamont-Hill & L. Vasudevan (Eds.), *Media, learning, and sites of possibility* (pp. 13–45). New York: Peter Lang.

Yin, R. (1993). *Applications of case study research.* Newbury Park, CA: Sage.

CHAPTER THIRTEEN

Embodying Dillard's Endarkened Feminist Epistemology

AMIRA MILLICENT DAVIS

A full moon is rising. Monday morning's lecture on the beginnings of the African slave trade awaits me, but only after I drum for Djibril's Sunday evening dance class, my church, and I can't miss service. I start the charcoal for the frankincense and myrrh. I blow the smoke from the sage bundle throughout the rooms, in the corners of my house, across my altars, around the sleeping bodies of my children and grands. There are candles to light, a bath of Epsom and sea salts to run. I choose five crystals to soak with—leopard and fire jasper for protection, turquoise for wealth and peace, citrine for mental and psychic clarity, and rutilated quartz as an accelerant. I check my inbox, "Mama Amira, are you going to submit an abstract for our book?" "Yes. Sorry for the delay. I'm running behind." The bath awaits. I sit in the warmth of its water and open myself to ideas, to words, theories, and concepts. For me, ritual is episteme and methodology.

AN ENDARKENED FEMINIST EPISTEMOLOGY

In her essay, "When the Ground Is Black, the Ground Is Fertile," Cynthia Dillard (2008) reflects on the Fourth Moment of qualitative research, described as a "crisis of representation" (Denzin & Lincoln, 2005). According to Dillard (2008), the crisis emanated from "hegemonic structures that have traditionally and historically negated and impeded the intellectual, social, and cultural contributions of marginalized communities" (p. 278). These structures also "negated the spiritual contributions of African ascendant people," which was particularly troubling given their worldview "places spirituality at the center of thought and discourse." This is especially true of "African and African feminist epistemological space."

Dillard's epistemological theory arose during the "Ninth Moment" of qualitative inquiry (2006 to the present), which is characterized by its inclusiveness of previously subjugated knowledges. This "Moment" emphasizes purposive, socially just research that rejects master narratives and epistemes in favor of decolonizing, emancipating methodologies, reclaiming indigenous knowledge while promoting interpersonal, communal responsibility (Denzin & Lincoln, 2005). An "endarkened feminist epistemology" asserts itself, first, as linguistically oppositional to conceptualizations of enlightenment that not only draw on a turn in Western intellectual development that supplanted superstition and religious doctrine with reason, but which also assumed a more advanced/superior epistemological perspective. In her articulation of an "endarkened feminist epistemology," Dillard theorizes how Black feminist thought has historically been constructed from the "cultural standpoint" of Black women who stand at the intersections of race, gender, class, and other identities that are oftentimes overlapping and competing. Dillard (2008) is interested in how their ways of knowing have critiqued oppression and enacted resistance. While emerging within a proliferation of Black women's gender theories, Dillard's concept reconnects Black women's feminist modalities to a motherland. Africa, as material and metaphoric mother, is the ground from which Black women emerge. Dillard writes,

> I seek in work on "both sides of the water," to open a way for relevant cultural connections and reciprocal possibilities for African people to address the very nature of domination and oppression of Black feminist and African-centered thought and indigenous cultural ways of knowing and being, through engaging indigenous and healing methodologies. (p. 281)

At the heart of Dillard's project is research that centers the need for Black people to craft theories and methodologies that explicate their lived experiences within oppressive structures while simultaneously creating modes for political engagement and personal and collective transformation. An "endarkened feminist epistemology" seeks not only to resist and transform social arrangements that violate civil and human rights, but it also serves as a healing methodology that emanates from the experiential knowledge of Africana people who express belief in a hierarchically arranged spirit world that encompasses the living, the dead, the universe, and all therein. Dillard says that this healing methodology is at once "intimately meditative," informed by the wisdom and advice of the ancestors and the Creator, and "faith-filled," meaning a methodology that is "prayerfully-attentive," expressing gratitude to the Creator and spirit world (p. 281). Dillard's epistemology is predicated on three key concepts: (1) spirituality, (2) community, and (3) activist praxis, meaning research in and on behalf of the African global community that is theorized from a critical Africana philosophical perspective (pp. 278–279).

As an epistemology of resistance (Medina, 2008), Dillard's subaltern voice rescues Black women's ways of being in and with the world from hermeneutical marginalization and silence. As more Black women enter academia and access what Audre Lorde (1984) calls the "master's tools," they claim and reshape them to suit their specific needs, which oftentimes are intimately tied with the needs of the larger, Diasporic African community. Africana feminist scholars such as Dillard serve as machete wielders and light bearers, clearing and illuminating hidden paths once obscured by Western patriarchal power.

For Black women scholars, reclaiming ancestral epistemologies has implications for the research process: the questions we ask, how we engage communities, as well as for teaching praxis: who and what we teach, and for our pedagogical approach: what methods will be used to transmit necessary information, encourage dialogue, and maximize possibilities for the co-creation of knowledge. In a time when the failures of patriarchy and capitalism are made obvious in the myriad calamities facing the planet, deploying the subaltern knowledge of Black women creates the possibility for animating a moral corrective for humanity.

> A new moon in Pisces. Mercury retrograde. Problems/delays in transportation and communications, but the possibility for do overs; rethinking the subconscious: retracing that which connects us to the primordial waters of the universe; return, recover, retrieve, rescue, restore, and redefine essences. Here I am. In the space behind my third eye where the stream of consciousness flows. I, as spirit, woman, and African, open myself to receive what the Ancestors and Divinities want me to speak into the world through the combined expression of Orò (the power of the word) and áṣẹ "life force and voiced power to make things happen." (see Thompson, 1984)

ENACTING AN ENDARKENED FEMINIST EPISTEMOLOGY: READING SIGNS AS WONDERS

On June 5–6, 2012, the planet Venus made its second and final trek across the sun until the year 2128.[1] The event brought out stargazers from around the globe, anxious to see this once-in-a-lifetime event. The ancients understood the connections between the movement of the planets and their impact on the earth and its inhabitants. The Yoruba of Southwestern Nigeria appeared to have meditated on Venus' movement across the sun and made the correlation between the planet Venus and the myth of the goddess Ọṣun's quest to save humanity.

> In the early days of the world, the Orișa became tired of serving Olodumare... the Lord of Heaven [who] was so distant.... When Olodumare caught wind of this attitude, [he] withheld the rain from the earth. Soon the world was encompassed by a staggering draught. The ground became parched and cracked. The plants withered and died without water.

> Then one day, the peacock, who was in reality Ọṣun herself, came to offer her services to save the world from this draught.... The little peacock flew off towards the sun and the palace of Olodumare.
>
> Ọṣun explained the state on earth and went on to tell Olodumare that she had come at risk of her own life so that her children/humanity might live.... The Lord of Heaven then turned to the peacock who was now a vulture, saying that her children would be spared and ordered the rain to begin again. Olodumare looked deeply into Ọṣun's eyes and into her heart, then announced that for all eternity she would be the Messenger of the House of Olodumare and that all would have to respect her as such.[2]

In June 2012, Venus and the sun weren't the only big stars in a planetary drama unfolding in the sky. Astrologers lit up the blogosphere with prophetic analyses of the three-year-long square dance between the planets Uranus and Pluto, set to commence on June 24, 2012. In a June 25, 2012, op-ed News.com article titled "Uranus and Pluto 2012: Mid-'60s Come of Age, Demand 'Report Card,'" Anne Nordhaus-Bike writes about the last time these two planets made contact in the mid-1960s:

> Uranus's electric, erratic nature and energy of sudden change, revolution, awakening, and genius combined with Pluto's deep, transformative nature and energy of destruction, evolution, surrender, and hidden power. Together, they created explosive energy that demanded change, and they ushered in a new historical cycle. In the decades since, the seeds Uranus and Pluto sowed at their conjunction have had opportunities to sprout and take root, and some have created tremendous change.

Currently, Uranus is in the independent, pioneering, martian/militaristic sign of Aries. Pluto in Capricorn speaks to deep changes (Pluto) in large structures (Capricorn) and secret machinations in high places, the Plutocracy. The unprecedented levels of state surveillance, making the private public, have recently been revealed in dramatic fashion. At the same time, r/evolutionary forces are using new technology (e.g., social media, computers, cell phones) for citizen journalism and popular education that promotes critical discourse. The dance between Uranus and Pluto will last until 2015 and indicates a time of dramatic transformations. The times offer an opportunity for creative imagining of ways to rescue humanity, urging us toward collective improvement and physical emotional, spiritual, and mental health. As Capricorn represents the patriarchal order, astrologers predict a challenge to the old patriarchy that will result in the re-emergence and reconnection with feminine principles that promote an ethics of care and interdependence.

During the mid-1960s, the world witnessed a shift as the result of energetic social movements among various marginalized groups: people of African descent on the continent and throughout the diaspora, women, antiwar protesters, and Latinos. Sixty years later, people across around the world are rebelling against neoliberalism, global capitalism, imperialism, and environmental destruction.

African America is witnessing the retrenchment to some of the primary gains made during the Civil Rights/Black Power era: the collapse of the Black middle class, double-digit unemployment, astronomical rates of Black male incarceration, the attack on public education, segregated neighborhoods, and the loss of voting rights. In addition to the failure of policies to mitigate Black suffering, state violence and repression is escalating. While intragroup violence is down from years past, media constructed Black criminality is used to justify the victimization of young Black men such that, according to the Malcolm X Grassroots Movement, an African American citizen is killed every 28 hours by policing forces.[3]

Meanwhile, Black mothers, once forced to reproduce the Western empire, are now being scapegoated as the reason for the social ills afflicting the Black community. For example, according to conservative pundit Bill O'Reilly, "the violent crime rate in the Black community is due to personal choices made by single Black mothers" (Webster, 2013). O'Reilly's reading totally obfuscates the history of racial and gender violence toward African American women that undermines their ability to mother. There has yet to be collective healing of the intergenerational trauma caused by the horrors of the Ma'afa.

In a time of such r/evolutionary change, is it possible to deploy an endarkened feminist epistemology as a restorative healing methodology for African America? What transformative energy can Black women derive from Venus'/Osun's trek across the Sun?

> July 21: a full moon in Aquarius. Mercury turned direct yesterday. Around the globe there were mass rallies to protest the killing of a Black woman's son/sun, Trayvon Martin. His crime, being a young Black boy wearing a hoodie in a place where he was perceived not to belong. His mother bears the pain of so many Black mothers before her who lost sons and daughters because 17th century slave codes made being off the plantation without a pass or daring to fight back punishable by death. The flash of the shooter's gun shed light on historical inequities while spotlighting this mother and the spirit of her dead child. And once again, Black life and the womb through which it comes is made spectacle.

OSUN AS ENDARKENED FEMINIST KNOWLEDGE

> The critical role of women as the vessels of new life was not lost on the architects of... ancient civilizations... in the Yoruban imagination women were reflective of the conduit of life, the stream of human consciousness... the maintenance of ethical and nurturing relations, and the deep feelings of love that sustain them. Thus the role of rivers, lakes, and streams in sustaining food production systems paralleled the roles of mothers as sustainers of humanity. [Women] therefore represented the possibility of renewal, redemption from injustice, reclamation of truth, and the forward flow of human society.[4]

Ọṣun's power is oftentimes reduced in Western translation as a river goddess, fertility goddess, and "the African Venus" (Murphy & Sanford, 2001). These concepts fail to fully express the "centrality and authority" of Ọṣun in Yoruba religious thought and the "multidimensionality" of her power, which is political, economic, divinatory, maternal, natural, and therapeutic (p. 1). Ọṣun transforms through "the simplest of natural substances," water and the mystery of birth (p. 2). Ọṣun rises quickly in defense of her children and conquers through the silent though persistent force of water with which she also heals. She is a warrior who fights for her children, vanquishing seen and unseen enemies. She is also a loving mother with a ready embrace. The Yoruba word *Ọṣun* means source. The metaphysical concept of Ọṣun is one of

> [a] perpetually renewing source of life... sweet water from dry ground, a mode of hope and agency in new and difficult situations, a way out of no way that has made life possible for her devotees in West Africa and throughout the African diaspora. (Murphy & Sanford, 2001, p. 8)

Ọṣun is also the leader of what the Yoruba call *Àjẹ́*, "people, particularly elderly women, who use power secretly" (p. 6). Within Western patriarchy, *Àjẹ́* are commonly identified by the pejorative term witches (Washington, 2005), however, Badejo (2001) notes that women who embrace the principles of Ọṣun worship individually and collectively become *Àjẹ́*, powerful beings who activate their *àṣẹ* to help others who consult them (p. 131). He goes on to say that "priestesses, devotees, and supplicants" of *Àjẹ́* use their "*àṣẹ* as artists, entrepreneurs, healers, educators, political power brokers, and social agents of change."

Ọṣun as a female archetype and the expression of *Àjẹ́* as a feminine force provide a paradigmatic structure for understanding the cultural importance of motherhood and the positive characteristics related to mothering to which women, especially women of African descent, can aspire. Reclaiming culturally accessible epistemes offers the possibility of restoring motherhood in African America as a legitimate source of identity and status for women, as well as a site of solidarity and social organization. Constructing an epistemological framework that centers ancient conceptualizations of mother in her material and metaphysical forms allows Black women as researchers, scholars, and educators to think beyond hegemonic patriarchal, Western discourses of motherhood, generally, and Black women's mothering in particular, to imagine ethical, sustainable interventions.

> It's the new moon, falling on the date of the New Year. Finally, I'm completing edits to this paper. In the interim, I've been able to bear witness to the ways Black mothers develop epistemes of survival and resistance within the context of multiple, interlocking forms of violence. I hear in their voices the mandate of Ọṣun and the collective charge of our

foremothers: "making a way outta no way." The Sun and Moon have joined together along with Pluto, animating Uranus' genius. While purchasing a sage bundle to cleanse tonight, a Fluorite gemstone called to me: the genius stone. I'm reminded that in order to transform civilization, we must overthrow patriarchal conditioning and allow the moral mother spirit to guide us back to our humanity. It is by reclaiming Mother, the divine feminine, that we reset our moral compass and recognize our relatedness to all that is, has been and will be. It is in the darkness of the moonless sky that we find the way forward.

SPIRITUALITY AS EPISTEMOLOGY AND METHODOLOGY: A CONCLUDING THOUGHT

As Venus made her way across the sun in June 2012, she recovered from ancient memory the story of the Yoruba goddess Ọṣun's quest to save humanity. The recovery of this African myth affords us the opportunity to imagine library praxis during a time of great planetary upheaval. From an African-centered perspective, spiritually is the essence of African identity. As an act of epistemic resistance, Dillard's endarkened feminist epistemology (2008) reclaims a spiritual praxis that has efficacy for political, social, and psychological regeneration. Dillard's articulation of an endarkened feminist epistemological framework operationalizes a pan-Africanist woman's unique standpoint within existing structures of power. It privileges spiritual and pre-cognitive ways of apperceiving and interpreting the world. Dillard's choice of the word *endarkened* recognizes the political nature of language, which has historically served as a powerful tool in the mental, spiritual, and intellectual colonization of African Americans and other marginalized peoples. Thus, to transform reality, both the language used to define and describe phenomena and the epistemes from which they emerge "must possess instrumentality" and be transformative (p. 279). The decolonization process requires that we adopt/appropriate non-Western vocabularies and epistemes.

Looking to Africa, the fertile ground from which the Africana identity emerged, for language, symbols, and hermeneutical perspectives, offers the possibility for library praxis. Looking to the skies, the planets and their movement, provides a text rich for reflexive theorizing. We hear and heed the call from contemporary scholars for the reclamation of ways of knowing that draw from the wellsprings of our cultural heritage. Citing educational scholar Joyce E. King, Dillard (2008) makes the point that it is incumbent upon Africana scholars to "recuperate identity, transform consciousness, and liberate methodologies from an African cultural and spiritual perspective" (p. 286). Cutting to the essence, Dillard goes further to cite from liberation theologist Gustavo Gutierrez's text, *We Drink from Our Own Wells: The Spiritual Journey of a People* in which he makes it plain: "our methodology is our spirituality." And so let it be. Àse!

REFERENCES

Badejo, D. L. (2001). Authority and discourse in the Orin Odun Ọṣun. In J. M. Murphy & MM-M. Sanford (Eds.), *Ọṣun across the waters. A Yoruba goddess in Africa and the Americas* (pp. 128–140). Bloomington, IN: Indiana University.

Denzin, N. K., & Lincoln, Y. S. (Eds.). (2005). *Handbook of qualitative research* (3rd ed.). Thousand Oaks, CA: Sage.

Dillard, C. L. (2008). When the ground is black, the ground is fertile. Exploring endarkened feminist epistemology and healing methodologies in the spirit. In N. K. Denzin, Y. S. Lincoln, & T. Smith (Eds.), *Handbook of critical and indigenous methodologies* (pp. 277–292). Thousand Oaks, CA: Sage.

Lorde, A. (1984). "The master's tools will never dismantle the master's house." In A. Lorde (Ed.), *Sister Outsider: Essays and Speeches* (110–114). Trumansburg, NY: Crossing Press.

Medina, J. (2008). *The epistemology of resistance. Gender and racial oppression, epistemic injustice, and resistant imaginations.* New York: Oxford University Press.

Murphy, J. M., & Sanford, MM-M. (Eds.). (2001). *Ọṣun across the waters. A Yoruba goddess in Africa and the Americas.* Bloomington, IN: Indiana University Press.

Nordhaus-Bike, A. (2012, June 25). *Uranus and Pluto 2012: Mid-'60s come of age, demand "report card."* OEN, OpEdNews.com. Retrieved from http://www.opednews.com/articles/Uranus-and-Pluto-2012-Mid-by-Anne-Nordhaus-Bike-120624-509.html

Thompson, R. F. (1984). *Flash of the spirit: African and Afro-American art and philosophy.* New York: Vintage.

Washington, T. N. (2005). *Our mothers, our powers, our texts: Manifestations of Àjẹ́ in Africana literature.* Bloomington, IN: Indiana University Press.

Webster, S. C. (2013, July 23). O'Reilly blames unwed black mothers for violent crimes. The Raw Story online. Retrieved from http://www.rawstory.com/rs/2013/07/23/oreilly-blames-unwed-black-mothers-for-violent-crimes/

ENDNOTES

1. The planet Venus is the Roman goddess of love, beauty, and harmony.
2. Oshún's Flight: How She Came To Be Messenger of Olodumare (God). orishanet.org. Oshun. Available at http://www.orishanet.org/oshun.html
3. Operation Ghetto Storm: 2012 Annual Report on the Extrajudicial Killing of 313 Black People. Malcolm X Grassroots Movement. Retrieved from http://mxgm.org/operation-ghetto-storm-2012-annual-report-on-the-extrajudicial-killing-of-313-black-people/
4. Facebook post by Dr. Kamau Rashid and Ogunsola Hammond, Conversations on the Divine Feminine, May 11, 2013.

SECTION III

Responsibility for Who and What as a Black Feminist Educator?

CHAPTER FOURTEEN

Black Girl Interrupted

A Reflection on the Challenges, Contradictions, and Possibilities in Transitioning from the Community to the Academy

MONIQUE LANE

Historically, the U.S. school system has overtly and covertly overlooked and subordinated African American female youth. Despite recent efforts toward urban school reform, there has been a general failure to examine the complex sociocultural contexts in which Black female students are situated and the ways in which their subordination is perpetuated in schools. While vestiges of a culturally responsive pedagogical movement are apparent in some schools, endeavors to engage urban African American female youth often translate into curricula that replicates and/or reinforces controlling stereotypical images of Black femininity—and therefore remains disengaging for these students. In this chapter, I use scholarly self-narrative to reflect on my trajectory from an urban Black girl—awkwardly ensconced in a matrix of race, class, and gender oppression—to a graduate student conducting dissertation research on the schooling experiences of African American female youth similar to my younger self.

I begin with a vignette that illustrates my struggle as an adolescent attending a large, academically underperforming urban public school and will describe how my experiences served as the impetus for returning to my alma mater as an English teacher to, in part, mentor African American female youth. As a theoretically informed curricular response to the rising academic disengagement and social alienation experienced by my young, African American female students, I sought to extend the work of Black feminist theorists by creating a critical and culturally relevant *safe space*[1] in my classroom. Hence, Black Girls United (BGU) was birthed.

In the final section, I will detail the trials I faced when my work with students in BGU was transposed into the world of academia. Specifically, I will address the tensions in managing the dual, competing interests of my two selves: the *homegurl* who values education as a vehicle for self-actualization and civic responsibility, versus the *researcher*, who is highly influenced by White hegemonic ways of knowing and doing. One of the major challenges I faced was representing participants' voices with dignity and accuracy, while responding to pressure from the academy to value quantity over quality. Drawing on Dillard's notion of "re-membering" the spiritual nature of education, the final section of this chapter discusses my efforts to move through and beyond these dualities to engage in research that pays the bills, rejuvenates the spirit, and nourishes the soul.

SCHOOL DAZE

It was a typical day in Honors 12th-grade English at King High School[2] in South Los Angeles in 1998. I had recently received acceptance to the University of California, Los Angeles (UCLA) for undergraduate admission and was anxious to take on the challenges and opportunities that college would present. Deeply proud of my accomplishment, I knew I would be the first person in my family and one of the few in my community to matriculate into higher education. Disengaged with our teacher's mechanistic application of the traditional curriculum and insulted by her low expectations, my peers and I participated in casual small talk—our usual escape from classroom boredom. Seemingly out of nowhere, our teacher rose to her feet from behind her desk and threw her arms up in frantic despair. Obviously frustrated by our inattentiveness, she cried out, "I really don't know why I waste my time with you guys! None of you are going to college! You aren't going to do anything productive with your lives!" The lunch bell rang, interrupting her rant, and like soldiers at war we all left—virtually unfazed by the tongue-lashing we had received from our drill sergeant. We had been exposed to multiple forms of racial stereotyping and deficit thinking expressed by many adults before; however, this particular incident epitomized our perception of teachers' opinions of urban youth of color.

As a high school student, I encountered various instances in which one or more dimensions of my identity were unmercifully attacked. In one typical day I occupied multiple spaces—each commingling race, class, and gender politics. In my classes, well-meaning yet misguided educators frequently trivialized my intelligence. In the hallways, teenage boys ogled and assaulted my maturing brown body via sexist epithets. Moreover, the ubiquity of reductive images of low-income

African American women in the media—that positioned us as icons of cultural deviation and pathology—had me convinced that I was a social leper, linked to a group of naturally inferior people. Despite my efforts at negotiating these offenses—a front of indifference, mean-muggin', and the seldom quick-witted counterattack—each interaction left an imprint of shame on my dignity, and the collective effect was a powerful strike against my humanity.

Lacking a formal space to critically analyze these experiences, I bore my stigma of shame in silence. The college-prep courses for highly gifted students traditionally disregarded oppressive social conditions; rather, they often reinforced them through curricula that valorized White middle-class norms. As such, I was young, gifted, and deeply embattled. There was, however, a glimmer of hope. I had big dreams. With my head buried in my books, I envisioned a revolution where young Black women unite—striking back against "the machine," to subvert the oppression that has so skillfully been woven into the fabric of American schooling.

THE RETURN TO KING HIGH SCHOOL

When I returned to King High as an English teacher my passion for education was raw. It was visceral. And it was palpable. My chief objective was to engage in transformative, humanizing education for *all* students. Like most Black female educators who identify as feminist, I understood the practice of teaching for the purpose of liberation is in direct conflict with the historic role of the institution as a source of oppression. This "political clarity" among Black feminist educators is grounded in the belief that we are "*ethically and ethnically*" accountable for preparing youth of color to transcend social injustices—a philosophy heavily reflected in our curricular choices (Beauboeuf-Lafontant, 2002, p. 77).

By my second year of teaching, I recognized similarities between my younger self and many of my African American female students. That is, traditional schooling environments had inculcated in Black girls a sense of powerlessness, isolation, and fear of external analytic expression—which was apparent in my day-to-day interactions with them. Having experienced and witnessed firsthand the marginalization that Black females endure in urban schooling spaces, I recognized the urgency to create an alternative setting where these young women could develop and exercise their critical consciousness and transformative agency.

After considerable reflection, I sought to extend the work of Black feminist theorists by creating a student organization that responded to the frustrations African American female youth were experiencing in school and in their respective communities. Moreover, my objective was to develop a space in which they could discover and celebrate the collective angle of vision that united them as young African American women. After a semester of developing my Black feminist pedagogical framework, Black Girls United (BGU) was birthed. During weekly lunches, BGU members used *critical ethnic literature*[3] to investigate and work toward resolving historical and contemporary issues facing the African American female population. Student-led discussions often resulted in meaningful community activities[4] that emerged organically from our conversations. Our shared objectives were to engender solidarity, self-love, and self-definition through dialogue, reflection, and critical analysis. By prioritizing sociocultural and academic concerns and empowerment of African American female students, this organization was uniquely poised to catalyze individual and collective changes I hoped would yield sustainable improvements in how young Black girls at King High experienced urban schooling.

After two years as BGU's faculty sponsor, I recognized three important recurring phenomena: (1) several students were developing an independent, self-defined standpoint; (2) African American females' individual and collective activism was generated and sustained; and (3) many participants demonstrated a strong desire to engage in critical analytical discussions. BGU functioned as an alternative and unorthodox setting within our mainstream urban schooling context; young African American women were afforded the opportunity to *collectively* read the world (Freire, 1973) and move toward transforming their place within it. The success of the program inspired me to return to graduate school and formally research, evaluate, and articulate the liberatory potential of Black feminist pedagogical practice in an urban educational context.

RE-MEMBER, RECENTER, AND REPEAT

I chose to enroll in the UCLA Urban Schooling Ph.D. program because of its commitment to improving the educational outcomes of Los Angeles's most underserved communities, and I was impressed by the number of faculty whose research interests were theoretically and pedagogically aligned with mine. There were great possibilities in transitioning from the community to the academy: I had the opportunity to contest the long-standing popular and scholarly narratives regarding the academic underachievement and cultural subjectivities of urban African American young women. Moreover, I could potentially influence the national debate on best teaching practices in urban schools and inform the preparation of future K–12 public school educators. I had an unabashedly *homegurl* mentality when I embarked on this journey. Not to be confused with the cliché loud talkin', self-indulgent, anti-intellectual Black female caricature that is plastered across American television and movie screens, a *homegurl,* by my definition, is the antithesis of this melodramatic portrayal. She is self-defining. She is resilient. She is driven by an intense love for family and community. Through her lens, a formal education is futile if it does not serve the interests of those who are most marginalized in our society. Essentially, a *homegurl* values education beyond the means of employability; it is a vehicle for self-actualization *and* civic responsibility. I entered my doctoral program with the ambitious intention of using my intellectual capital as such. Regrettably, two years into my studies, I realized my vision had somehow gone awry.

After completing coursework, the next course of action was to establish my dissertation study's design. I was certain of the "what" of the investigation: I was going to research the role of Black feminist pedagogy in the racial/ethnic and gender identity development of students in Black Girls United. Furthermore, I was interested in how a shift in individuals' racial and gender identities influences their orientation toward school. The unanswered question was with what means to ascertain this information. Consequently, I ran into one of the greatest challenges in my doctoral program: *the methods conundrum*. Graduate students faced immense pressure to engage in solely quantitative or mixed methods research. Pressure emanated from various sources, including distinguished faculty members and fellow students. It was considered universal knowledge, part of the "not-so-hidden curriculum," that quantitative studies are often perceived as more reliable and generalizable as specified by classic scientific research standards.

As an impressionable, budding scholar concerned with the marketability of my research in the academic economy, I obsessed over whether my dissertation would rival extant educational literature, my ability to acquire fellowship opportunities, and the degree to which my methodological choices could influence eventual job opportunities. I concluded that a mixed methods study would increase my chances of success at all three of my aforementioned anxieties. It was official; my *researcher* identity had emerged. Success in the academy—as measured by White hegemonic ways of knowing and doing—was equated with my ability to achieve wealth and superstardom as a university professor. The sociopolitical concerns and interests of research participants were overshadowed by my personal crusade for economic and professional gains. I was rapidly losing sight of my *homegurl* sensibilities; they had become a faint glimmer at the end of a long, windy tunnel.

The challenges I faced negotiating the competing dualities of my *homegurl* and *researcher* identities is a common struggle among scholars of color. Universities have historically existed as racialized, cultured, gendered, classed, and highly political spaces, and non-White graduate students have endured various instances of marginality at the crossroads of our multiple identities. Dillard (2008) documents this phenomenon and encourages researchers to *re-member* the "things that we've learned to forget" (p. 89). She calls for individuals to recall racial/cultural, spiritual, and/or political expertise to guide us in conducting ethical, empowering research.

As Dillard explains, a principled and liberatory approach to research necessitates that educators draw on the Spirit within—namely, the concrete experiences of our everyday lives that serve as the basis of our current wisdom, and the ways in which we make sense of the world (Dillard, 2002, 2006). Embodying these experiences, Dillard purports, is key to working in concert *with* research participants, and ultimately engaging in the kind of transformative education that serves the greatest good. For me, this meant "wandering back into a familiar context," and reclaiming my purpose in the academy (Dillard, 2008, p. 89).

I stumbled upon Dillard's concept of *re-membering* through an experience I had with a former member of Black Girls United. As I developed my dissertation research proposal, I met with a handful of students to gauge their willingness to participate in the study. One student, Ashanti, experienced a tragic accident in her family that occurred just one week prior to our meeting. Her female cousin was murdered in a drive-by shooting while standing outside of an acquaintance's home. On the day we met for lunch my intentions were to briefly check in with Ashanti regarding her emotional state and then proceed with the business of my dissertation. With pen and notebook in hand, I was in full *researcher* mode when I met her in the parking lot. The original motivation behind our meeting was lost when I looked into her eyes; she was still visibly shaken, and undeniably heartbroken.

My lunch with Ashanti ultimately served a much greater purpose than to advance my research objectives. In that meeting, she and I embodied Black feminist praxis as we explored the dialectic of our oppression and our activism as African American women. We spoke about love. We shared stories about death and familial cycles of pathology. We disclosed our fears and shared feelings of powerlessness. And we challenged each other to look to Spirit to reclaim our agency in times of sadness and despair. *Re-membering* these stories and cultural experiences with Ashanti reified my purpose for entering into academia: to use education as a liberatory tool to subvert the oppressive conditions under which many urban African American female students exist. Currently, the systematic ways in which schools disengage Black girls through disempowering and de-humanizing pedagogies and curricula is reproduced in their subjugated labor positions, and racial and spatial isolation to urban ghettos. Ashanti's cousin was a disturbingly frightening reminder of this fact.

Later that afternoon, I concluded that my *homegurl* and *researcher* identities were not adversaries. Admittedly, the *researcher* in me was self-serving, pushy, and determined—however, this state of being also equipped me with the necessary knowledge and adeptness to navigate the competitive, alienating world of academia. My *homegurl* sensibility, on the other hand, functioned as a constant reminder to the *researcher* of the unyielding passion from which my scholarship emerged, and my commitment to continually engage in work that is in service of others. My mind, body, and spirit were fully reengaged in the dissertation process when I recognized the transformative potential of oscillating between these two dispositions. My challenge was to develop an innovative and empirically sound methodological framework representing the voices of participants with dignity and accuracy.

CONCLUSION: TACKLING THE METHODS CONUNDRUM— A CRITICAL RACE FEMINIST AUTOETHNOGRAPHY

I decided to use an autoethnographic approach in my dissertation to document the effects of Black feminist pedagogy on my BGU students' identity development. Similar to other qualitative methods, autoethnography relies heavily on storytelling to assist in the interpretation of social interactions (Spry, 2001). Autoethnography is distinctive because through public exposure of personal narratives, a powerful process of self-investigation occurs. During this process, the *autobiographical* and *personal* links to the *cultural* and *social* (Ellis, 2004, p. xix). The act of self-narration fosters critical interpretation and eventual transformation of personal as well as broader social and political circumstances. In my dissertation, the documentation of the effects of my teaching practice were connected to a larger sociopolitical project. Through public, narrative disclosure of students' engagement with Black feminist pedagogy, my research aims to subvert the historically oppressive means by which African American female youth are schooled.

The autoethnographic tradition derives from the long-standing convention of personal storytelling in the fields of anthropology and feminist ethnography (Jirousek, 2006). As an extension of critical race theory, *critical race feminism* complicates the feminist practice of autobiographical storytelling within autoethnography through the centering of *non-White* racialized female experiences (Delgado Bernal, 2002; Evans-Winters & Esposito, 2010). Although historically concentrated on legal policies affecting people of color, critical race feminism has more recently been extended to include challenges to educational policies and research methods. As such, the autoethnography draws on critical race feminist philosophy to denaturalize Eurocentric notions of femininity within educational research practices while illuminating the "indivisible oneness of racialized femininity" within educational experiences of young *Black* women (Muhammad & Dixson, 2008, p. 176). As African American female youth authoritatively utilize their collective voice in the narrative articulation of their differential schooling experiences, the hierarchy of knowledge claims is inverted, and the "multiple layered realities in which Black girls exist" becomes the focus (Evans-Winters & Esposito, 2010, p. 22).

Resolving *the methods conundrum* was one of many victories that I have notched in pursuit of my doctorate degree. Moving through and beyond the duality of the *homegurl* and the *researcher* provided me the opportunity to engage in scholarship that fills a tremendous void in educational literature. It critically addresses what young Black women want, need, and can benefit from in urban schooling contexts. Furthermore, this work uses student voices to interpret how African American females are situated in schools—positioning them as experts of their own sociopolitical location and empowering them as co-participants in the effort to radically transform U.S. public education.

Throughout various instances of my graduate career, I have made choices that serve as a brazen affirmation of my love for self *and* community. In these difficult times, I have relied on Dillard's notion of *re-membering* in order to "heal the depth of conflict and differences" that reside from within (2008, p. 92). To *re-member* is to reconnect with Spirit—and the racial, gendered, and cultural knowledge that collectively operate as a magical lifejacket in the most turbulent waters. I have learned that trusting in my experiential wisdom will invariably guide me back to shore, where I become centered in my most authentic self. It is only then that I can engage in an educational research praxis that pays the bills, rejuvenates the spirit, and nourishes the soul.

REFERENCES

Beauboeuf-Lafontant, T. (2002). A womanist experience of caring: Understanding the pedagogy of exemplary Black women teachers. *The Urban Review, 34*(1), 71–86.

Collins, P. (2000). *Black feminist thought: Knowledge, consciousness, and the politics of empowerment* (2nd ed.). New York: Routledge.

Delgado Bernal, D. (2002). Critical race theory, Latino critical theory, and critical raced-gendered epistemologies: Recognizing students of color as holders and creators of knowledge. *Qualitative Inquiry, 8*(1), 105–126.

Dillard, C. B. (2002). Walking ourselves back home: The education of teachers with/in the world. *Journal of Teacher Education, 53*(5), 383–392.

Dillard, C. B. (2006). When the music changes, so should the dance: Cultural and spiritual considerations in paradigm "proliferation." *International Journal of Qualitative Studies, 19*(1), 59–76.

Dillard, C. B. (2008). Re-membering culture: Bearing witness to the spirit of identity in research. *Race and Ethnicity in Education, 11*(1), 87–93.

Ellis, C. (2004). *The ethnographic I: A methodological novel about teaching and doing autoethnography.* Walnut Creek, CA: AltaMira.

Evans-Winters, V. E., & Esposito, J. (2010). Other people's daughters: Critical race feminism and Black girls' education. *Educational Foundations, 24*(1/2), 11–24.

Freire, P. (1973). *Pedagogy of the oppressed.* New York: Continuum Press.

Jirousek, L. (2006). Ethnics and ethnographers: Zora Neale Hurston and Anzia Yezierska. *Journal of Modern Literature, 29*(2), 19–32.

Morgan, J. (1999). When chickenheads come home to roost: My life as a hip hop feminist. New York, NY: Simon & Schuster.

Muhammad, C. G., & Dixson, A. D. (2008). Black females in high school: A statistical educational profile. *The Negro Educational Review, 59*(3–4), 163–180.

Shakur, A. (2001). Assata: An autobiography. Chicago, IL: L. Hill Books.

Spry, I. (2001). Performing autoethnography: An embodied methodological praxis. *Qualitative Inquiry, 7,* 706–732.

ENDNOTES

1. Patricia Hill-Collins defines a *safe space* as a setting in which Black women are allowed to freely engage in critical discourse around relevant issues (2000, p. 110). Within these spaces, Black women's self-defined, group standpoint emerges.
2. This school has been given a fictitious name.
3. *Critical ethnic* literature includes texts written by Black women and women of color that challenge traditional representations of non-White women in popular literature and in dominant media. Some examples include *The Autobiography of Assata Shakur* and *When Chickenheads Come Home to Roost*.
4. Community activities included neighborhood protests, collective health/fitness undertakings, and engagement with local women's organizations apart from King High School.

CHAPTER FIFTEEN

"Oh, You'll Be Back"

Bridging Identities of Race, Gender, Educator, and Community Partner in Academic Research

BILLYE SANKOFA WATERS

"I remember myself as surrounded by extraordinary adults who were smarter than me. I was better educated, but I always thought that they had true wisdom and I had merely book learning. It was only when I began to write that I was able to marry those two things: wisdom and education." —*Toni Morrison (in Lanker, 1989)*

INTRODUCTION

Knowledge of self is most often articulated through intricate constructions of race, gender, class, religion, sexuality, and ability. (For the focus of this chapter, I will only directly address the first two.) These categories, which have traditionally been understood as immutable binaries, are named through scientific and academic research and are therefore problematic in that they position living bodies as aggregated data before the bodies have fully articulated self-awareness. Post-conventional approaches in research have complicated these fixed ideas with factors such as historical space and cultural practices. According to Patricia Hill-Collins (1989/1995), the primary tenet of Black feminist thought[1] is that lived experience is the criterion for meaning and credibility. This privileges *wisdom* before *knowledge*. Additionally, the lens of an endarkened feminist epistemology, as articulated by Cynthia B. Dillard (2008), allows me to explore the struggle and desire for my research coparticipants to see the "solid, taken-for-granted nature of my African American identity" (p. 87) as sister, daughter, and othermother (Hill-Collins, 2004). It is at these critical nexuses of knowing that researchers have the opportunity for more nuanced ways of transmitting knowledge as well as transformative practices in the academy and society.

In this chapter, I first unpack my positions as a Black woman from Chicago who is trained as a qualitative researcher. Second, to further examine the relationship of Black women as *subjects* of research, I revisit a project I began in 2010 titled, *We Can Speak for Ourselves*. Essential to this journey was a Black feminist lens, which provided the activist orientation, interview protocol, and space for poetry. I conclude with an application of the work of Cynthia B. Dillard (Okpaloaka, 2000, 2008, 2011) to further explore wisdom, healing, and reciprocity in academic research.

IDENTIFYING EDUCATOR

I first began my work in education as a tutor and mentor in the Chicago Public Schools (CPS) and later as a director of an afterschool program where I began to focus on the needs of adolescent Black girls. The environment often created a tension steeped in self-identity, hormones, and academic ambition. I created and facilitated peer groups for the girls, recognizing some of the same questions, arguments, and identity concerns I had 20 years prior. There were no magic recipes—I worked tirelessly with other "Black girls" to build ideas and projects that we either had or wanted to have when we were growing up. They kept me buried in ways to grow us as a group, continually feed their hunger, and build upon their resiliency. *They made me go to graduate school.* Furthermore, these relationships set the stage for my master's thesis and I felt like they were doing the work with me.

As I moved through my program that espoused an orientation toward social justice, I was baffled at the pockets of resistance to my topic: Black girls. One professor commented, "Well, White girls have had it hard too. Why don't you write about that as well?" This professor—who had had an impressively extensive library on feminism, yet no texts that included the lives and voices of Black women—stood in agreement with others who accused Black students of "oppression bias" (Richardson, 2013), also referred to as "me-search" (McLean, 2014). I am grateful that as a very young scholar I had the support of other critical senior faculty members who encouraged me to press forward.

The most important push came February 2009 when a friend called me early in the afternoon. I listened as she explained through a hoarse throat that one of our former students, age 11, had killed herself the night before. This young girl, Alissa, had been in the midst of completing a homework assignment when she wrote that she didn't want to be a burden anymore and used a jump rope to strangle herself in her bedroom closet. Where many of us hear the screams of our Black girls—despite statistics of progression and promotion—many more are still silenced within the walls of higher education. The professor and Alissa pushed my Black feminist baby steps into leaps and bounds. I realized that my presence represented both an appeasement of the historical order as well as a threat and I had to decide if my work would temper or tip the scale. I realized power in the works of Audre Lorde (1977/2007) who is often quoted in this regard: "what I most regretted were my silences. To question or to speak as I believed could have meant pain, or death. But we all hurt in so many different ways, all the time, and pain will either change or end. Death, on the other hand, is the final silence" (p. 41). Alissa presented me with the opportunity to not allow her silence to be in vain. I found bridges with the community works Project Butterfly and Little Black Pearl; I culled wisdom from the research and creative work of Rebecca Carroll (1997), Michelle Cliff (1980), Venus Evans-Winters (2011), Iris Jacob (2002), and Joyce Ladner (1995) as a formidable start.

IDENTIFYING FEMINIST RESEARCHER

I entered graduate school with two goals: one, learn how to teach teachers, and two, acquire and create tools to facilitate the development of positive identities of Black girls (because that's what good educated Black girls do—give back). Instead, I began the discovery that I was in fact *so* privileged with the proverbial village of Black women doctors, administrators, artists, activists, scholars, and mothers that I neglected to realize how these rights and gifts manifested while the battles press on. Much like the research I engaged, I collapsed the experiences of Black women within Black power or feminism and did not fully understand the frontline wars of Black women for and by us. In fact, a Black woman had not even been allowed to enroll at my graduate alma mater until 44 years prior to my acceptance.[2] So, while I could recite speeches of Sojourner Truth, quote Harriet Tubman, and was intimately familiar with the American women's suffrage movement, it wasn't until I began reading the speeches of Maria Miller Stewart (1803–1880), Frances E. W. Harper (1825–1911), and Anna Julia Cooper (1858–1964) in 2008 that my spirit shifted and I *suddenly* became both a woman and a feminist.

Asserting my identity as a Chicago native, poet, and feminist, my work as a scholar within a university with very high research activity (RU/VH), Southern institution enabled me to investigate and blend the duality of my positions while unknowingly engendering a healing process for myself and my coparticipants—Black women and mothers.

> The summer of 2010, I was granted the opportunity to work in Chicago for a 10-week Education fellowship and was assigned to a K–8 charter school on the South Side to

> develop a Parent University.³ I was keenly aware that I was not a (birth) mother. This distinction seemed important to make so the women I worked with understood I had not positioned myself as a "parent expert" and I gave them the space to approach me as they saw fit. Some related to me as a researcher—Sonia asking me point blank—"I want to know what *you* are reading"; some related to me as another warm body in action; and others related to me as a sister and a daughter. (Rhodes, 2012, p. 41)

Toward the end of our first meeting, I candidly admitted to them, "I know who you are but I don't see you women in my research." Proverbial light bulbs burst as I continued, "I think I want to do my dissertation here." They began to celebrate as I told them I needed to pray about it and confer with my advisor. But there was a shared energy that was incredibly powerful. Maya made an on-the-spot declaration: "Oh, you'll be back."

Journaling throughout the process was absolutely necessary to capture both the shifts in my perspectives—as well as the mothers'—and the relationships that were created. I wrote about how my presence transformed the space of the school and challenged my assumptions as both an insider and outsider. I was initially asked to publically journal (blog) as part of the fellowship requirements, but I continued to do so privately when my contract was complete.

> I was able to write more about the women themselves—how I saw them in their beauty and in their flaws. I wrote about how many times I felt like I was in the way. I wrote about how angry I was about some of the administration decisions that were made. I wrote about times I felt like "The Spook Who Sat By the Door."⁴ I wrote about the discomfort of these women trusting me with personal experiences that I knew I would choose, shape, and present to a public audience.... I also wrote about my own mother—a lot. (Rhodes, 2012, p. 56)

Cynthia B. Dillard (2008) reminds us, "cultural memory is at least part of what these scholars of color raised up in these studies and in their ongoing quest to be 'seen' and 'heard' and 'unlimited' in the myriad ways they approach their questions, their scholarship" (p. 89). Thus, this work is important because while the work of mothers I knew seemed effortless, it was absolutely backbreaking and nameless. *We Can Speak for Ourselves* created a stage to not only share the women who affected our lives across generations, but to righteously tell their truths and complexities along with how we continue the work of self-identification and actualization for our children. Our voices became a declaration to "poignantly express the need of African-American woman to honor our mothers' sacrifices by developing self-defined analyses of Black motherhood" (Hill-Collins, 1990/2009, p. 187). This understanding of motherwork or othermothering—which "can be done on behalf of one's own biological children, or for the children of one's own racial ethnic community, or to preserve the earth for those children who are yet unborn" (Hill-Collins, 2004, p. 48)—introduced me to a quilt of literature with many patterns, while reaffirming the carefully stitched pieces in every patch of my life. This was the guiding post in developing my interview protocol where I posed conversation pieces such as "How did your mother raise you?" "How did you come to the decision of motherhood?" "Where do you take risks with your child?" and "When did you learn you are Black?"

There were beautiful rhythms in the way that each woman performed her story. I attempted to capture this in the text through punctuation and formatting and maintained the use of first person as they were speaking to a direct audience. At any point of tension or light heartedness, there is a lot of laughter, pauses for self-reflection or assessment and quite a few "mmhms" from me. I shared my research with them along with my deep appreciation for Audre Lorde (1977/2007) noting: "for women… poetry is not a luxury. It is a vital necessity of our existence. It forms the quality of the light within which we predicate our hopes and dreams toward survival and change" (p. 37). We operated in the same space that Dillard articulated in conversation: "what I am struck by are the limits of the language of research to really accommodate what I experience and hear and see as the '*data*' of our stories" (Okpalaoka & Dillard, 2011, p. 68). Therefore, as a woman and an artist, the inclusion of poetry in this project was just as important as the theoretical framework and analysis. Poetry created a space to fully express ourselves and allowed us to actively create community.

CONCLUSION

I grow from a legacy that prides itself on education and accountability; however, the schooling process—much regarded as a gatekeeping system—immerses students in world inside itself, predicated on separation rather than inclusion. This is most evidenced in the scientific and philosophical language we employ that does not reflect the poetic, guttural, silent, and rhythmic nuances of "others," but only responds to a so-called standard Eurocentric articulation of thought. Such communication does not highlight intellect as much as it speaks to the protection of a ruling class (West, 1982/2003). So this is where I tread my path—on the paths of the "first," "one of the few," or the "only" (Hill-Collins, 1990/2009)—to open the narrow discourses of academia with the fullness of my living people. Responding to the reflections of Alice Walker (1983), engaging research with and for the communities I am part of means I am "involved in work [my] soul must have" (p. 241). I share my story, the stories of my girls, the stories of my mothers, "as a way to both stand in solidarity with and to bear witness to the collection of research[ed subjects]" (Dillard, 2008, p. 88). This chapter is cradled by the work of Cynthia B. Dillard—which espouses an endarkened feminist epistemology—with great respect to the cultural mores of wisdom, healing, and reciprocity.

WISDOM

In "Re-membering Culture: Bearing Witness to the Spirit of Identity in Research," Dillard (2008) explores the intrinsic awareness of "African ascendant women" (Okpalaoka & Dillard, 2011, p. 65). In this way, I am mindful as a feminist researcher to call on the African gifts of oral tradition and griots not simply for the goal of record keeping but for protecting, preserving, restoring, and learning. These stories are then shared within these respective academic cannons toward both a sacred and global wisdom, which is neither visible nor hyper-visible, but rests with the responsibility of agency and service. During her 2009 doctoral defense of Black women Freedom School teachers, Kristal (Moore) Clemons stated, "You can't be a Black woman in the academy if you don't know what's happening in the streets." *We* validate our work (Stanfield, 1985) by returning to our histories and our memories. "They are inspirational, breathing new life into the work of teaching, research, and living. They are memories that transform; a place within and without that feeds our ability to engage new metaphors and practices in our work" (Dillard, 2008, pp. 90–91). Recalling the words of Toni Morrison that introduced this chapter, we build both wealth and wisdom through the fluidity of our experiences across geographies and generations. We do not educate simply for the acquisition of social and cultural capital; we do not engage scientific inquiry to conquer. We do this work for full spiritual and community health, understanding our connectedness as a whole rather than accomplishing individual quests.

HEALING

Inextricably tied to the journey of health is the process of healing. While I act in service to holistic development and well-being of those I share community with, as a researcher I must always ask: Where do I do harm to myself and Black women or where am I complicit in harm that has already been done? This was most noticeably brought to my attention during the first parent meeting I had with my project coparticipants:

> Upon seeing [Deja], I thought she was one of those parents who made you want to walk in the opposite direction upon approach. She was out of breath when she reached the doorway, and her unkempt hair was barely tucked under a baseball cap. She sat her McDonald's bag at the meeting table and began to complain about her ongoing job search…. What took me back the most was when Deja pulled reports and articles from her bag addressing teacher retention, student success… literature to underscore current challenges in the classroom, the school at-large, and how the parents present could organize themselves to be more involved.

I felt ashamed for how I initially judged her. I thought she was there only to complain. I thought she was there to tell us how bad the teachers were. I thought she was there to explain to us that her child wasn't a problem, the school was. I translated her rushed appearance and relaxed tongue as unmotivated and confrontational. As a "good researcher" and community member, I didn't even realize I was coming in with such a strong bias. (Rhodes, 2012, pp. 10–11)

What I learned in this space was to listen; I learned to be vulnerable and ask questions rather than confirm assumptions—good or bad. I had to open a space where questions could be asked of me. I learned to back off; my help is not always warranted, welcomed, and in those spaces where I may feel rejected is an opportunity for me to reflexively investigate my positionality and performance. What Deja showed me that day was that she was absolutely comfortable in her skin, which inadvertently made me uncomfortable in mine. Healing was able to take place when I asked myself "Why?" Therefore, I believe the first and most important step in identifying *spaces* of healing is understanding who we are as individual bodies before we can understand our relationship to one another and propose strategies; each of us must "know our role." In this way, we are able to better craft our own gifts and talents to configure how they contribute to the whole. This is an active, everyday choice each of us has to make.

RECIPROCITY

Finally, as we respond to ourselves and to one another through wisdom and healing, we act as change partners to both receive and give. A transformative moment for me as a new graduate student was when Bettina Love presented research from her dissertation during an 2009 American Educational Studies Association (AESA) meeting and concluded with: "these girls gave me a PhD; I had to ask myself, what am I giving them?" I fully understood that *my girls* gave me the courage to even enter the academy; the women of *We Can Speak for Ourselves* gave me a host of more daughters and sons as well as prepared me for my own. I acknowledge how incredibly privileged I am in the work of the latter; not every project yields long-term relationships, nor should they be built on this premise. However, these women's stories are as fresh and active to me as my own. I share them as an intentional act of both sense-making and "quilt-making" (Walker, 1983, p. 239). We have shared names and histories that now include one another. The heart of my work aligns with this statement: "An endarkened feminist epistemology articulates how reality is known when based in the historical roots of global Black feminist thought and when understood within the context of reciprocity and relationship" (Okpalaoka & Dillard, 2011, p. 65). Therefore, my research honors the work of Black women by telling our names, so that we no longer assign anonymous tags such as "Some Nigger"[5] or "an anonymous Black woman" (Walker, 1983, p. 239) to our images and life's work. My research honors the work of Black women by creating collaborative spaces for us to speak for ourselves. My research honors the work of Black women by keeping the promise: "Oh, you'll be back," by not only returning, but also realizing that I have never left.

REFERENCES

Carroll, R. (1997). *Sugar in the raw: Voices of young Black girls in America.* New York: Three Rivers Press.

Cliff, M. (1980). *Claiming an identity they taught me to despise.* Watertown, MA: Persephone Press.

Hill-Collins, P. (1995). The social construction of black feminist thought. In B. Guy-Sheftall (Ed.), *Words of fire: An anthology of African American feminist thought* (pp. 338–357). New York: New Press. (Original work published 1989)

Hill-Collins, P. (2004). Shifting the center: Race, class, and feminist theorizing about motherhood. In E. N. Glenn, G. Chang, & L. R. Forcey (Eds.), *Mothering: Ideology, experience, and agency* (pp. 45–66). New York: Routledge.

Hill-Collins, P. (2009). *Black feminist thought: Knowledge, consciousness, and the politics of empowerment.* New York: Routledge. (Original work published 1990)

Dillard, C. B. (2000). The substance of things hoped for, the evidence of things not seen: Examining an endarkened feminist epistemology in educational research and leadership. *International Journal of Qualitative Studies in Education, 13*(6), 661–681.

Dillard, C. B. (2008). Re-membering culture: Bearing witness to the spirit of identity in research. *Race and Ethnicity in Education, 11*(1), 87–93.

Evans-Winters, V. (2011). *Teaching black girls: Resiliency in urban classrooms.* New York: Peter Lang.

Jacob, I. (Ed.). (2002). *My sisters' voices: Teenage girls of color speak out.* New York: Henry Holt and Company.

Ladner, J. A. (1995). *Tomorrow's tomorrow.* Lincoln, NE: University of Nebraska Press.

Lanker, B. (1989). *I dream a world: Portraits of Black women who changed America: Photographs and interviews by Brian Lanker.* New York: Stewart, Tabori and Chang.

Lorde, A. (2007). Poetry is not a luxury. In A. Lorde (Ed.), *Sister Outsider* (pp. 36–39). Berkeley: Crossing Press. (Original work published 1977)

Lorde, A. (2007). The transformation of silence into language and action. In A. Lorde (Ed.), Sister Outsider (pp. 40–44). Berkeley: Crossing Press. (Original work published 1977).

Lorde, A. (2007). The master's tools will never dismantle the house. In A. Lorde (Ed.), *Sister Outsider* (pp. 110–114). Berkeley: Crossing Press. (Original work published 1979)

McLean, S. A. (2014, March 7). "Me-search": When white people justify their colonial white gaze. [Web log post]. Retrieved from http://decolonizeallthethings.wordpress.com/2014/03/07/me-search-when-white-people-justify-their-colonial-white-gaze/

Okpalaoka, C. L., & Dillard, C. B. (2011). Our healing is next to the wound: Endarkened feminism, spirituality, and wisdom for teaching, learning, and research. *New Directions for Adult and Continuing Education, 131*, 65–74. doi:10.1002/ace.422

Rhodes, B. N. (2012). "We can speak for ourselves": Parent involvement and ideologies of Black mothers in an urban community (Doctoral dissertation). Retrieved from ProQuest. (Publication Number 2763014011)

Richardson, W. (2013, July 1). Oppression bias and the struggles of a Black sociologist. [Web log post]. Retrieved from http://sociologicalimagination.org/archives/13511

Stanfield, J. H. (1985). The ethnocentric basis of social science knowledge production. *Review of Research in Education, 12*(1), 387–415.

Walker, A. (1983). *In search of our mothers' gardens: Womanist prose*. San Diego, CA: Harcourt.

West, C. (2003). A genealogy of modern racism. In L. Cahoone (Ed.), *From modernism to postmodernism* (pp. 298–309). Malden, MA: Blackwell. (Original work published 1982)

ENDNOTES

1. The tenets of Black feminist thought are (1) lived experience as criterion for meaning, (2) the use of dialogue in assessing knowledge claims, (3) the ethic of caring, and (4) the ethic of personal responsibility.
2. Women had been provided various forms of conditional enrollment since 1897. However, it wasn't until 1972 that Title IX banned all sexual discrimination in admissions and women were admitted on equal terms with men. Also of note, 1955 marked the enrollment of the first Black students (three men) to the university; Karen Parker followed in 1963 as the first Black female; and in 1969, Dr. Roberta Jackson was hired by the School of Education as the university's first Black, tenured professor. Retrieved from http://womenscenter.unc.edu/about/womens-history-unc/.
3. Parent Universities are designed as a theoretical space to instigate parent involvement.
4. *The Spook Who Sat By the Door* (1969/1989) is a work of fiction by Sam Greenlee that describes a Black male who uses his skills and training as a government agent to develop young men on the South Side of Chicago as "Freedom Fighters."
5. This refers to a postcard of a young Black girl photographed circa 1900 where the bottom caption reads: "Just a nigger." Charleston, S.C. Image can be retrieved via http://www.blackhistory101mobilemuseum.com/.

CHAPTER SIXTEEN

Lessons Learned Through Double-Dutch

Black Feminism and Intersectionality in Educational Research

CORRIE L. THERIAULT

THE LESSONS OF DOUBLE-DUTCH

I have vivid memories of jumping double-dutch with my friends in my neighborhood. It was certainly not for the faint at heart and we were proud to be the select few who could do it. I grew up in a predominately White area, where jumping rope singularly was the preferred method. I cannot pinpoint where we learned the lesson of double-dutch but I remember this experience as a turning point in the construction of my identity. Here, I entertained the notion that despite my marginal position, despite being different from the perceived norm, there existed some resemblance of positive self-worth. We could do something *they* could not, or possibly would not, do. Often, and typically for an audience, we displayed skill, patience, and teamwork combined with the friendly competition we had with one another. We sang the words to the *Double-Dutch Bus* (Smith, 1981) and danced to it knowing we also held membership in this special club.

Much like the stories shared in Gaunt's (2006) *The Games Black Girls Play: Learning the Ropes from Double-Dutch to Hip Hop*, we made up and sang many chants to help us keep time but to us, the rhythms and beats were equally important. Love (2012) discussed the importance of the beat in relation to hip hop but her sentiments extend to this form of expression as well. She noted the beat of a song speaks to the listener and that these patterns "are powerful, soulful, endearing, and rebellious all at the same time" (p. 89). The lyrics and beats that we knew, and could therefore adjust and emphasize freely, were sung in solidarity and helped shape our identity and voice. One such chant was:

> Down in the meadow where the corncobs grow
> a grasshopper jumps on an elephant's toe.
> The elephant cried with tears in his eyes,
> why don't you pick on someone your size?
> Unknown Author

We said this chant, and others like it, with a sense of ownership and pride but we also knew that not reciting them while jumping could be costly. One moment out of sync, one moment where the beat was off, could equate to weeks of pain. Being slashed by two ropes in your face, your ankle, or your hip was a known risk. We knew this risk was substantial. Making an error with two ropes caused more pain than the one rope *they* used. Double the lesson learned. Double the pride. We had to negotiate two ropes that in essence mirrored a kinetic Venn diagram. Each rope represented its own place in the sport while together they delivered a much different opportunity. My sister jumpers and I knowingly shared these risky yet rewarding moments. My sister scholars and I continue this exercise today. Through the lens of double-dutch, we can "consider the ways in which these facets of identity are navigated within racialized spaces, as well as the ways in which such negotiations are understood by particular scholarly approaches" (Hentges, 2007).

BLACK FEMINISM, INTERSECTIONALITY, AND EDUCATIONAL RESEARCH

The art of jumping through hoops and negotiating multiple moving targets is not germane to the sport of double-dutch. The bobbing and weaving Pardlo (2008) referenced in the opening poem occurs in many contexts and appears frequently in the intersection of Black feminism and educational research. Dillard and Okpalaoka (2011) argued that "racism, power, and politics profoundly shape our research and representations, especially as scholars of color" (p. 147). It is necessary then to have a theoretical approach that challenges the existing nature that is oppressive and patriarchal (Murray-Johnson, 2013) while allowing social scientists a way to reference more than one way of seeing and knowing. It is essential to think about questions of power, justice, and equality in relation to research centered on history and experience (Mohanty, 2003; Oleson, 2011).

This idea of intersectionality has multiple interpretations. Crenshaw (1989, 1991) suggested this term as a way to join forces with competing sensibilities and

McCall (2005) defined it as the "relationships among multiple social dimensions and modalities of social relations and subject formations" (p. 1771). It lends itself to the notion that we are multifaceted with layers, or ropes, that intertwine and intermingle. Sometimes these ropes meet at a specific space while they can also appear to be separate entities in another. These areas of our identity center us and although seemingly opposite, always function as one. Patricia Hill-Collins (1998) argued these layers "mutually construct one another" (p. 62). Within the contested layer of race and ethnicity, for example, Black feminist educational researchers often grapple with multiple aspects of physical identity:

> age
> multi-racial
> skin tone (light or dark)
> hair (relaxed or natural)
> attire (ethnic or Eurocentric)
> place (northern or southern)
> status (tenure-track or non tenure-track)

In addition to these racial matters of identity, Black feminist educational researchers also navigate matters of perception:

> How will my skin tone be received?
> Will I be considered a sell-out?
> Will I inspire other young women?
> Will they think I am [too] powerful?
> How will my race affect my data collection and findings?

Black feminist educational researchers must also concern themselves with matters of power, sexual identity, religion, etc. Even if all of these areas are considered, we jump in our studies knowing our identities are complex and evolving and we also accept the risk of being perceived as something or someone other than who we are.

STEPPING INTO SOLIDARITY

Through Black feminism and intersectionality, I am able to conceptualize my positionality and reflect on my negotiation of the ropes during my own research experiences. In 1989, hooks called for Black women to create a model of feminist theory and scholarship that widens options and "enhances our understanding of black experience and gender" (p. 182). One particular moment of research stands out as a time that I was confronted by the intersectionality of multiple identities. As part of a funded project, I was hired to visit several afterschool programs across the state. The purpose of this study was to explore the methods of care, culturally relevant pedagogy (CRP), and character education in a federally funded afterschool program. I visited many elementary, middle, and high schools but in this case, I visited a middle school sponsored by, and designed to mirror, Historically Black Colleges and Universities (HBCU). I was excited about the prospects of this day. I graduated from an HBCU and have fond memories of the opportunity it afforded me as a young Black woman.

Walking the halls of the school, I remember feeling a sense of community and camaraderie. Knowing that my lived experience was in conjunction with what this afterschool program was attempting to accomplish offered a sense of purpose to my work. At the time of this visit, I was eight months pregnant with my youngest son but, in my perspective, I could have easily been mistaken for a woman carrying quadruplets. I felt very large and uncomfortable but I was determined to complete this portion of the study. It was an interesting time in my life to say the least but I was looking forward to it.

The program I was asked to observe was created to increase Black girl empowerment and centered on Black feminism as well as Ladson-Billings's (1994) framework of CRP. The mission of the program required the program staff and teachers to be intentional in their use of students' backgrounds and experiences as assets in their afterschool lessons and activities. They were also charged with creating an atmosphere that would be intriguing to young Black girls while also playing an integral role in improving their proficiencies in mathematics, reading, and science. Although someone else from my research team could have visited this school, I was determined to connect with this center myself. This day, the day I chose to visit, the females were in the gym stepping—practicing for an upcoming exhibition. Chilisa and Ntseane (2010) argued that an aspect of Black feminism/activism is to recognize "sayings, proverbs, rituals and songs from our research respondents as part of the missing literature that has been muted by Euro-Western methodologies largely dominated by male thought" (p. 621). Stepping, like double-dutch, is another form of expression that involves rhythm, timely body movements, and precision. "Frequently coupled with songs, chants, and verbal calls, stepping is a vibrant performance practice that has been shaped by the experiences of blacks" (Branch, 2005, p. 316). With this knowledge, I waddled into the gym and smiled when I saw them stepping because I pledged a Black sorority and recognized some of the elements of their show. For a moment, I was mentally transported to my college days of carefully chosen uniforms, step show practices, and homecoming competitions. I realized that telling this story of history and cultural meaning was just as important to me as the opportunity to view its development.

I was hired as an educational researcher and program evaluator but I was identifying with this group of girls in a way that extended beyond my research agenda. Johnson-Bailey (2010) considered this to be the work of reciprocity and relationship in research. My multiple identities wanted to share my HBCU and stepping experience with these young Black women. The double-dutch ropes in my brain were turning and I was jumping between and betwixt these identities all at once. The Black feminist framework allows Black women to reject dominant narratives that suggest singular identities and serves as a space to "question methods that distance the observer from the object of study, thereby denying a facet of the social construction of knowledge" (Rosser, 2008). I observed the girls carefully, paying close attention to the facilitator's instruction and the reactions of the students while simultaneously and discreetly, learning the routine. I walked around in my role of careful observer but could not ignore my past.

I felt at ease at my HBCU. I write that the school is *mine* and I know I was just one of the many students who went there, but I was made to feel special and important. Perhaps it was because I grew up in a predominately White neighborhood but for whatever reason, I thrived in this environment. Pledging and stepping only added to the sense of acceptance and family-like atmosphere I experienced. It was apparent to me why this afterschool program chose to function in this manner. It validated, affirmed, and appreciated when the world often does not.

Momentarily forgetting that I was eight months pregnant, while remembering precious moments from college, I jumped behind the tallest girl in the line (lines are situated from shortest to tallest and I am 5'10") and began to recite the words, move to the beat, and demonstrate my commitment to Black feminism and intersectionality. As an educational researcher, this posed a risk for me. I recognized that my position situated me in a place of authority and that jumping out of this boundary could influence the study. Although the students and staff in the program cheered and seemed to enjoy my impromptu demonstration, I realized that who I was would always play a role in my research. Later, long after I dealt with the physical consequences of stepping while largely pregnant, I realized my analysis and interpretations centered on constructions of identity, activism, and Black feminism and its relation to the program's mission and overarching goals. It took this study for me to understand that collecting data and subsequently analyzing the results, served as my new form of double-dutch. I respected the risks involved and knowingly journeyed toward the space in between the researcher and the researched. The cultural connections and balance of power involved in this study were a lesson learned for me and resulted in an analysis that benefited the program and surrounding community.

WHO GOT NEXT?

When enjoying our time jumping double-dutch, there was often a line of people waiting to join us. The self-imposed leader (often the same person every time for the purposes of structure) would always determine who was next to jump. She would ask, "Who got next?" and whoever was going to risk everything to jump in would make their presence known by loudly affirming, "Me… I'm next." This act of acknowledgment, stepping to the plurality of the ropes, is essential for the next jumper, or in this case, the next Black feminist educational researcher. Moving forward, it is my hope that educational research is conducted in a manner that is fearless. Black feminist researchers need to challenge conventional methods, norms, and traditions that have historically led to studies that are neither *for* us nor *about* us. Our research agendas need to shift from those immersed in the custom of perish or publish. Instead, research projects should aim to uplift and empower people and communities outside of academia. Our "work within the field needs to be more impactful, meaningful, and exact various forms of social justice" (King-White, 2013, p. 296). Negotiating the often murky terrain of educational research can be challenging but knowing that others have successfully paved the way through Black feminism is empowering.

Those of us that have walked this path should expect others to follow. It is our responsibility to encourage their journey through guidance and honest explanation. Black feminist theory tells us that we have an obligation to reflect on the wisdom before us but we must also share said pieces of knowledge with those coming behind us. "So wisdom, from an endarkended/Black feminist standpoint, encompasses a set of experiential principals or 'lessons' arising from Black women's experiences" (Okpalaoka & Dillard, 2011). This work has to be an "integral part of our scholarship if we are going to have politically relevant scholarship and education" (Ali, Mirza, Phoenix, & Ringrose, 2010).

The art of double-dutch requires lessons in risk, training, and advancement. These lessons translate well into the next phase of this work. Integral to the success of future Black feminists in educational research is the uphill battle to "value the lives, stories, and interests of black women in academic spaces" (Alexander-Floyd, 2010, p. 810). There is risk involved. The ropes in a research journey may harm you but the ultimate goal is the end result of empowerment and activism.

> I can do a tap dance
> I can do a split
> I can do the polka just like this!
> Unknown Author

As the double-dutch chant above notes, I can metaphorically do a tap dance, a split, and the polka and will show you, often without having being asked, what I can do. I am multi-faceted and I am constantly evolving. I can negotiate intersecting identities in educational research because I have followed the footsteps of my sister mentors: Hill-Collins, Dillard, Evans-Winters and hooks, just to name a few. They have shown the way, which in turn, has made it easier for me, and others, to jump between the contested lines. So the question is, Who got next? Who will be the next generation of jumpers, willing to brave new ground and, like double-dutch, become a site of resiliency and empowerment? This work must be done. The words of another phenomenal woman of color may be used for inspiration in times of fear:

> When I dare to be powerful, to use my strength in the service of my vision, then it becomes less and less important whether I am afraid. (Lorde, 1997, p.13)

Moving the legacy forward is essential and continuing the work of Black feminism in educational research will advance the ideologies that the adolescent game of double-dutch teaches.

REFERENCES

Alexander-Floyd, N. G. (2010). Critical race black feminism: A jurisprudence of resistance and the transformation of the academy. *Signs: Journal of Women in Culture and Society, 35*(4), 810–820.

Ali, S., Mirza, H., Phoenix, A., & Ringrose, J. (2010). Intersectionality, Black British feminism and resistance in education: A roundtable discussion. *Gender and Education, 22*(6), 647–661.

Branch, C. D. (2005). Variegated roots: The foundations of stepping. In T. Brown, G. Parks, & C. M. Phillips (Eds.), *African American fraternities and sororities: The legacy and the vision*, 147–162 (Dillard and Okpalaoka). Lexington: University Press of Kentucky.

Chilisa, B., & Ntseane, G. (2010). Resisting dominant discourses: Implications of indigenous, African feminist theory and methods for gender and education research. *Gender and Education, 22*(6), 617–632.

Crenshaw, K. (1989). Demarginalizing the intersection of race and sex: A Black feminist critique of antidiscrimination doctrine, feminist theory, and antiracist politics. *University of Chicago Legal Forum*, 139–167.

Crenshaw, K. (1991). Mapping the margins: Intersectionality, identity politics, and violence against women of color. *Stanford Law Review, 43*(6), 1241–1299.

Dillard, C. B., & Okpalaoka, C. (2011). "The sacred and spiritual nature of endarkened transnational feminist praxis in qualitative research." In N. K. Denzin & Y. S. Lincoln (Eds.), *Handbook of qualitative research*. Thousand Oaks: CA Sage.

Gaunt, K.D. (2006). *The games Black girls play: Learning the ropes from double-dutch to hip-hop*. New York: New York University Press.

Hentges, S. (2007). "Othered" girls: Growing up between two worlds. *Feminist Collections, 28*(4), 18–22.

Hill Collins, P. (1998). Intersections of gender, race, and nation. *Hypatia, 13*(3). 62–82.

hooks, b. (1989). *Talking back: Thinking feminist, thinking Black*. Boston: South End Press.

Johnson-Bailey, J. (2010). Learning in the dimension of otherness: A tool for insight and empowerment. *New Directions for Adult and Continuing Education, 126*, 77-88.

King-White, R. (2013). I am not a scientist: Being honest with oneself and the researched in critical interventionist ethnography. *Sociology of Sport Journal, 30*, 296–322.

Ladson-Billings, G. (1994). *The dreamkeepers: Successful teachers of African American children*. San Francisco: Jossey-Bass.

Love, B. L. (2012). *Hip hop lil sistas speak: Negotiating hip hop identities and politics in the new south*. New York: Peter Lang.

McCall, L. (2005). The complexity of intersectionality. *Journal of Women in Culture and Society, 30*(5), 1771–1880.

Mohanty, C. T. (2003). *Feminism without borders: Decolonizing theory, practicing solidarity.* Durham & London: Duke University Press.

Murray-Johnson, K. K. (2013). Cultural (de)coding and racial identity among women of the African diaspora in U.S. adult higher education. *Adult Learning, 24*(2), 55–62.

Okpalaoka, C. L., & Dillard, C. B. (2011). Our healing is next to the wound: Endarkened feminisms, spirituality, and wisdom for teaching, learning, and research. *New Directions for Adult and Continuing Education, 131*, 65–74.

Olesen, V. (2011). Feminist qualitative research in the millennium's first decade: Developments, challenges, prospects. In N. K. Denzin & Y. S. Lincoln (Eds.), *Handbook of qualitative research*, 129–146. Thousand Oaks: Sage.

Pardlo, G. (2008). Double-dutch. *American Poetry Review, 37*(4), 29.

Rosser, S. V. (2008). Gender inclusion, contextual values, and strong objectivity: Emergent feminist methods for research in the sciences. In S. N. Hesse-Biber & P. Leavy (Eds.), *Handbook of emergent methods.* New York: The Guilford Press.

Smith, F. (1981). *Double-dutch bus.* UNIDISC Music.

CHAPTER SEVENTEEN

Responsibility, Spirituality, and Transformation in the (For-Profit) Academy

An Endarkened Feminist Autoethnography

QIANA M. CUTTS

> I use the term "endarkened" feminist epistemology to articulate how reality is known when based in the historical roots of Black feminist thought, embodying a distinguishable difference in cultural standpoint, located in the intersection/overlap of the culturally constructed socializations of race, gender and other identities, and the historical contemporary context of oppressions and resistance for African American women. (Dillard, 2006, p. 3)

In *On Spiritual Strivings: Transforming an African American Woman's Academic Life*, Dillard (2006) argued for the decentering of traditional epistemological stances in support of a more culturally indigenous epistemology. Further expounding on her earlier work (Dillard, 2000), Dillard explored the "endarkened" feminist epistemology (EFE)—an epistemology that celebrates Black women's ways of knowing, teaching, and researching in the academy. An EFE also values our experiences and voices, focuses on reciprocity and relationships, and uses stories to heal and affirm while nurturing spiritual and community connections (Okpalaoka & Dillard, 2011). Dillard (2006) identified the following six assumptions of EFE:

1. Self-definition forms one's participation and responsibility to one's community.
2. Researching is both an intellectual and a spiritual pursuit, a pursuit of purpose.

3. Only within the context of community does the individual appear (Palmer, 1983) and, through dialogue continue to become.
4. Concrete experience within everyday life form the criterion of meaning, the "matrix of meaning making" (Ephraim-Donker, 1997, p. 8).
5. Knowing and research are both historical (extending backward in time) and outward to the world: To approach them otherwise is to diminish their cultural and empirical meaningfulness.
6. Power relations, manifest as racism, sexism, homophobia, and so on structure gender, race, and other identity relations within research.

These assumptions are not used to replicate the White male epistemological domination by encouraging a mirrored version from the Black women perspective. Instead, the assumptions highlight power relations, validate the work of Black women, and support multiple ways of researching, teaching, and being.

An EFE is methodologically aligned with African oral traditions and uses narratives and "life notes" to communicate Black women's experiences. Dillard (2006) maintained that "life notes refer broadly to constructed personal narratives such as letters, stories, journal entries, reflections, poetry, music, and other artful forms" (p. 5). Keeping with the methodological authenticity of EFE, in this chapter I use poetic life notes to explore my experiences with responsibility, spirituality, and transformation in the for-profit academy.

BLACK TEACHERS ARE RESPONSIBLE TEACHERS

Life Notes Poem One: We Are Responsible

Black woman academic
    I am
Responsible
to my community
    of Black women
Academics and
Mothers
Wives
Sisters—We are.
Responsible

For Each Other.

The first assumption of EFE emphasizes a strong self-identity as a prerequisite to community engagement (Dillard, 2006). Exploring my identity as a professor in a for-profit setting has been challenging. Having attended and taught in both not-for-profit and for-profit settings, I know there are challenges in both settings. However, the stigmas associated with for-profit universities are overwhelming. For example, many for-profit universities are perceived as "diploma mills" and criticized for unethical practices regarding recruitment, instruction, etc. (Asimov, 2010).

As a professor, I combated the for-profit stigmas by committing myself to being responsible for my students' successes. Black teachers' responsibility for their Black students extends beyond instruction (Hilliard, 1998). In addition to educating, Black teachers inform, awaken, transform, mediate, support, advocate, and nurture (Foster, 1997; Irvine, 1989; Maylor, 2009). Black teachers hold high expectations and utilize culturally responsive teaching strategies (Irvine, 2003). Black teachers are role models, cultural translators, social justice advocates, and African-centered. This level of self-identity and responsibility aligns with Dillard's (2006) first assumption of EFE.

While much of the discussion on the responsibility of Black teachers reflects literature focusing on students in K–12 settings, it is my argument that the same level of responsibility exists for Black teachers in higher education. In the for-profit university, most of the students in my courses are Black women. Therefore, I feel an inherent responsibility to and for my students. Black women in the academy face a number of challenges as faculty and students (Cutts, Love, & Davis, 2013). Ladson-Billings (2005) noted the academy is a privilege and burden for Black women. As faculty or students, we are privileged to be in the academy but are burdened because Black women's competence, research interests, and belonging are constantly challenged or questioned (Berry, 2004; Ladson-Billings, 2005). These explorations of the academy as a privilege and burden reflect the experiences of the authors in traditional universities. However, there are specific considerations for Black women in the for-profit academy. Specifically, I used EFE to examine the following questions: What are the academic experiences of Black women students in the for-profit academy with an open enrollment policy? What challenges are made regarding Black women's competence, research interests, and belonging in the for-profit milieu? As a professor, how did I self-identify to participate in and be responsible to the community of Black women at the university?

As previously noted, Cutts et al. (2013) and Berry (2004) indicated that Black women face some challenges in higher education. Yet, the challenges situated in Black women's identities as Black and female were not as significant in my for-profit setting. The majority of the students and many faculty members were Black women. Therefore, my students were in classes with students and professors that looked like them and possibly shared some similar cultural experiences. My students' challenges centered on balancing their life roles as students, educators, wives, mothers, etc. They were concerned with their pending financial responsibilities as many of them accrued massive debt in hopes of advancing their careers.

They were challenged by our program's lack of mentoring and support related to publishing and presenting at conferences. As a Black teacher, I was responsible for supporting students as they worked through these challenges. I supported my students in two specific ways: establishing and promoting critical friends groups (CFGs) and mentoring.

Research suggests that CFGs and mentoring play major roles in the experiences of doctoral students. Critical friends groups (CFGs) often are teacher and administrator professional learning communities (Curry, 2008; Fahey, 2011), but recent focus has been on the use of CFGs for students in graduate programs (Costantino, 2010; Cutts et al., 2013). Within the CFGs I facilitated, the students assisted one another with the research process, provided a listening ear, scheduled writing days, attended one another's defenses, etc. Instead of using their CFGs to combat institutional racism, my students used their CFGs to support their goals of successfully writing and defending a final dissertation and to process academic, professional, and personal changes in their lives.

Mentoring, particularly for students of color, has also been explored (Davidson & Foster-Johnson, 2001; Davis, 2007; Grant & Simmons, 2008; Hopwood, 2010). Watching students connect as critical friends was rewarding and further supported the need for peer and faculty mentoring. In my efforts to mentor students, I read numerous drafts of their work; scheduled meetings with the CFGs and individual students; advocated their concerns to colleagues and campus administrators; encouraged them to submit proposals to conferences and attended their presentations; listened to them discuss their challenges; noted that their tears were not signs of weakness; offered words of encouragement and affirmation; and encouraged them to be empowered. As a responsible Black teacher, I provided mentoring that focused on academic and professional preparation and included an element of "emotional support, understanding, or *sistering* (relationships with other caring and nurturing women of color for social, professional, and spiritual support with networking opportunities)" (Grant & Simmons, 2008, p. 509). Therefore, my identity as a professor has been influenced by mentoring, supporting, and *sistering* my Black women students. I am because they are.

UNMASKING THROUGH SPIRITUALITY

Life Notes Poem Two: Revising Dunbar

I wear the mask for pain it hides
It preserves my façade and my tears it dries
Beyond this mask there is no smile
Empowered to some, faking good all the while
And counting resilience casualties…

With the second assumption, Dillard (2006) maintained that research aligned with an EFE seeks to produce knowledge and explore truth. She also suggested that "All research is a social construction and a cultural endeavor" (p. 3). Because the focus of this chapter is on teaching, I apply these contentions to teaching. For me, teaching is a spiritual process—a participatory act concerned with knowledge, truth, social construction, and cultural exploration. Teaching nurtures my spirit. Dillard explained that there are three main conditions that exist within the spiritual foundation of research (and teaching).

1. Senses of self and purpose are examined as the research or teaching is implemented.
2. Researchers and teachers are susceptible on various levels (and these vulnerabilities should be challenged).
3. Research [and teaching] is reciprocal and caring supported by three factors.

While I consistently made every effort to examine my sense of self and purpose as a Black teacher and to be reciprocal and caring in my approach, I often struggled with the concept of being empowered and "stepping out on faith" (p. 21). Only after a student questioned my empowerment did I consider an analysis of my vulnerability and revisit the concept of un/masking through spirituality and the EFE lens.

In an email, a student asked, "How do you stay empowered?" Her question forced me to consider whether I was empowered or "faking good," a phrase a counselor used to describe clients that pretended to be happy to be viewed favorably. Empowerment, or resilience as these terms are often used synonymously, is a process. "Resilience refers to a *dynamic process encompassing positive adaptation within the context of significant adversity*" (Luthar, Cicchetti, & Becker, 2000, p. 543; emphasis in the original). Okpalaoka and Dillard (2011) reminded me that my empowerment and resilience were only as strong as my healing. For example, Dillard explained that to seek healing, we should:

> Speak words in ways that have love at the center, especially love of yourself. And speak them because (and Maya Angelou comes to mind here) we have the responsibility, once we have learned something or have healed something, to go and teach, to heal someone else. We "fight the fight" by showing up healthy, strong, whole, with a great sense of what OUR part of the work is, our purpose for being here at this moment on this Earth in these bodies. (p. 69; emphasis in the original)

The spiritual process of healing is a prerequisite for being empowered and resilient. To be empowered and resilient *or* teach and heal someone else, I had to first be healed.

In exploring my empowerment and resilience, I reflected to my dissertation research when I first considered the importance of spirituality and healing in higher education. During the emotional healing after my mentor made his physical transition while in Egypt, Rodriguez (2006) prompted me to explore healing and unmasking as necessary processes. In "Un/masking Identity: Healing Our Wounded Souls," she maintained that "Oftentimes, masking ourselves allows us to survive" (p. 1069). Paul Laurence Dunbar (1869) also communicated this sense of survival in his poem, "We Wear the Masks." When we mask ourselves we merely survive. We do not live authentically. As I reflected on the work of Rodriguez and Dunbar, I questioned the relationship between masking and un/masking. I wondered whether Black women in the academy could emotionally afford to engage in consistent masking. My experience has taught me that we cannot. How do we begin the process of un/masking? How do we heal? According to Dillard's (2006) third assumption of EFE, we continue to become or heal through dialogue within the community context. Similarly, Okpalaoka and Dillard (2011) suggest that we initiate the healing process by speaking our truths and exploring our healing and self-affirmation in safe spaces. Being in the company of authors in this book is a safe space. Surrounding myself with other Black women scholars cultivated a safe space. Looking in the mirror and speaking my truths, apprehension, and affirmations are safe spaces. These safe spaces navigate the spiritual healing process.

Black women often experience spiritual crises in the academy (Cozart, 2010). My spiritual crisis was "concerned with inner connectedness, meaning and purpose in life. It is described as a universal concept that unites all beings to the creative force" (Agyepong, 2011, p. 177). Midway through my fourth year in the for-profit academy, I encountered a spiritual crisis that challenged my healing. Impromptu administrative changes in the academy left me in a position of decreased salary. The reliance of my department on my qualitative "expertise" and ability to work with the most difficult students had become extremely overwhelming. I had grown weary of being guarded about my sexual orientation. I had more to do as a writer, researcher, and scholar, but the for-profit academy bound my hands with students that sought mentoring from me. In addition, being committed to the responsibility to and for my students as a Black teacher had challenged my commitment to self-care. Finally, I started to question my position as a faculty member in the academy. Previously, I had not been concerned with transitioning to a not-for-profit university because my work was highly regarded in my for-profit setting. However, after four years, I longed for a change. I was spiritually drained and in need of jolt to my spirit, which would revive my empowerment. Writing was my jolt.

Life Notes Poem Three: Writing Is Spiritual

When all avenues to sustain and support them have failed many Black women in the academy depend on their spirituality as a source of strength which enables them to invent ways to survive the oppressions they have to deal with such as the forces of racism, ethnicity, gender and class biases. (Agyepong, 2011, p. 179)

> Writing is Spiritual.
> Pressing of keys or stroke of the pen
> Sends me into hallelujah praise dance
> Heart beats faster and then
> Eyes fill with tears because un/masking
> Is a process
> Star gazing replaced with self-hazing
> Mirror staring and daring to be
> Honest
> Because Writing is Spiritual
> > my savior, my creator
> On many occasions when I couldn't speak
> Words
> Putting them together on screen or paper
> Writing has always been
> > my savior, my creator
> Writing is Spiritual
> > and sends me to corners
> > places were I
> > reflect and cry
> > and live.
>
> Writing is Spiritual…

The healing powers of speaking out through writing are discussed by a number of authors (Holt, 2003; Khaxas, 2011; Lorde, 1984; Reed-Danahay, 1997; Richardson, 2000). Writing contributed significantly to my un/masking and resuscitated my spirituality. Writing is "the courage to try out in [my mind] what freedom would feel like, what it would taste like to live [life for myself]" (Khaxas, 2011, p. 33). With writing, the spirit showed up.

RESEARCH, TEACHING, AND LIVING AS TRANSFORMATION

The fourth, fifth, and sixth assumptions of EFE focus on experiences, knowing and research, and power relations. Collectively, the six assumptions inform my transformation. Transformation is a continuous process that helps teachers nurture their spirits and educate their students (Hilliard, 1998). As a graduate student, I was transformed through the mentoring and work of Baba Asa Hilliard III (Cutts, 2009). As a faculty member and Black woman, I was transformed through applying EFE's assumptions of being responsible and unmasking through spirituality and healing. An EFE posits that telling, connecting, being whole, and seeking truth are valued (Dillard, 2006). These areas are addressed through transformational dialogue where Black women use our stories to "talk back" (hooks, 1999). I talked back through dialogue with other Black women who are critical friends, mothers, daughters, and sisters.

Through an EFE, I examine my experiences, knowing, and research and challenge how power relations shape my ways of being in the academy. My spirituality suffered as I questioned my professional identity, research interests, and sense of place. One day, these questions festered and I posted to Facebook that I was not being productive because I was taking time to relax. The relaxation, I wrote, was "good for my spirit." Dillard (2013, personal communication) responded to the post: "Then to heck with productivity: You are doing EXACTLY what you need to be doing for the REAL you, Qiana Cutts!" The REAL me had a place in the academy. I embrace healing, remain responsible to my community, and resist power relations. I use an EFE "to resist and transform those social arrangements [and seek] political and social change on behalf of the communities we represent" (Dillard, 2006, p. 27). We Black women will not be denied.

Life Note Poem Four: The Finale—Ode to Dillard's (2006) A Final Note

Trepidation and private conversations [thoughts]
Public spaces for race, class, gender
In teaching and research and leadership
I was
A decontextualized outsider-within
The academy trained me well…
In search of "legitimate" teaching and research
Disconnection of
    raced/gendered/classed/sexualized lives
    communities/families/selves
I could not breathe…
Contradiction, exaggerations
Yet faith prevails
From alienated positionalities
Transformation
Radical (self-care) and transformative feminist politics
Becoming whole, authentic, empowered
To foster responsibility in teaching, researching
In and of and for and with
Our communities
    With EFE—the REAL me.

I am transformed and healed.

REFERENCES

Agyepong, R. (2011). Spirituality and empowerment of Black women in the academy. *Canadian Woman Studies, 29*(1–2), 176–181.

Asimov, N. (2010, December 1). For-profit colleges: Debt, not diplomas. *San Francisco Chronicle*, p. A1.

Berry, T. R. (2004). Why are all these White women trying to run my life? One Black woman's experience toward earning a doctorate. In D. Cleveland (Ed.), *A long way to go: Conversations about race by African American faculty and graduate students* (pp. 47–57). New York: Peter Lang.

Costantino, T. (2010). The critical friends group: A strategy for developing intellectual community in doctoral education. *i.e.: inquiry in education: 1*(2). Retrieved from http://digitalcommons.nl.edu/ie/vol1/iss2/5

Cozart, S. C. (2010). When the spirit shows up: An autoethnography of spiritual reconciliation with the academy. *Educational Studies, 46*, 250–269.

Curry, M. (2008). Critical friends groups: The possibilities and limitations embedded in teacher professional communities aimed at instructional improvement and school. *Teachers College Record, 110*(4), 733–774.

Cutts, Q. (2009). *To be African or not to be: An autoethnographic content analysis of the works of Dr. Asa Grant Hilliard, III (Nana Baffour Amankwatia, II)*. Retrieved from ScholarWorks at the Department of Educational Policy Studies at Georgia State University.

Cutts, Q., Love, B., & Davis, C. (2013). Being uprooted: Autobiographical reflections of learning in the [New] South. *Journal of Curriculum Theorizing, 28*(3), 57–72.

Davis, D. J. (2007). Access to academe: The importance of mentoring to black students. *The Negro Educational Review, 58*(3–4), 217–231.

Davidson, M. S., & Foster-Johnson, L. (2001). Mentoring in the preparation of graduate researchers of color. *Review of Educational Research, 71*(1), 549–574.

Dillard, C. (2000). The substance of things hoped for, the evidence of things not seen: Examining an endarkened feminist epistemology in educational research and leadership. *Qualitative Studies in Education, 13*(6), 661–681.

Dillard, C. B. (2006). *On spiritual strivings: Transforming an African American woman's academic life*. New York: State University of New York Press.

Dunbar, P. L. (1869). We wear the mask. In *Lyrics of Lowly Life* (p. 167). New York: Dodd, Mead, and Company.

Ephirim-Dunker, A. (1997). African spirituality: On becoming ancestors. Trenton, NJ: African World Press.

Fahey, K. M. (2011). Still learning about leadership: A leadership critical friends group. *Journal of Research on Leadership Education, 6*(1), 1–35.

Foster, M. (1997). *Black teachers on teaching*. New York: New Press.

Grant, C. M., & Simmons, J. C. (2008). Narratives on experiences of African-American women in the academy: Conceptualizing effective mentoring relationships of doctoral student and faculty. *International Journal of Qualitative Studies in Education, 21*(5), 501–517.

Hilliard, A. G., III (1998). *SBA: The reawakening of the African mind*. Gainesville, FL: Makare Publishing Company.

Holt, N. L. (2003). Representation, legitimation, and autoethnography: An autoethnographic writing story. *International Journal of Qualitative Methods, 2*(1). Article 2. Retrieved from http://www.ualberta.ca/~iiqm/backissues/2_1/pdf/holt.pdf

hooks, b. (1999). *Talking back: Thinking feminist, thinking Black.* Boston, MA: South End Press.

Hopwood, N. (2010). Doctoral experience and learning from a sociocultural perspective. *Studies in Higher Education, 35*(5), 829–843.

Irvine, J. J. (1989). Beyond role models: An examination of cultural influences on the pedagogical perspectives of Black teachers. *Peabody Journal of Education, 66*(4), 51–63.

Irvine, J. J. (2003). *Educating teachers for diversity: Seeing with a cultural eye.* New York: Teachers College Press.

Khaxas, E. (2011, December). Writing for our lives: Women claiming power of the pen. *Sister,* 32–33.

Ladson-Billings, G. (2005). *Beyond the big house: African American educators on teacher education.* New York: Teacher College Press.

Lorde, A. (1984). *Sister outsider.* Berkeley, CA: Crossing.

Luthar, S. S., Cicchetti, D., & Becker, B. (2000). The construct of resilience: A critical evaluation and guidelines for future work. *Child Development, 71*(3), 543–562.

Maylor, U. (2009). "They do not relate to Black people like us": Black teachers as role models for Black pupils. *Journal of Education Policy, 24*(1), 1–21.

Okpalaoka, C. L., & Dillard, C. B. (2011). Our healing is next to the wound: Endarkened feminisms, spirituality, and wisdom for teaching, learning, and research. *New Directions for Adult and Continuing Education, 131,* 65–74.

Palmer, P. (1983). *To know as we are known: Education as a spiritual journey.* San Francisco: Harper.

Reed-Danahay, D. (1997). Introduction. In D. Reed-Danahay (Ed.), *Auto/ethnography: Rewriting the Self and the Social* (pp. 1–17). Oxford: Berg.

Richardson, L. (2000). Writing: A method of inquiry. In N. K. Denzin & Y. S. Lincoln (Eds.), *Handbook of qualitative research* (2nd ed., pp. 923–943). Thousand Oaks, CA: Sage.

Rodriguez, D. (2006). Un/masking identity: Healing our wounded souls. *Qualitative Inquiry, 23*(6), 1067–1090.

CHAPTER EIGHTEEN

Why We Matter

An Interview with Dr. Cynthia Dillard (Nana Mansa II of Mpeasem, Ghana, West Africa)

BETTINA L. LOVE AND VENUS E. EVANS-WINTERS

BL: In your opinion, why is a book like this necessary?
CD: There are three reasons why this book is important. First, this book begins to center the work of the early feminists of color in such a way that it doesn't forget the true legacy of Black feminism. That's an important piece. Often when you see edited volumes, they are just about what is happening today but they fail to lean on what has happened in the past. So I think that's one of the things that this book does beautifully. Second, I think it takes up the current conditions of Black womanhood, Black feminism, and Black womanism in really interesting and complex ways. So it takes today's sister, today's theories, today's ideas, today's current events, today's material conditions and lays them at the feet of these grandmothers of color, again in ways that honors the long struggle of Black feminist struggles and contributions. Finally, I think *Black Feminism in Education: Black Women Speak Back, Up, and Out* makes more complex the idea of Black feminisms (with an "s"), taking up the whole notion of identities in different and interesting ways. Many of these new articulations start gendered and raced studies in Black girlhood. Many of us who were in the first wave or second wave of Black feminism didn't do that work as we were still trying to articulate the field of Black feminism! So I think that's what's different about this book, what's important about this book, what's new about this book.

BL: How does this book expand traditional educational research?
CD: Just the fact that you have gathered together some 25 black women and men is itself an interesting and important piece. It's really a radical kind of move, in the spirit of Akasha Hull, Patricia Bell Scott, and Barbara Smith's *But Some of Us Are Brave*. We don't have a lot of texts that collectively speak back in such provocative and courageous ways. This is a radically endarkened text in that it's gathered together brilliant new wave Black feminists and put them together in one volume. I think this volume also works and represents new ways of Black feminist theorizing: These authors are playing with ideas of multiple and shifting identities, of sexualities, of global being. And they are theorizing in contexts that are new and exciting such as social media and digital literacies. So in that sense, in a time of increased standardization and narrowing of diversity in the academy, these Black women and men scholars begin to stretch Black and endarkened feminisms in education with/in/and against the field, creating what might be thought of as maybe the fourth (and new) wave of endarkened feminisms.

BL: So what do you think is the importance of this book to the field of education? There are only a few Black feminists in the field of education who scholars can lean on who are actually in education identifying themselves as Black feminists. What do you think the book means for the field of education?
CD: What this book does is to center education certainly but in a way that still raises up Black feminist/womanist legacy. So for those of us in the second wave of Black feminisms, our work was about theorizing and speaking out loud Black women's epistemology, our realities and identities, in a very transdisciplinary way. What I mean is that our focus in theorizing didn't allow us to live within disciplinary boundaries: What we cared about was the articulation of our endarkened realities. If you were in education (like me), or sociology (like Patricia Hill-Collins), or liberal arts (like Beverly Guy-Sheftall), what mattered most, if you were a Black feminist/womanist at that time, was speaking the truth of your realities and locations. That was most central. What this book does is to both continue and extend this legacy: The recognition that for Black women, these disciplinary boundaries had not been created for us, don't contain us, and are often not useful for us. If we *need* something in sociology, we're grabbing it and putting it to work. If we need something in women's studies, we're grabbing it and putting it to work. As so many of the authors gathered in this volume are located in the field of education, this is one of the first pieces that I've seen where contemporary Black feminists and Black womanists speak back to education particularly. For example, those who are talking about Black girlhood and those who are talking about how we walk through these halls of academies as Black women scholars are speaking about the ways that our exclusions, our inclusions, our potentials as Black women are shaped by the education that we have received *and* the same education that

we, as scholars, have the opportunity—and the responsibility—to transform. That the field of education gets foregrounded in this way has usefulness for everybody! I want to go to the question about what have we yet to understand in the field!

BL: Okay.
CD: So again I begin my thinking grounded in the "first wave" of Black feminists that included sisters like Barbara Smith, Alice Walkers, bell hooks, Akasha Hull, Patricia Bell Scott, and Beverly Guy-Sheftall. These sisters were really pioneers in the field that brought the second wave, the wave that came with me. In our wave, there were very few of us in the field of education. And that's the niche that this book fills. There's still a lot of theorizing to do relative to education as a field that Black womanism, Black feminism, endarkened feminisms have yet to do, like the scholarship here on Black girls, for example. How do we think about the foundational work of Black feminism and these works in relationship to Black girlhood? I think another thing is that we still don't have a tie as strongly as I'd like to see it between African cultural traditions and what we've traditionally called Black feminism or Black womanism that was grounded in the U.S. context and our struggles as Black women on this continent. What I tried to do in marshaling the notion of endarkened epistemologies and feminisms was to make that link more explicit, to answer questions like: What is African about us as Black women, as Black feminists? How can our feminisms, as Black women thinkers and doers be "endarkened," placed within and against the traditions of our African ancestors and heritage contexts? I think this might be my own personal bias but one of the things I love about this text and one of the things I think that still needs to be articulated is this idea of spirituality. As Black women in academic spaces, we tend to talk and dance around it, but we don't really try to theorize through a lens of spirit or spirituality, given the way Black bodies, minds, and spiritualities have been marginalized and trodden upon. Another topic that needs additional inquiry and theorizing for this generation of Black womanist and feminist thinkers is to articulate Black feminism and womanism in this time of social media. As Black people generally, and Black women particularly, we know very little about what social media is doing *to* us, for us, with us, against us. This is exploration that still needs to happen in the field of Black women's studies and particularly in education. Another thing I would love to see are more pieces that are place-based, very much like your work, Tina, that take context and location up in substantive articulations of what Black womanism or endarkened feminist epistemologies look like in Atlanta or Baltimore, Seattle, Canada, Mexico, or Ghana, wherever. So the notion of place in endarkened scholarship, particularly in education, would be something that I would love to see more of. Finally, I would wish for additional research on the what of Black feminist/womanist/endarkened methodology. Said another way, what are the methodologies that we might use in research that are

Black feminist and what makes them Black feminist? What makes particular research methods endarkened? So I think that's something we haven't yet articulated well across disciplines and certainly within education. I think Robin Boylorn's new book helps us greatly. But it's the question of articulating Black feminist methods operationally: If I were to do a study with young Black girls, what makes my methods Black and feminist? What would make my work as a researcher Black and feminist besides being a Black woman? That's the challenge as I work with students, you know? They say, "Dr. Dillard, how do we put this (Black or endarkened feminism work) to work?" I think we're starting to see some of that here but mostly as autoethnographic pieces. So I'm wondering if there might be a way for this new wave of endarkened feminist scholars to really think about what research and methods for inquiry would look like.

BL: I like that. That is definitely missing. Where would you like to go next?
CD: Where would I like to go next? The other piece that still hasn't been yet articulated that is very interesting to me is the connection between endarkened feminist/Black feminist/womanist research in education and Black women across the globe. So as a sister in the United States, in what ways would the very notion of Black feminism/womanism be changed if I were in conversation and relation with sisters in Nigeria, the Caribbean, and Canada? How can I understand us in *relation*? Said another way, how does my experience and marshalling of an endarkened feminism map on to, shift from, connect to, inform work from these sisters' articulations and theorizations? And I think that's something we don't see much, that is, collaborations for example between a sister in Canada who's articulating an endarkened feminism (like Afua Cooper) who does this amazing work on Black women and the history of Canada, and somebody's work here in the United States in a way that begins to examine our more global Black connections, our places of difference in relation. So I think that's another thing that hasn't been yet articulated. But I think it's possible and has been the work I have certainly tried to also forward. And I look at the gathering of scholars in this volume and I think there are some who are particularly situated to make these global links, to (re)member us from continent, to diaspora, and back again.

VE: At your qualitative talk last year something that I picked up on was that there's a new generation of young scholars, junior faculty, and graduate school students, who don't know the legacy of Black feminism. What I got from your talk is the students have to be vested in the legacy. For example, they need to know who taught Patricia Hill-Collins, who influenced bell hooks.
CD: Sure. I may be to these new young Black feminist women what bell hooks, Beverly Sheftall, the Combahee River Collective, or Ruth Catlett was to me. But there are young Black women who don't even know about the Combahee River

Collective or Ruth Catlett. I think that hurts. We've forgotten the legacy—or maybe never knew it! If we go to the core of that, Venus, part of what you're saying is that we have a bad case of amnesia, right? We don't *know*. We have amnesia about the history of our people generally, but certainly Black feminist scholars more particularly—that is always problematic in my mind. That you don't know the earlier articulations of what you are trying to articulate today dishonors our history, culture, being. It is incumbent upon this generation of scholars, if for no other reason than respect, to lift up the voices of those that have come before them in order to truly make sense of their own. These sisters have got to move out of the practice of sampling! It's like what you would do in music: You sample beats. The problem (whether in music or in scholarship) is that you don't have any idea what the rest of the song is, or who made it, or its place in the legacy! Part of the work is to keep trying to remind this generation that there are sisters and brothers whose work informs their own, who have made their work even possible. So whether it is through our everyday practices, our pedagogy, inquiry, or through our biographies, we're, you know, standing on someone. But it's through the kind of work that we continue to do that we both center Black feminist thought traditionally, but then also push it forward. In African tradition, naming is an important heritage tradition. In my mind, there should be no one who would call themselves a feminist/womanist who has not read Barbara Smith, or Asa Hilliard, or even Gloria Anzaldúa, for that matter. Now, if they haven't read them (given the exclusions and racism in the curriculum of public education systems throughout the United States), they should be on a mission and have a desire to do that for themselves. That's what it means to be educated. And it seems to me that part of the good work of this book is that it reminds us that Black feminist legacies are ours and are important to our lives.

VE: I agree.
CD: This lack of depth points to a lack of proper education for Black folks—and to some extent, it's indicative of the ethos of this particular generation. For example, you can like something on Facebook. It's a real quick gesture and you are done. But this idea that there are folks' work you're standing on takes time and energy to acknowledge and understand. It's incumbent upon you if you're going to call yourself an endarkened or Black feminist/womanist that you also are responsible *to* the legacy that comes before you and then responsible in extending that legacy, too.

BL: I think that takes us to another one of the questions. Where do you see this field going in the next 5 to 10 years? What would you like to see?
CD: Let me start with some of the challenges. I think they can really be summed up in a question that I've been thinking about a lot myself and am trying to take up in this next iteration of my work on endarkened feminisms, particularly in

education. That question? *Who are the Black women we carry within us whom we still don't know?* How do their lives inform our own and our work? So, for example, there are Black feminists/womanist scholars in Canada doing really exciting stuff but we don't necessarily bring them to bear in U.S. feminisms. Likewise, who are the African, Caribbean, Mexican feminists who are doing work that could inform our own? So I think that's one of the biggest challenges we have in the field: the rather ethnocentric nature of our work as U.S. Black feminists/womanists/endarkened thinkers. How do we (re)member ourselves as Black people of the world generally, and Black women of the world more particularly? Frankly, in these neoliberal, ego-driven times, many of us are dealing with the conflict and tension between responding to the reward systems in the academy that we are required to respond to, and actually being about the work centrally of (re)membering who we are as Black people and why we are: To make sure that our sisters are thriving, to make sure that we're articulating ourselves clearly, authentically, and responsibly, and to make sure that we haven't forgotten the brilliant legacy that we're a part of as Black people. And I think that raises another challenge, too, for Black feminist scholars today: the Ubuntu nature of our work. So, if I take up this notion that I exist because of all the Black feminists (and other feminists of consciousness) before me, and the Black feminists now, and the Black feminists to come, both the lack of depth and heritage knowledge *and* the attention to the individual ego (versus the attention to the community) is problematic. I actually think that's the biggest challenge this generation of scholars will have because there's a big tension particularly when you're in the academy. But I think you can respond to the tensions in different kinds of ways, with different kinds of choices. My work, as a scholar, has been to attempt to articulate a very different way of thinking about education, an education that centered on Blackness, on Black womanhood. It was a narrative that sought to articulate who we are as a global Black community including our culture, our styles of learning, our way of thought and being. But I think your generation has the challenge of dealing within that tension of the individual and the community, the ego and the community. Frankly, I don't know where that's going to land! But I continue to see young sister scholars who are brilliant but are so overly concerned about their performance of self, so concerned about being *with* someone because of what that someone can provide, so concerned about standing in the light of fame (without credentials to do so), so concerned with trying to attach themselves to others so that, by association, they are seen and perceived to be powerful. In that way, the collection of young Black feminist/womanist scholars in this book gives me a great deal of hope.

BL: What new frameworks or authors are you reading right now that inspire you?
CD: This is one of my favorite questions because it got me thinking about what is important to me right now. I think in the tradition of M. Jacqui Alexander's

Pedagogies of Crossing, that I'm really interested in trying to *weave us back together*. In that spirit, what are the pedagogies, research methods, ways of being/gathering, that might happen that weave us back together as Black women from here and there, from south and north? So, you take a book like Paule Marshall's *Praisesong for the Widow* and you look at the ways in which the key character was so deeply changed by her engagements with the continent, African understandings, and African cultural traditions. I'm wanting to think more about those connections as a way to influence education. So how do we (re)member more clearly who we are as African people? That is what's interesting me right now. I think what this book and what this generation of scholars gives me in this next iteration of endarkened feminist work is a kind of courage. You all know how to play and push in a way I think many of us don't know how to do! These new articulations are embodied and courageous and sexy and sensual and full of art in a way that rings differently than early Black feminisms! Look at early Hill-Collins, bell hooks, and others: While articulations of bodies as art, bodies involved, aesthetics, music, and dance are mentioned and explored, they weren't theorized with sensuality at the core. This generation—those gathered here—makes me ask a different question of my work: What would happen if African traditions (because that's what they are) were really enacted in this next iteration of my own work? The central notion of (re)membering isn't just a cognitive one: It's about how bodies (re)member, how Black women's bodies (re)member, how we engage *our* art in ways that resonate with Blackness and transform not just us but the field of education. And there are a number of young scholars who inspire me and are really interesting to me and whose work, while outside of education, also informs education. So right now I'm reading for example a book by Susanna Morris about the Black family, Black feminisms, and the paradoxes of respectability, right? And so I'm like, this is cool because earlier Black feminist scholars had the challenge of being respectable as well. I mean we had to be "right" in the academy and we were concerned about the academy. But it makes me want to (re)think some earlier notions about how this generation is pushing the academy in a very interesting way. I'm also reading a number of Nigerian authors right now, to answer the question of knowing and understanding my sisters' works and their worlds. I am particularly interested in reading those folks who are trying to understand the connection between here and there (continent and diaspora). So I just finished reading Chinwe Okpalaoka's *(Im)migrations, Migrations and Relations*, published in my Peter Lang series on Black Spiritualities and Indigenous Thought. I have written a number of pieces with her, but this book on immigrations and migrations helps me to complicate the place of movement in Black women's lives and scholarship, and the role of place in shaping our cultural beings as African people. She helps me to even trouble this notion of weaving Black identity and the huge role that location and nation play in how we understand Blackness. Being able to see ourselves as African might free us to see the globe as our playground! I look at Chimamanda Adichie's book *Americanah* and the ways, again, the sisters here and there are working (and making VERY messy!) notions of relationship with self, ideas of nation, concepts of partnership, Black identities, everything. Tina, your own work on hip-hop inspires me. And you know you're going to have to at some point write about the spirit/spirituality of hip-hop. There is no question to me that there is a connection between spirituality and hip-hop. It's these kinds of boundaries, that have not been brought together before, that are so important. Also reading this sister Taiye Selasi who wrote a book called *Ghana Must Go* again, a novel weaving the histories of/between her own homelands of Nigeria, Ghana, and the United States. It is just blowing my mind. So that's all the long way of saying I'm using these new voices to try to understand what Du Bois said long ago, you know: What is it that we can feel between these places better than we can understand (at this point)? I'm trying to understand *that*. Because to be Black and live within that legacy is bigger than what we've articulated up to now. And I think Black women in particular will continue to say something really profound about Blackness, about Black womanhood and about humanity. Any works that help us think ourselves back together again are what I am interested in. Anything that can heal these breaks and splits between us.

BL: So I have one last question. At AERA, Ed Brockenbrough asked you a question about critical race theory. I think it was your answer to him that is still sticking with me. You said it's important for us to write dangerously. What would be your advice to me, to Black women in the field? How do we write dangerously?
CD: Well, this notion of writing dangerously I garnered from Haitian writer Edwidge Danticat. I mean it's not a simple notion but this is the simple answer to your question. If you write for your sisters, if you write for the world as an act of healing (which in itself is an act of revolution), you would have to write with all Black folks in mind. So this idea of writing dangerously is about writing to save people's lives. Now whether we're writing in education or we're writing outside of education doesn't really matter. But writing dangerously is this idea that you're not writing for that next promotion or only to publish in some prestigious journal that will bring you accolades: You are writing because somebody *needs* to read those words to be alive, to be okay, to be enough, to heal. So that's the spirit I think I'm trying to argue here and what I have tried to do in my own academic journey. There are certainly other articles or books I could have written throughout my career than about endarkening our epistemologies, or about spirituality, or about transforming our academic lives as Black women. But then when I get those emails, notes, or letters that say, "I stayed in the academy because of this," "I changed my framework because of your work," "I feel more of myself because of what you wrote," or "I feel more courageous because of your words," then I know that's the piece I *needed* to write, the one I want to leave behind. So I think that's

the kind of dangerous creation I'm talking about: Articles and books and ways of walking that have the potential to save somebody's life in their truth-telling about Black life, Black womanhood, and Black cultural traditions. And to create such texts means that this truth-telling is *foregrounded* as the intention versus tenure and promotions or being famous (whatever that is). If tenure and promotion and fame come as a result of creating dangerously, what a fabulous blessing! But if they don't, that makes them no less worthy to create. The primary reason we have been blessed with these academic lives from a spiritual perspective is to heal ourselves and others. One way to do this is to provide texts that push us all to heal. And I think *Black Feminism in Education: Black Women Speak Back, Up, and Out* begins to do that. The way that you have gathered together these brilliant women and men who are, in the best of our traditions, telling stories about their lives/work in the fields of education is noteworthy, maybe even epic. It is a foregrounding of Ubuntu (I exist because you exist) and therefore I have to take care of you. Despite the ego-driven Western spaces we exist within, this is a decidedly endarkened feminist and womanist text. And that is a model for us all.

Contributors

Denise Taliaferro-Baszile is Director of Diversity Initiatives and Associate Professor in the College of Education, Health and Society at Miami University. Her research interests are in the history, politics and philosophy of race and its impact on curriculum and pedagogy.

Philip Bostic is a doctoral student in Curriculum & Instruction at the University of Wisconsin-Madison. His areas of interest are multicultural teacher education, deep education, change theory, and transdisciplinarity in education. He is a former Milwaukee high school teacher.

Ruth Nicole Brown is an associate professor of Gender and Women's Studies and Education Policy, Organization and Leadership at the University of Illinois Urbana-Champaign. Her most recent book, *Hear Our Truths: The Creative Potential of Black Girlhood* (University of Illinois Press, 2013), is an ethnographic account of the creative processes Black girls use to create a sense of belonging and power through creativity, spirituality, memory, and performance.

Angela N. Campbell is Assistant Professor of Education at Cabrini College. She earned a Ph.D. in Urban Education with an emphasis on the social context of education and adolescent gender identity development from Temple University. As a teacher educator, she uses her work to cultivate student voice and empowerment. As a scholar activist, she is committed to training a new generation of teachers to use holistic methods to inspire student engagement, create purposeful cultural and historical connections in the learning process, and to produce equitable and socially just educational experiences for all students.

Lara Chatman does work on African American women and mentoring, multicultural/diversity education, and minority student retention. She uses critical race counterstorytelling to share and analyze African American women's experiences in pursuing advanced degrees at predominately White institutions. She is known for her abrasive and sassy talks on and about African American students thriving in inhibited college environments and *Uncourageous Talks on Diversity and Race*.

Qiana M. Cutts is a professor, writer and spoken word artist. Drawing from education, mental health and women's studies, her research focuses on educators and the lived experiences of Black girls and women. As a queer Black woman from the rural South, Dr. Cutts also examines constructions of geographic identities and redefines traditional notions of the "Southern Belle" through poetry and spoken word.

Amira Millicent Davis is an independent scholar, mother, community-othermother, and artist whose work is focused in underserved African American communities. Dr. Davis has received funding for several community-based, supplementary education programs that focus on art, literacy, history, and social justice for youth and families. Dr. Davis' research interests include Black women's gender paradigms, Africana feminist performance pedagogy, critical theories of race and gender, and popular education. She received an EdM in Curriculum and Instruction and a PhD in Educational Policy Studies with a concentration in African American Studies from the University of Illinois-Urbana.

Adrienne Duke is a doctoral candidate in Human Development and Family Studies at the University of Wisconsin-Madison. Her areas of interest are positive youth development in minority youth, girls' development, and participatory action research.

Venus E. Evans-Winters is an Associate Professor of Education, and faculty affiliate with Women & Gender Studies and Ethnic Studies at Illinois State University. Her research and writing interests are school resilience, Black girls' and women's educational development across the African Diaspora, critical race theory and feminism(s), and critical methodologies in educational research and discourse. This recent White House invitee to the White House Research Conference on Girls, is the author of *Teaching Black Girls: Resilience in Urban Classroom* and *(Re)Teaching Trayvon: Education for Racial Justice & Human Freedom* as well as several academic journal articles and book chapters.

Roberta P. Gardner is an Assistant Professor in the Department of Curriculum and Instruction at the University of Mary Washington. Her trans-disciplinary literacy research explores relationships among social positioning, and educational equity, particularly in relation to issues of race, class, gender and place-based identity contexts.

Kyra D. Gaunt is an ethnomusicologist specializing in the politics of voice and body in Black girlhood studies. She is a TED Fellow and the author of *The Games Black Girls Play from Double-Dutch to Hip-Hop*, winner of the 2007 SEM Alan Merriam Prize from The Society for Ethnomusicology. Her latest research on YouTube, digital self-presentation and Black girls who twerk explores cognitive and media ecological fitness to help teen/adolescent produsers affected by intersectional discrimination learn more about ownership of their digital selves in a hyper-networked world still digitally divided by race, sex, gender, age, and money.

Lisa Hobson is Associate Professor of Educational Leadership at Prairie View A&M University and has served in the professorate since 1999. She holds a Ph.D. in Educational Administration from the University of Wisconsin-Madison with a minor in Curriculum and Instruction. Her research areas include: leadership and organizational development, teacher leadership, urban school leadership, student retention, and student engagement.

Adonica Jones-Parks is an educator with almost twenty years of experience in teaching and educational leadership in K-12 public education. Dr. Jones-Parks is Founder and CEO of The Write Touch Consulting, which is committed to standing in the gap for children to increase academic achievement and opportunities for reaching their highest potential. Dr. Jones-Parks earned her Doctor of Education degree from Miami University, Oxford, Ohio.

Monique Lane's collective ten years of experience as an educator in Los Angeles public high schools has informed her research on the intersections of Black feminism, critical pedagogy, and the educational empowerment of urban African American female youth. She recently earned her Ph.D. from UCLA's Graduate School of Education & Information Studies' Urban Schooling Program, and currently works at Columbia University's Teachers College as the Minority Postdoctoral Research Fellow. Dr. Lane's research has resulted in several emerging publications and numerous invited lectures and presentations.

Bettina L. Love is an award-winning author and Associate Professor of Educational Theory & Practice at the University of Georgia. Dr. Love is a sought-after public speaker on a range of topics including: Hip Hop education, Black girlhood, queer youth, Hip Hop feminism, art-based education to foster youth civic engagement, and issues of diversity. In 2014, she was invited to the White House Research Conference on Girls to discuss her work focused on the lives of Black girls.

Karla Manning is a doctoral student in Curriculum & Instruction at the University of Wisconsin-Madison. Her areas of interest are multicultural teacher education, visual and cultural studies, media literacy studies. She was a high school English teacher in Chicago Public Schools and has also taught ESL in South Africa.

Ezella McPherson is the Director of the Titan Success Center at Indiana University South Bend. Her expertise is African American Education, science, technology, engineering, and math (STEM) education, and equity in K-20 schools. In 2015, she became principal investigator for a college persistence grant that will fund two summer programs serving low-income and minority collegians.

Carla R. Monroe currently serves as an Associate Editor for Intercultural Education and her research generally addresses issues of race, culture, gender, and immigration. Her previous scholarship has appeared in journals such as *Educational Researcher, Urban Education, Race Ethnicity and Education*, and the *Journal of Teacher Education*. She is also the Guest Editor of a forthcoming issue of *Theory Into Practice* which focuses on colorism in education. In 2006 she was selected as a Social Context of Education Research (SCER) Fellow for Division G of the American Educational Research Association.

Lameesa W. Muhammad is an English Teacher at an urban high school in Cincinnati and also an Adjunct Assistant Professor at the University of Cincinnati. Dr. Muhammad has worked in the public and private sector in educational settings at the elementary, secondary, and post-secondary levels in regular and special education classrooms as well as in the social service field in the areas of addiction and recovery, mental health and wellness, and shelter and housing for adults and children over the past 20 years.

Darlene Russell is Professor of English Education and Critical Pedagogy at William Paterson University, and author of *Seeing the Invisible: Reading Literature Through Critical Lenses*. As the founder of Nurturing Culturally Responsive Equity Teachers (NCRET) Research Project, Dr. Russell and NCRET scholars have presented at several national conferences. She has conducted teacher-training sessions on critical literacy to teachers in Rwanda, and served as a research consultant for a gender equity research project with the National University of Rwanda (NUR) and Kigali Institute of Education (KIE).

Kyra T. Shahid is an emerging scholar with a concentration in race, spirituality, and higher educational leadership and a practitioner in the areas of diversity and inclusion. Shahid serves as Assistant Director for the Center of Student Diversity at Mount St. Mary's University in Emmitsburg, Maryland.

Corrie L. Theriault is the Director of Collaborative Graduate Programs and an Associate Professor of Educational Research at Kennesaw State University. Dr. Theriault has served as an evaluator for many local, state, national and federally funded projects. Her research interests include emergent qualitative methods, program evaluation, and culturally relevant pedagogy.

Andrea L. Tyler is the Director of Graduate Student Services at Tennessee State University. Dr. Tyler's research foci include graduate school access and outcomes; student and faculty voice, mentoring relationships; race/gender/class equity in postsecondary education, and identity formation among marginalized populations, particularly African American females and first generation.

Billye Sankofa Waters is an interdisciplinary scholar trained in Education, Writing, and Black Studies. Her intellectual and ethical commitments have allowed her to engage projects that range from penning the poetry collection, *Penetrated Soul*; directing an afterschool program of an urban charter school; founding Sunflower Seeds Studio; and co-creating an ethnographic study with Black mothers. She currently teaches at Northeastern University where she develops the social justice and research curricula, in addition to conducting doctoral-level writing workshops.

Tuwana T. Wingfield is a third year doctoral student in the Educational Administration and Foundations higher education program in the College of Education at Illinois State University. She received her graduate degree in social work at the University of Chicago, School of Social Service Administration and is a licensed clinical social worker in the State of Illinois. Her areas of interest are feminisms, critical theories, culturally responsive education, social justice, identity development, mentoring, and research methods in education.

ROCHELLE BROCK &
RICHARD GREGGORY JOHNSON III,
Executive Editors

Black Studies and Critical Thinking is an interdisciplinary series which examines the intellectual traditions of and cultural contributions made by people of African descent throughout the world. Whether it is in literature, art, music, science, or academics, these contributions are vast and far-reaching. As we work to stretch the boundaries of knowledge and understanding of issues critical to the Black experience, this series offers a unique opportunity to study the social, economic, and political forces that have shaped the historic experience of Black America, and that continue to determine our future. Black Studies and Critical Thinking is positioned at the forefront of research on the Black experience, and is the source for dynamic, innovative, and creative exploration of the most vital issues facing African Americans. The series invites contributions from all disciplines but is specially suited for cultural studies, anthropology, history, sociology, literature, art, and music.

Subjects of interest include (but are not limited to):

- EDUCATION
- SOCIOLOGY
- HISTORY
- MEDIA/COMMUNICATION
- RELIGION/THEOLOGY
- WOMEN'S STUDIES

- POLICY STUDIES
- ADVERTISING
- AFRICAN AMERICAN STUDIES
- POLITICAL SCIENCE
- LGBT STUDIES

For additional information about this series or for the submission of manuscripts, please contact Dr. Brock (Indiana University Northwest) at brock2@iun.edu or Dr. Johnson (University of San Francisco) at rgjohnsoniii@usfca.edu.

To order other books in this series, please contact our Customer Service Department:

(800) 770-LANG (within the U.S.)
(212) 647-7706 (outside the U.S.)
(212) 647-7707 FAX

Or browse online by series at www.peterlang.com.

www.ingramcontent.com/pod-product-compliance
Ingram Content Group UK Ltd.
Pitfield, Milton Keynes, MK11 3LW, UK
UKHW022239230426